Past

Past in the Making

Historical Revisionism in Central Europe
after 1989

Edited by Michal Kopeček

Central European University Press
Budapest New York

© 2008 by Michal Kopeček

Published in 2008 by

Central European University Press

An imprint of the

Central European University Share Company
Nádor utca 11, H-1051 Budapest, Hungary
Tel: +36-1-327-3138 or 327-3000
Fax: +36-1-327-3183
E-mail: ceupress@ceu.hu
Website: www.ceupress.com

400 West 59th Street, New York NY 10019, USA
Tel: +1-212-547-6932
Fax: +1-646-557-2416
E-mail: mgreenwald@sorosny.org

ISBN 978-963-9776-04-3 paperback

MINISTRY OF CULTURAL HERITAGE

Published with the support of the Culture 2000 programme of the
European Union, the National Cultural Fund, Hungary, and the Hungarian
Ministry of Cultural Heritage.
The editing was completed in 2007.

Library of Congress Cataloging-in-Publication Data

Past in the making : historical revisionism in Central Europe after 1989 / edited
by Michal Kopecek.
    p. cm.
A collection of papers from the international workshop, held in Prague in
Oct. 2006.
Includes bibliographical references and index.
ISBN 978-9639776029 (cloth) – ISBN 978-9639776043 (pbk.) 1. Europe,
Central–History–20th century–Historiography. I. Kopecek, Michal. II. Title.

DAW1032.P37 2007
943.0009'04072–dc22

                              2007016920

Printed in the USA

Contents

Preface

*"Some of us might have noticed we had stopped going in a straight line
and were turning in a circle. It also struck me several times
that time was fading in the pale light, turning more translucent,
losing its color and taste again, and I was horrified by that."*
Jáchym Topol, *City Sister Silver* (1994)

The year 1989 is usually considered a watershed in the history of Central and Eastern Europe, and rightly so. It not only marks a basic change in the organization of political, economic, and social life, but also serves as an elementary signpost in the making or remaking of individuals' life stories—a basic orientation point in the chaos of the running waters of time. Just as there are multiple stages and periods in an individual's life, the different time-lines overlap in the social space and collective consciousness, resulting in a multiplicity of time experience and significance—captured so imaginatively in the novel, *City Sister Silver,* a brilliant story of dislocation and bewilderment following the demise of the state-socialist monolith by the Czech writer Jáchym Topol. This temporal fuzziness and diversification successfully discredits the naïve linear model of history and challenges the simplified politico-economic story of the fall of an authoritarian, collectivist regime and the (re)turn to free liberal democracy.

The new era in Central and Eastern Europe, which started in late 1989, is characterized by multiple "posts" (denoted by, in particular, the coincidence of the period of post-Communism with the high point of globalizing post-modernism), with all the possible consequences that this overlapping has for the ways in which the history of the last 60 years or so has been reflected on, commented on, and elaborated in the countries concerned. For it is not merely political expediencies in combination with the allegedly neutral curiosity of historical scholarship that shape the general outline of the historical image of the authoritarian and totalitarian past. In fact there are many more players from civil society in the game now, free to express themselves and to propose projects at will (if they manage to collect the necessary funding). It is a state of affairs that has altogether changed the not-so-old situation in this part of the world: the basically transparent (if often misleading) contraposition of the official state-funded machine producing historical legitimacy against the smaller, rather than larger, circle of dissidents, émigré writers and independent-minded activists. It is the unprecedented pace of technological progress, along with the overall social and cultural decentralization that, under the banner of the "cultural memory," shatters the old hierarchies of academic historical knowledge and breeds an unequalled democratization, which goes hand in hand with a loss of balance—whether real or merely perceived—in historical representation. The critical appraisal of the collective memories within national historical cultures that started in France some three decades ago—a process that Krzysztof Pomian captures in one of his essays as the way "from history as a part of memory, to memory as an object of history"—has found fertile soil all over Europe and, in the last decade, is gaining remarkable currency in Eastern Europe.

This collection of papers goes back to a small but lively international workshop, "Historical Revisionism in East Central Europe after 1989," held in Prague in October 2006. Shortly before the workshop started, the French National Assembly, despite opposition from the EU Commission and from within the government itself, passed a controversial bill criminalizing the denial of the genocide of the Armenians committed by the Ottoman state in 1915. Ironically that happened the same day the great Turkish writer Orhan Pamuk (known for his critical views on the Turkish state's handling of the "Armenian question," which led to his prosecution in his own country) was awarded the Nobel Prize for Literature. In December, not long after the Prague workshop, the notorious Teheran Holocaust Conference sponsored by the government of the Islamic Republic of Iran was held, with a clear anti-Israeli political agenda cloaked in an archetypal revisionist challenge to the undeniable historicity of the Nazi Final Solution. A month later, on January 19, Armenian Turkish journalist Hrant Dink, another prominent Istanbul critic of the Turkish official politics of history, was assassinated in front of his newspaper offices by a fanatical defender of the allegedly insulted Turkish national identity. These highly politicized events, which received dense media coverage, framed our workshop in time, as it were, and underlined the topicality and complexity of our subject, which clearly reaches beyond academic debates and historiographical interpretations. It also reminded us that despite the epistemological and ontological relativism of our age, which in its most radical forms tends to relegate history to the rhetorical realm of mere story-telling, in the political and social reality virtually all over the world historical representation remains a very material and contested, nay, bloody business.

In Central and Eastern Europe the concept of "revisionism" itself has a variety of meanings and historical layers, with a long and convoluted intellectual and political genesis. It was the anti-Versailles and anti-Trianon territorial revisionism of Germany, Hungary, and ultimately also the Soviet Union—quite rightly a nightmare for the neighboring states established after 1918—which was to underpin the whole of interwar European diplomacy, which in the end proved too feeble to contain its powerful energies. While many of these energies were dissipated during the war, the bogey of revisionism, now qualified with predicates such as imperialist or militarist, was incorporated into communist anti-Western propaganda from the outset of the Cold War. Besides, the ambitious communist ideological project, along with various political expediencies, led to an appropriation of the symbolic force of the notion of "revisionism" for internal diversification. Using terminology drawn from older disputes and clashes within the socialist movement, first the Soviet ideologues and then their local counterparts started to fight so-called "Marxist revisionism" in its own sphere of influence, beginning with the 1947 Soviet–Yugoslav split, through the suppression of the 1956 Hungarian Revolution, up to the consolidation after the 1968 Prague Spring. To be sure, none of these historical forms of "revisionism" in Central Europe was directly addressed in the Prague workshop presentations. Nevertheless, aware of the fact that the "memory of language" is far from innocent, we were not surprised to be asked by our colleagues or by dispassionate observers what kind of "revisionism" we were actually speaking about this time.

The tricky notion of historical revisionism served as a catchword and organizational key of the workshop, which aimed both to explore the scale, depth, and meaning of it in the national and regional histories of Central Europe, and to reconsider the value of the term itself. Far from being restricted to small groups of "deniers," historical revisionism seems to feature strongly in the public historical discourses of many countries and regions nowadays. With spectacular trials and heated debates around Holocaust-deniers, the term has become stigmatized, and is used to describe suspect historical works dealing with the Holocaust and the Third Reich. In a broader sense, however, historical revisionism in the realms of modern and recent history has galvanized political and historical debates, both within national communities and at the international level, on virtually all continents, e.g., Holocaust worldwide, the US role in the Cold War, the "positive value" of French colonialism, and Japanese or Russian history textbooks, to give only few prominent examples. In the eyes of some observers the specter of historical revisionism is haunting the old continent and indeed the whole world.

Central Europe with its Nazi, fascist and communist past not only fails to stay aloof, but in many ways lies at the center of the debate, if only from the historical point of view. No doubt the Holocaust is, and will remain, the principal indicator of the accountability of any historical portrayal of the 20th century, as well as the nemesis, to use Frank Ankersmit's metaphor, of a radical epistemological critique of historical knowledge, which claims that the historicity of the past is a mere pragmatic convention or rhetorical figure. Beyond that, however, in the local context of individual national cultures, revisions of the recent past and the very notion of historical revisionism acquire connotations and peculiar meanings, which draw on respective national histories or their specific parts rather than on a general European historical narrative.

Where is the line between legitimate reexamination of historical interpretations, and attempts to rewrite history in a politically motivated way that downgrades or denies essential historical facts? What are the layers and instruments of the contemporary debates about historical revisionism involving not only academia and the mass media, but also decentralized grassroot initiatives empowered by the Internet, cheap digital storage, and recording facilities? How does the international debate about ethnic cleansing and the expulsion of the German population during and after Second World War, and the thesis that "expulsion equals genocide," resonate in different Central European countries? What tensions arise from the juxtaposition of politically motivated moral condemnations of totalitarian regimes with a value-restrained academic discourse of social and cultural approaches in recent historiography? How do the more or less traditional "national historical narratives" react to the spill-over of international and political controversies into their sphere of influence and intellectual orbit?

It is not the purpose of this volume to give a systematic, well-knit set of answers to these questions, which were raised in the first announcement of the workshop. The contributions range from general accounts of the epistemological background of recent historical revisionism, and articles concentrating on the relationship between historical scholarship, politics, and popular historical consciousness, to focused analyses of particular debates or social-cultural phenomena in individual countries. Both its thematic scope and its geographical range are far from being complete in any sense, even though considerations of both played a certain role in the composition of the workshop program and the subsequent volume. It is hoped by the authors that their essays will lead to a lively exchange of ideas and encourage further inquiry, and thus prolong in some way what they experienced during a sunny October weekend in Prague back in 2006.

Michal Kopeček, Prague, March 2007

Historiographic Revision and Revisionism

The Evidential Difference

AVIEZER TUCKER

The debate between historians and revisionists such as Holocaust deniers rests on a number of issues in epistemology, the branch of philosophy that deals with the nature of knowledge and how it is acquired: What is historical knowledge? How can we know if we possess the historical truth? What is the difference between a historiography that merely sympathizes with bizarre extremist politics and revisionist historiography that also fabricates misrepresentations of the past?

Historiography, our beliefs about the past, history, is in constant flux; our beliefs are constantly being revised. In that sense, all historians who conduct research are "revisionists." Had historiography not been subject to constant revision, there would have been little for historians to do beyond transmitting received wisdom to yet another generation. Historiography is a progressive and innovative discipline composed of various dynamic research programs precisely because it is capable of revising itself, constantly improving itself, expanding knowledge and becoming relevant in new historical contexts. Broadly, there are three types of historiographic revision:

Evidence-driven revision results from the discovery of new evidence. New evidence may reduce the probabilities of hypotheses about the past that once had sufficiently high probability to be considered part of our knowledge of the past, or it may increase the probability of hypotheses that had low probabilities or were not even considered at all. New evidence that is more likely to support a new hypothesis than an older one causes a revision in historiography. Hypotheses that explain a broader range of evidence and lead to the discovery and explanation of new evidence are preferred to hypotheses that explain a narrower range of evidence. Progress in the history of historiography usually follows innovations that allow historians to utilize new types of evidence, such as the discovery of the archive as an evidential treasure trove in the first half of the 19th century, or the later discoveries that led to the widespread use of non-documentary evidence such as material remains or bureaucratic records that can be used to generate quantitative historiography. The search for new theories and methods that can generate new evidence and new knowledge of the past is sometimes motivated by new interest in aspects of the past that once received little attention, such as the history of childhood or women, which had not been considered significant for historians in previous generations.

Significance-driven revision results from changes in what historians consider significant in history. At the very least, historians must choose which of the many probable propositions about the past which they derive or may derive from the evidence is worth mentioning. Some wish to present their knowledge of the past in a structured manner to create a narrative of past events. Selection and structuring require a sense of the meaning or significance of the historical process. This perception of significance is revised as a result of historical changes. For example, historical changes lead historians to search for precedents to better understand their present. The emergence of totalitarianism in the 20th century led to greater interest in the Anabaptist experiment with totalitarianism in 16th-century Münster. Contemporary terrorism has led to examinations of anarchist terrorism at the start of the 20th century. Since historical processes take time, the significance of some events and their outcomes may become patent only long after their occurrence. Historians can present such a retrospective understanding of processes only after they are completed; nobody could have written of the Hundred Years War before it was over, a fuller understanding of the significance of the US support for anti-Soviet resistance in Afghanistan during the 1980s only emerged after the attacks against the United States in 2001. Ethical consequentialists, who measure the moral value of action according to its consequences, may also be inclined to revise their moral evaluations of historical actions and the agents who performed them according to their significance in retrospect.

Value-driven revision takes place when historians reevaluate the historical events and processes they describe and explain. This may result either from new evidence that leads to a reevaluation of past events, or from a revision in the system of values that historians employ to evaluate historical events, actions, and actors. For example, the historiography of art, literature, philosophy, music, or architecture has never stopped revising its evaluations of works of art, literature and philosophy. Such reevaluations keep historiography relevant.

Readers of scientific historiography, especially those who read more than a single interpretation of similar evidence, can easily distinguish revisions that are due to different systems of values or considerations of significance from those that result from different evidence. Revisionist historiography shares with *revised* historiography the revision of historical significance and system of values. However revisionist historiography is distinct from revised historiography in being immune to the effects of new evidence. One of the chief revisionist strategies has been to "make fuzzy" epistemological issues, to make the distinction between evidence-based probable knowledge of history and fiction vague and unclear. It blurs the border between historiographic truth and falsehood by claiming there can be more than a single "true" historiographic narrative. Historical events like the Holocaust may then be "true" for some people, and "not true" for others. If historiography is reducible to the political, social and other values, interests and affiliations of the people who write it, the Holocaust may be a part of the narratives of some communities, but not of others. I demonstrate in this article that revisionist historiography can easily be distinguished from historiographic revisions. Revisionist historiography is uniquely founded on the penchant for therapeutic values over cognitive values. Revisionist attempts to confuse knowledge with fiction are founded on bad philosophy, invalid arguments and misunderstandings of contemporary epistemology and philosophy of science. We have very good reasons to believe in the historical truth of the Holocaust and to trust the methods that historians have been using to infer it.

A distinctively philosophical approach is required to debate revisionism because ordinary historical arguments are insufficient to combat the second line of defense of revisionists. When historians prove *using evidence and standard historiographic methods* that there was a Holocaust, the revisionists can and do fall back on disputing the epistemic standards of mainstream historiography; for example, by claiming that the political or ethnic biases of most historians, their "victors' justice," prevent them from seeing what the revisionists consider their "truth." Arguably, historiography is written by the winners, and the vanquished Nazis may have their narrative as well, which may be just as legitimate. Though Holocaust deniers are neo-Nazis and/or anti-Semites of various shades who do not usually belong to the academic mainstream, the philosophical underpinnings of their attack on the *epistemic* foundations of our knowledge of the Holocaust are shared by some academics, who are neither right-wing political extremists, nor racists. Relativist and skeptical philosophers such as (the liberal) Richard Rorty or (the Marxist) Hayden White, both of Stanford

University, claim that it is impossible to prove the probability of the historical truth of the Holocaust, or for that matter any other historical event.

The apparent plausibility of this second line of defense of revisionism is founded on the false assumption that there are only two philosophical options: obsolete positivism or post-modern skepticism about our knowledge of the past. True, the 19th-century positivist "view from nowhere" notions of objectivity and truth that are referred to occasionally by historians have become obsolete in contemporary epistemology and philosophy of science, and for good reasons: all knowledge, most notably scientific knowledge, is theory- and value-laden. Most contemporary philosophers consider objectivity a form of inter-subjective perspective rather than truth independent of any viewpoint. However, progress in the philosophical understanding of knowledge and objectivity does not imply that "anything goes," or that "truth is in the eye of the beholder"—an attitude that some philosophers call "perspectivism," introduced by Nietzsche and upheld by Rorty. Instead of absolute truth, science (including historiography), expects its practitioners to achieve the best explanation of the evidence, the explanation that makes the evidence most likely and the explanatory hypothesis most probable. What historians consider knowledge, like scientific hypotheses, is just highly probable; historians offer *fallible* probable knowledge.[1] Every science, including historiography, is value-laden. However, values are divided into cognitive values (precision in description of the evidence, simplicity of structure, scope of explanatory power, internal consistency and diligence in the search for evidence) that allow choice between competing hypotheses or theories, and other values that do not increase the probability of the truth of the propositions as they are attached to – moral or political values for example. Historiographic revisions are distinguishable from illegitimate revisionist historiography by their adherence to truth-conducive scientific cognitive values, and by their acceptance of a hierarchy of values according to which cognitive values take precedence over other value judgments in historiography.

I have argued elsewhere[2] that consensus among historians, in a uniquely heterogeneous, large and uncoerced group, is a likely indicator of knowledge because shared knowledge rather than any complex set of biases is a more probable explanation of such a uniquely heterogeneous consensus (there is no competing heterogeneous consensus on inconsistent beliefs). I also argued that such a uniquely heterogeneous consensus in historiography emerged following the introduction around the turn of the 19th century of a new paradigm that came to be associated with Ranke. I argued that this paradigm is marked, in addition to shared cognitive val-

ues, by the inference of common causes, events in the past, from information preserving similarities between their contemporary effects, the evidence. But it is possible to prove the existence of such a heterogeneous
community of historians who share cognitive values, theory-laden methods and consequently likely knowledge of the past *via negativa* by examining beliefs about the past and historiographic cognitive values that are
outside the heterogeneous consensus and are best explained by the biases
of homogenous communities.[3] Dissenting historiographies include for
example, "revisionist" historiography of the Holocaust; 19th-century nationalist historiographies that "discovered" ancient national sagas; the
changing Bolshevik historiographies of their revolution, and conspiracy
theories.

The best explanation of the shared beliefs of homogenous communities
that dissent from the uniquely heterogeneous historiographic consensus is
their particular biases. A uniquely heterogeneous community of historians,
Jewish and Gentile, German and British, right-wing and left-wing, agree
that there was a Holocaust. "Revisionist historians" who deny it compose a
homogeneous community composed exclusively of Nazis or Nazi sympathizers. There is a wide and uniquely heterogeneous consensus over the
historiography of early medieval Europe that is agreed on by historians of
all European national identities and by historians who are not Europeans or
do not have any national identity. The "historians" who affirmed the authenticity of various forged national sagas, from those of the Scottish "sage"
Ossian to the alleged Czech medieval heroic sagas, shared single national
identities, and fervently so. A uniquely heterogeneous consensus on the
historiography of the Soviet Union evolved as evidence became available to
historians of all nationalities and all political opinions with the exception of
orthodox, Moscow-oriented communists. Advocates of mutually inconsistent Bolshevik historiographies (as these historiographies kept being revised
from purge to purge) were either orthodox communists or Soviet subjects
who were coerced into toeing the party line.

Revisionist historiography usually relies on *therapeutic values* instead
of the standard consensus-generating cognitive values that historians of
diverse backgrounds agree on. Therapeutic values rate historiographic
propositions according to their effect on the psychological well-being of
their intended audience. Frequently-used therapeutic values in historiography include: the denial of historical guilt, for instance through denying
the Holocaust; the promotion of self-respect, for instance via national
myths; and the elimination of a sense of alienation and absurdity, for instance through conspiracy theories:

The conspiratorial world view offers us the comfort of knowing that while tragic events occur, they do at least occur for a reason, and that the greater the events, the greater and more significant the reason. Our contemporary world view, which the conspiracy theorists refuse to accept, is one in which nobody—not God, not us, not even *some* of us—is in control. Furthermore, the world (including the people in it) is uncontrollable, irrational, and absurd in a way illustrated by the plays of Eugene Ionesco and Samuel Beckett.[4]

Probable historiographic knowledge may sometimes have therapeutic effects for some groups. For example, a member of a racially discriminated-against community, such as African American, may develop higher self-esteem if she learns of achievements of her forbears, e.g., of the ancient cultures of Africa and the contributions of African Americans to science and technology that clearly refute dominant racial stereotypes which may have lowered her self-esteem and confidence. But the scientific cognitive values of historiography are indifferent to their therapeutic effects. For example, a member of an unsuccessful or backward community may wish to believe his situation is the result of a global conspiracy against his people directed by some group of people he considers to be better off than he is. Such faith in a conspiracy theory has a therapeutic value because it shifts the responsibility for perceived misery onto someone else and releases the believer from self-inspection, self-criticism that might well lead to an acknowledgement of a need to reform and change his culture. But scientific historiography may discover that there is no evidence of any plan against his people and much evidence against it; nobody actually even noticed the unfortunate group, let alone conspired against it. Often, human misery has no larger meaning and nobody benefits from it. The cognitive values of scientific historiography allow the therapeutic chips to fall as they may.

The distinction between scientific and therapeutic historiography is indicated by the difference in the communities that accept them. Historiography founded on scientific cognitive values is accepted by a large, uniquely heterogeneous and uncoerced community. Historiographies founded on therapeutic values are accepted by particular homogenous communities that are clearly identifiable according to their problems and grievances; Holocaust denial is popular among neo-Nazis who dislike the guilt which the Nazis, and by implication their admirers and supporters, have borne, and who have a political interest in dissociating Nazism from mass murder. Particular national historiographic myths are promoted by nationalists of particular national identities who suffer from a deficit in heroic prestige; faith in conspiracies is promoted by particular groups of people who share a sense of helplessness and meaninglessness as the world changes and passes them by. There has always been a market for therapeutic historiography because people and their institutions will always pay to promote, read, or hear therapeutic accounts of their collective, or for that matter personal past. The psychological equivalent of revisionist historiography would be therapies that would convince the patient that whatever personal failings they have, or social mess they have created for themselves, are the fault of someone else and that they have just been passive victims. Undoubtedly, such therapy may be effective in improving self-esteem, relieving guilt and instilling a sense of self-righteousness. However, the positive therapeutic effects of this narrative do not contribute anything to its probability. The abusive behavior of some parents may indeed be responsible for the character flaws of their offspring; their anxieties, inhibitions or obsessions; and, most significantly, their abusive behavior towards others. However, despite the therapeutic benefits of convincing adults that their parents worshipped Satan and engaged in child sacrifice and sexual abuse, and despite the therapeutic recovery of alleged "suppressed memories" of Satanic rituals and sexual abuse, there is little evidence that would make these narratives of abuse historically probable.

Inconsistencies between therapeutic and scientific cognitive values manifest themselves in social conflicts between homogenous therapeutic communities and members of the uniquely heterogeneous historiographic community that share cognitive values. During the 19th century various forged "ancient" poetic documents surfaced in Europe, but were exposed despite their therapeutic value for nationalist causes. The poems of the "Scottish Homer," Ossian, were exposed in the early 19th century as having been written in the 18th century by James Macpherson. In Bohemia, Tomas G. Masaryk participated in exposing similar "ancient" Czech poems as forgeries. The universality of the cognitive values of scientific historiography is demonstrated by Masaryk's dual role as the foremost leader of the Czech national movement who became later the first president of Czechoslovakia, and as a professional philosopher and the chief opponent of the forgeries.

Legitimate historians, like Masaryk, accept a hierarchy of values, according to which their scientific cognitive values take precedence over the therapeutic values and needs of their political, national, class, ethnic, gender, racial, religious and/or other group(s). We may want to believe that a group with which we identify has always been virtuous and faultless and that whatever blemishes we find in our group are the product of the evil that was done to us unjustly by some other class, or gender, or political, national, ethnic, racial, religious and/or other group(s). But if this involves overriding the critical cognitive values of the historiographic community, this is exactly what the uniquely heterogeneous historiographic community should not let us believe in. Bluntly, but truthfully:

> ... the final and really meaningful distinction is not between feminist and non-feminist, or Marxist and non-Marxist, but between competent historians and incompetent ones. Those who put political programmes and slogans before the much more difficult task of patient analysis of the evidence are among the incompetent ones: they may be in fashion, they may briefly provoke useful controversy, but in the slow accumulation of knowledge, their work is unlikely to have great significance.[5]

Legitimate historiography is marked by the precedence of critical cognitive values over other values, not by the absence of other values that generate different historiographic interpretations. Indeed, the presence of values in historiographic interpretation is inevitable.[6] As long as the hierarchical precedence of cognitive over other values is preserved, legitimate historiography can accommodate myriad different and conflicting values and the ensuing interpretations.

Historiographic interpretations are affected by moral and aesthetic values, by the affiliations, political biases and perspectives of the historians who write them. This is the main reason for the differences between historiographic interpretations of similar historical processes and events. Yet, an excessive emphasis on the differences between historiographic narratives may overshadow the broad agreements among historiographic interpretations, made possible by shared cognitive values and a hierarchy of values that give precedence to cognitive values over other values. Once the requirements of the cognitive values are satisfied, there is ample space for personal interpretations, perspectives, value judgments and interpretations of the meaning and significance of historical processes. For example, legitimate Marxist historiography shares its cognitive values with the rest of the politically uniquely heterogeneous historiographic community and gives them precedence over the political values of Marxism.[7] When the Marxist historian David Abraham published a book supporting the marxist thesis that the rise of the Nazis was underwritten by German big capital, but violated the cognitive values of historiography by playing fast and loose with the evidence, another Marxist historian, Henry Ashby Turner, who agreed with the thesis, effectively excommunicated Abraham and his book for violating the cognitive values of the historiographic community, Marxist or not.[8] Philosophers of historiography have been debating whether historiography should or should not be value-laden.[9] Once we understand the hierarchy that gives precedence to consensus-generating cognitive values over other values that divide the historiographic community, it becomes clear that value-laden historiographic interpretation is inevitable, but hierarchically inferior to its scientific core.

The difference between scientific and therapeutic historiography, between historiography that makes revisions according to the evidence and revisionist historiography that ignores the evidence, can be illustrated by comparing Holocaust-denying revisionist fabrications of the past, and its "contextualization" in Ernst Nolte's interpretation. The therapeutic–political purposes of both are similar: the denial of Nazi or German guilt for the crimes committed by Nazis, Germans and their allies during the Second World War, and the dissociation of Nazism, or German nationalism, or radical nationalism, from crimes against humanity in order to facilitate their resurgence. The revisionists ride roughshod over the cognitive values of scientific historiography and fantasize a Western conspiracy to fabricate evidence for the Holocaust, construct the remains of the concentration camps, write the documentation generated by German bureaucracy and contemporary eyewitnesses, and arrange for people to play the role of survivors who would offer oral evidence for the Holocaust. Nolte, by contrast, did not deny the relevant evidence that led to the historiographic consensus concerning the events of the Holocaust. His interpretation of the Holocaust varies from that of many other historians, amounting to a high-brow version of "Springtime for Hitler," the imaginary Max Bialystock and Leo Bloom production of a Broadway musical about Hitler that concentrates on his virtues in Mel Brooks' movie and play *The Producers.* Though morally deviant, this version of Nazi history still does not require the violation of the basic cognitive values of the historiographic community. Nolte constructed a comparative theoretical model that subsumes Nazism under a more general model of 20th-century totalitarianism, with the therapeutic effect of denying the moral uniqueness of Nazism. Nolte emphasized aspects of the Third Reich that were not evil, as the Bialystock and Bloom production does not neglect to mention that the Führer was an excellent dancer. Nolte considered Bolshevism as one of the causes for Nazism. Thus, he considered Nazism a response to, and a bulwark against, the spread of Communism. The therapeutic effect is in shifting responsibility from the German perpetrators to their nasty neighbors in the east.[10]

Nolte's interpretation resembles the speech of a defense attorney who mitigates after the court has convicted his client. He claims that the defendant grew up in a tough criminal neighborhood, he also did good deeds for the community, and was provoked by the crimes of others. Nolte's causal connection between Bolshevik and Nazi totalitarianism is surely weak and Bolshevism was neither a sufficient, nor a necessary cause of Nazism, but it does not blatantly violate the cognitive values of scientific historiography by ignoring or fabricating evidence. At most, Nolte's opponents can claim that he is a lousy historian, as Bialystock and Bloom's "Spring Time for Hitler" was a lousy musical, but not a fabricator. The arguments of Nolte's opponents such as Christian Meier and Jürgen Kocka, for the uniqueness of the Holocaust and the peculiarities of National Socialism, resemble those of the prosecution when it argues for the incomparable severity of the crime, for the absence of extenuating circumstances. Yet, what is interesting in this *Historikerstreit* is not the predictable disagreements on the interpretation of recent history, which have obvious implications for contemporary political debates, but rather that both sides were able to agree on so much and remain within the bounds of a united historiographic community.[11]

To take another example closer to home, the outcomes of the collapse of Communism led to a flurry of conspiratorial interpretations of the collapse and the revolutions. To take just a single representative example from this genre, "the Dolejší Analysis" (1991) is a conspiracy theory about the Czechoslovak dissident movement of Charter 77 and the 1989 Velvet Revolution. Dolejší's hypothesis was that the Charter 77 movement was invented and run by the communist secret services, the StB. The results of the Velvet Revolution, according to Dolejší, reflect a deal between the leaders of Charter 77 and their former handlers from the secret services that would allow both groups to share the post-communist spoils of power of wealth with immunity. Dolejší's evidence was the social and institutional continuity in the composition of most of the Czech and Slovak elites after the Velvet Revolution. In politics and the media, where there was a marked replacement of elites, some former Charter 77 dissidents were indeed, initially, the beneficiaries. Dolejší assumed that the high positive correlation between the winners of the process of transition after 1989 and pre-1989 conflicting communist and dissident elites must have a conspiratorial explanation. The therapeutic value of this conspiracy theory lies in absolving the larger Czech public of complicity with or responsibility for the outcomes of Communism and the results of the Velvet Revolution. If Charter 77 was a communist front organization all along, it was right and prudent to avoid joining it prior to 1989, and ordinary people who did not become involved with dissent have nothing to be ashamed of. If the outcome of the Velvet Revolution is the result of a deal between elites, ordinary people are neither responsible for it, nor obliged to strive and struggle to improve the results of this political revolution so as to try and wrestle control over their own lives in a new democracy away from the post-communist elite and its bureaucracy, because everything is a done deal anyway, the result of hidden machinations behind the scenes. It is all somebody else's fault and nothing can be done to change it. Yet, despite the helpless passivity of the common people, the political world is still meaningful rather than absurd, since the evil conspiracy of the communist elite lurks behind everything. The therapeutic effects of this conspiracy theory do not detract from its probability. However, the main problem with this conspiracy theory, which does greatly reduce its probability, is the absence of corroboration. There is not a shred of documentary evidence or oral testimony about communist manipulation of the leadership of Charter 77, or about any deal along the lines of immunity in exchange for replacement of the political elites, as was the case in transitions in Latin America and South Africa. We know of such deals there because they generated documentary and other evidence, and the terms of the transition included a variety of explicit constitutional safeguards to protect the old elite from prosecution and to enable it to maintain its power. But in the post-communist case, on the one hand the *nomenklatura* was too used to relying on Soviet assistance to be able to threaten alternative elites with a civil war or a military coup once Soviet assistance was withheld, while on the other hand, the political opposition was too small to actually attempt a social revolution and the replacement of all institutional elites. A more plausible explanation, which makes the evidence of the continuity of elites more likely, explains a wider scope of evidence, and is founded on a diligent search for further evidence in other post-totalitarian countries such as Germany or other post-communist countries (three cognitive values). It is that since totalitarianism is marked by the active elimination and then prevention from the emergence of alternative elites, once it collapses, there are few alternative elites available to challenge and replace the totalitarian one, consequently there is always a spontaneous continuity of elites from totalitarian to post-totalitarian societies, with or without a conspiracy. As practically the only alternative political elite in the Czech lands, the 2,000 signatories of Charter 77 were the only alternative elite able and willing to receive the keys in 1989. But the political dominance of this elite was brief, as new elites have emerged from within the "gray" professional classes that had been politically passive prior to 1989. The relative tolerance of Charter 77 during the late seventies and eighties in comparison with the physical elimination of political opposition during the terror of the fifties that Dolejší cited as evidence for secret police control over Charter 77 was in fact common to all late totalitarian regimes after the Khrushchev period and the deal which members of the Communist elites made with each other to restrain violence for mutual protection.

As many philosophers have noted,[12] there is no *a priori* proof that discredits all conspiracy theories, the attribution of a secret plan to a small group of people who attempt to influence large scale historical events via covert action. Conspiracies can and often do happen in history. The distinction between revisionist and legitimate conspiratorial historiographies lies in their relationship with the evidence, not in the content of their theories. The evidence for revisionist conspiracy theories usually consists of correlations between the attributed interests of small groups and large scale historical events, without evidence for the mediating intermediary actions and processes that should have connected the motives of the small group with the large scale historical events. Without such intermediary stages, it is easy to attribute all deaths of property owners to conspiracies by their inheritors, usually their children. As Keeley and Basham noted,[13] conspiracy theories, like good scientific theories in that respect, tend to unify all the evidence, with the particular twist that they consider the absence of evidence that would support the conspiracy theory, and even evidence that seems to contradict the theory, as evidence of the conspiracy, of its ability to conceal relevant evidence and fabricate evidence that appears to falsify it. Keeley suggested that conspiracy theories are akin in this respect to universal skepticism about knowledge, introduced by Descartes' hypothesis of a demon that controls all our sense data in order to deceive us, thereby explaining all our sensations and beliefs. Keeley then suggests that conspiracy theories may be dismissed and ignored on similar grounds to universal epistemic skepticism, as having low prior plausibility. I would add that universal skepticism, like revisionist conspiracy theories, is unfruitful as it does not lead to any new discoveries, nor can it predict or explain precisely why reality is as it is.

Keeley concluded that conspiracy theories prefer "an almost nihilistic degree of skepticism" to "absurdism."[14] Basham replied to Keeley that the four standard arguments against conspiracy theories, their unfalsifiability, the uncontrollability of human affairs by a small number of conspirators who should keep their conspiracies secret, the positive evidence for the trustworthiness of public institutions and public information, and the *ad hominem* accusation that conspiracy theorists are paranoid, are not sufficient to exclude conspiracy theories in general. Unfalsifiable theories can be true, some institutions can and do keep conspiracies secret, public institutions, especially in illiberal states, are not trustworthy, and paranoids may be persecuted. I think that the problem with Keeley's formulation of the problem is in its bivalent choice between universal skepticism and absurdity. Absurdity is a reflection on the teleological state of the universe, namely the absence of a *telos*, a meaning or end to the historical process. True though this existentialist world view may be, it is not an *explanation* of the world, it is a reflection on its state of meaninglessness. Conspiracy theories on the other hand are primarily an explanation of the way the world is, as caused by the interests or motives of a small group of people. This small group imposes its interests clandestinely on the world and consequently the end of the historical process corresponds with its interests. Proper competitors to conspiracy theories would then be alternative explanations of the historical evidence for conspiracy theories, most notably the positive correlations between historical events and processes and the interests and motivations of small social groups. The comparative evaluation of such competing explanations of such evidence would require additional evidence for intervening stages between the explanations, be they conspiracies or unintended consequences of complex interactions between social groups and the evidence. Conspiracy theorists would have to explain the absence of such evidence by the same old conspiracy, while alternative explanations would usually be able to come up with evidence for the unintended processes that lead to correlations between events and interests. *Ceteris paribus* scientific cognitive values would decree that the theories with the broadest scope of evidence, which are also fruitful and precise in being able to lead to the discovery of new evidence and predict some of it precisely, would be preferred to their inferior alternatives.

The skeptical philosophy of historiography denies the scientific cognitive values of the uniquely heterogeneous, uncoerced and large historiographic community and their hierarchic precedence over non-cognitive values. Instead, it endorses value pluralism and denies the precedence of cognitive values over other values. If skeptics interpret historiography as having the form of a narrative, they would claim that one narrative is as good as another, and therefore there is no substantial difference between historiography and fiction. For Hayden White, "historical narratives ... are verbal fictions, the contents of which are as much invented as found and the forms of which have more in connection with their counterparts in literature than they have with those in the sciences."[15] White concluded that the choice between competing historiographic narratives is undertaken on aesthetic grounds, and claimed that the existence of the Holocaust is dependent on political interpretation.[16] Spitzer claimed that the guilt or innocence of Trotsky is dependent on moral values rather than on historical evidence.[17]

As a description or explanation of historiography, skepticism is manifestly inconsistent with the history and sociology of historiography. The existence of an uncoerced uniquely heterogeneous community of historians that reached consensus on many beliefs and cognitive values for over two centuries must be an incredible mystery for the skeptics. Yet, clearly, historians do think they can prove that there was a Holocaust and that Stalin and his minions were suffering from paranoid delusions. Skeptics would find this consensus puzzling. Had the skepticism been right, historiography should have been sociologically as fragmented as literature or art are.

The skeptical interpretation of historiography is founded to a large extent on pre-scientific historiography and philosophy of history, prior to the emergence of uncoerced uniquely heterogeneous consensus in historiography.[18] Scientific cognitive values and the resulting historiographic beliefs did not come to dominate historiography overnight. They emerged first in Germany at the turn of the 19th century, initially in biblical criticism, philology and textual criticism and only later in historiography with Ranke, and traveled westward during the 19th century. Pre-scientific historiography, written for example by Gibbon, Macaulay and Michelet, was sometimes well-written and consequently had a wide reading public and a market niche during the 19th century even if it did not adhere to the new Rankean standards. But contemporary historians regard such historiography as pre-scientific, or even "prehistoric," to use Elton's phrase.[19] The conflation of a historiography constituted of scientific, cognitive values with pre-critical historiography is underlaid by an even deeper misunderstanding of the nature of historiographic research, a confusion of historiography with textbooks about the past. Literary critics may claim that there is nothing outside the text, that the text is all we have. But in historiography, including the historiography of literature, we certainly have far more than self-contained historiographic texts. The text refers through footnotes to evidence. The historian infers historiography from evidence, and documents it by means of the footnote. The alternative is the therapeutic invention of historiography, preferring therapy to truth, and concluding with "Springtime for Hitler."

NOTES

1 A. Tucker, *Our Knowledge of the Past: A Philosophy of Historiography* (Cambridge: Cambridge University Press, 2004).

2 Ibid.

3 G. G. Iggers, *New Directions in European Historiography* (Middletown CT: Wesleyan University Press, 1985), pp. 9, 11, 26.

4 Brian L. Keeley, "Of Conspiracy Theories." *Journal of Philosophy,* Vol. 96, No. 3 (1999): 124.

5 A. Marwick, *The Nature of History*, 3rd edition (London: Macmillan, 1993), pp. 329–330.

6 I. Berlin, "Historical Inevitability" in *Four Essays on Liberty* (Oxford: Oxford University Press, 1969), pp. 41–117.

7 Iggers, ibid. pp. 123–174.

8 R. J. Evans, *In Defense of History* (New York: Norton, 1999), pp. 100–110.

9 W. H. Dray, *Philosophy of History*, 2nd edition (Upper Saddle River NJ: Prentice Hall, 1993), pp. 46–54.

10 S. Brockmann, "The Politics of German History." *History and Theory*, Vol. 29, No. 2 (1990): 179–189; C. Lorenz, "Historical Knowledge and Historical Reality: A Plea for 'Internal Realism.'" *History and Theory*, Vol. 33, No. 2 (1994): 297–327.

11 Brockmann, ibid.

12 Ch. Pigden, "Popper Revisited, or What Is Wrong with Conspiracy Theories?" *Philosophy of the Social Sciences.* Vol. 25, No. 1 (1995): 3–34; B. L. Keeley, "Of Conspiracy Theories." *Journal of Philosophy,* Vol. 96, No. 3 (1999): 109–126; B. L. Keeley, "Nobody Expects the Spanish Inquisition! More Thoughts on Conspiracy Theory." *Journal of Social Philosophy,* Vol. 34, No. 1 (2003): 104–110; L. Basham, "Malevolent Global Conspiracy." *Journal of Social Philosophy,* Vol. 34, No. 1 (2003): 91–103.

13 Ibid.

14 B. L. Keeley, "Of Conspiracy Theories." *Journal of Philosophy,* Vol. 96, No. 3 (1999): 125.

15 H. White, *Tropics of Discourse* (Baltimore: Johns Hopkins University Press, 1978), p. 82.

16 H. White, *The Content of the Form* (Baltimore: Johns Hopkins University Press, 1987).

17 A. B. Spitzer, "John Dewey, The 'Trial' Of Leon Trotsky And The Search For Historical Truth." *History and Theory,* Vol. 29, No. 1 (1990): 16–37.

18 H. White, *Metahistory* (Baltimore: Johns Hopkins University Press, 1973).

19 G. R. Elton, *The Practice of History* (Glasgow: Collins, 1969), p. 14.

From Revisionism to "Revisionism"

Legal Limits to Historical Interpretation

VLADIMIR PETROVIĆ

Contrary to radical postmodern approaches, there are limits to the representations of the past. Even if one subscribes to the trend which sends the traditional distinctions between facts and values, description and interpretation, to the junkyard of historiography, several rather lively "reality checks" ought to be taken into account, both within the craft and outside it. However, one might embrace the postmodern argumentation insofar as it indicates the fuzziness of the distinction between scholarly and unscholarly historical interpretations. It might even seem that apart from risking the collective rage of fellow historians, or breaking certain rules of formal logic and elementary physics, not much remains to differentiate between advancing a preposterous argument and suggesting a bold historiographical hypothesis. In the light of those epistemological uncertainties, the proposed subtopic, focusing on the "border between legitimate reexamination of historical narratives and attempts to rewrite history in a politically motivated way that downgrades or denies essential historical facts," stands out as an interesting but by no means easily approachable problem.

Indeed, how does one cross the limit? By borrowing and adjusting the title from the famous conference on the Holocaust in history, organized in 1990 by UCLA under the disturbing name "Probing the Limits of Representation," this paper carries the gist of that gathering into the legal realm, in an attempt to examine the involvement of the courts in distinguishing between legitimate and illegitimate historiographical interpretations.[1] The paper analyzes the ways in which various legal proceedings are influencing the demarcation between revisionism (reexamination of views on the past) and "revisionism" (denying the mass crimes of the 20th century). The workshop on revision of Central European history lends itself very well to such scrutiny, as Holocaust denial stands out as both the most malignant and the most persistent tendency among the "revisionist" projects. The attempts to revise this part of Central European history have attracted considerable legal attention and brought the heavy hand of the law into an issue whose sensitivity challenges the traditional notions of value-free historical scholarship. In order to contribute to the understanding of such a development, this paper revisits the inherent connection between historical revision and the law. The emergence of revisionism through criticism of the Versailles treaty is examined, as well as legitimate and less legitimate forms of revisions of the Nuremberg and other Second World War-related trials. The paper further sketches the variety of legal reactions to certain revisionist attempts, arguing that this activity has significantly contributed to shaping the border between revisionism and "revisionism." The dynamics of this demarcation are scrutinized in different legal contexts typical of various national jurisdictions. The impact of this courtroom activity on historiography is illustrated, and some possible avenues are indicated for coping with this process, through which the edges of credible academic discourse are cut, for better or for worse.

1. HISTORICAL REVISION BETWEEN NONCONFORMISM AND DENIAL

Ambiguities surround the term revisionism, loaded with meanings, denoting both legitimate reassessment of the past and illegitimate manipulation of it. Setting the terminology straight by differentiating between revisionism (provocative, controversial nonconformist questioning of entrenched beliefs) and "revisionism" (denial of crimes, distortion of the truth apologetic of extreme policies) would seem sensible, but it is a surprisingly slippery task.[2] The border between the two is in fact unstable, and powerful instruments outside academia often tip the balance, the primary example being the law; across the world a number of self-proclaimed revisionists are caught up in the webs of legal proceedings. Some of them are in jail. *Freedom for Europe's Prisoners of Conscience!*, demands Mark Weber, head of the USA-based revisionist Institute for Historical Review, commenting on the imprisonment of some of the leading figures of contemporary revisionism, such as Ernst Zündel, David Irving and Germar Rudolf, claiming that they are victims of suppression of the freedom of academic expression.[3] However, there is more to it. More than simple victims of crime of thought, revisionists operate, and have always operated, at a sensitive junction between history and law. The current wave of their legal predicaments might be seen as one stage in the long-lasting, structurally-entangled relationship between revisionism and the law, central to the understanding of both legitimate and illegitimate revisionist undertakings.

How did this connection emerge? To begin with, revisionists (legitimate as well as illegitimate) need to have something to revise. Any subject of their revision is more than just a conventional scholarly interpretation of the past. They challenge something bigger—the "official" truth, a paradigm sanctioned by political authorities, guarded by legal decisions and maintained by the majority of allegedly opportunistic academics. This dynamic is typical of revisionist discourse and makes it easy to differentiate between a regular scholarly debate, conducted in the form of an informed dialogue between academics, and a politically saturated exchange. High-profile legal proceedings and landmark courtroom decisions, as examples of a legally imposed truth, are thus prone to becoming a starting point of their revision. The term was in fact used for the first time to describe intellectuals who were fighting for the revision of the Dreyfus case. It also entered historiography in a similar context, as it was initially used to describe the activities of a number of interwar historians (Sidney Fay, Harry Elmer Barnes, Charles Beard, Alfred von Wegerer, Pierre Renouvin...) challenging the famous Article 231 of the Versailles Treaty.[4] According to this and related parts of the Versailles Treaty, Germany was solely responsible for the outbreak of the war, and revisionist historians attempted to show that this decision rested on a highly selective and misguided historical interpretation. To counter it, they launched a scholarly debate (known as *Kriegsschuldfrage*—the Question of War Guilt) which is in fact still open and remains a valid subject for research.[5] Nonconformism towards governmental narratives and suspicion towards propaganda were typical features of early revisionism.

Structurally similar, albeit manifestly very different developments occurred in the aftermath of the Second World War, whose juridical follow-up was much more thorough and took on various forms of legal and extra-legal retribution.[6] The criminalization of Nazi Germany, and its allies and collaborators, resulted in a number of proceedings, in the course of which more and more factual knowledge was gathered about the atrocious aspects of *Neuordnung Europas*. Following defeat on an unprecedented scale, the Third Reich was dismantled, its archives seized and utilized to furnish evidence for the trials to come. In the midst of this frenzied activity stands the Trial of Major War Criminals before the International Military Tribunal in Nuremberg (20 November 1945–1 October 1946). The protagonists of the great trial had no doubts about the historical importance of their work. "We cannot here make history over again. But we can see that it is written true," concluded Telford Taylor, one of the prosecutors.[7] His colleague, Robert Kempner, dubbed the proceedings the "greatest historical seminar ever held."[8] Nuremberg stands for the quintessential attempt at what might be called juridical memory making, namely the attempt to influence collective memory via high-profile proceedings in which law, politics, memory and history intertwine in a memorable public event, producing a particular outlook on the past.

As the years went by, it became clear that Nuremberg had left an ambiguous legacy. On the one hand, it was hailed as a new beginning for international criminal justice. Not only did it inspire subsequent proceedings against Nazi war criminals, but it has certainly assisted the creation of the ad hoc International Criminal Tribunals for Yugoslavia and Rwanda, and ultimately, the emergence of the International Criminal Court. On the other hand, being the first of its kind, conducted in the haste of an immediate postwar context, the proceedings at Nuremberg created a number of questionable precedents in international criminal law. Procedural faults were legion, and easy targets for barrages of political, legal and historical criticism. Skeptical voices labeled it an exercise in victors' justice, and yet another imposition of the official truth. Various aspects of the proceedings were scrutinized and directly or indirectly criticized by reputed legal scholars, political scientists and historians. As early as 1961, A. J. P. Taylor provoked lively debate with his *Origins of the Second World War*. His interpretation of the causes of the war was very remote from the framework offered by the Nuremberg Judgment, and was boldly subtitled *A Revisionist View*.[9] Many serious studies of the Nuremberg proceedings since then have maintained a critical edge towards what Mark Osiel recently named called "Nuremberg's conspiratorial outlook on history." Michael Marrus concurs that "as most of the historians would agree... this interpretation has not withstood the research of a subsequent generation of scholars."[10] Nuremberg is indeed a topic on which reasonable, well-informed people have many doubts.

Fishing in this murky water was bliss for the newly emerging, significantly different brand of revisionism. It is no wonder that most researchers into the history of Holocaust denial usually single out Maurice Bardéche's book *Nuremberg or the Promised Land* (1947) as its point of departure.[11] Without the benefit of much scholarly argumentation, but with a very clear political agenda, authors like Bardéche set out to undermine the impact of the postwar trials and revise their findings. Criticizing Nuremberg alongside well-reputed scholars gave the new revisionism badly needed legitimacy. However, unlike benevolent critiques, they were using selective, guided attacks in order to exculpate the Nazi policies that were buried in the Nuremberg trials. Shielded to some extent by the Cold War-generated equation of the crimes of Communism with those of National Socialism, they produced many frighteningly successful distortions of otherwise convincing arguments. The participation of Soviet representatives in the Nuremberg proceedings prompted the revisionists to claim that the trial was not only victors' justice, but not justice at all. The inability of the Nuremberg prosecutors to establish the exact number of murdered Jews was misused for repeated reductions of the death toll. The nonexistence of the written order signed by Hitler regarding the Final Solution of the Jewish question was evoked as an argument *ex silentio* that he knew little or nothing about the death camps.[12] The attack on the Nuremberg and related trials lay at the heart of what Pierre Vidal-Naquet labeled "an assassination of memory" and Deborah Lipstadt calls a "growing assault on truth and memory."[13]

The new revisionists consciously promoted themselves as inheritors of interwar revisionism. The presentation of the Institute for Historical Review states: "Devoted to truth and accuracy in history, the IHR continues the tradition of historical revisionism pioneered by distinguished historians such as Harry Elmer Barnes, A. J. P. Taylor, Charles Tansill, Paul Rassinier and William H. Chamberlin."[14] However, the differences were striking. Unlike the interwar debate on the question of German guilt, which did advance factual knowledge on the outbreak of the First World War, and did contribute to a wider understanding of causality in history, the new revisionism had far less to offer. Whereas the interwar revisionist historians were questioning the dictum of a peace treaty, which was a political imposition in a legal document, postwar revisionists were attacking the core of postwar legal proceedings. Whereas most other scholars concentrated on criticizing the concept of crime of conspiracy and crimes against peace as defined at Nuremberg, new revisionists extended this skepticism to investigations into crimes against humanity and war crimes, casting doubts on their findings. Academic nonconformism in the spirit of "speaking the truth to power" was transformed into an outright denial of human suffering. Suspiciously, among the ranks of the new revisionists one could seldom find reputable professional historians; instead, mavericks of different brands took over the floor. Nevertheless, in the light of the deepening crisis of historical scholarship shaken by relativism, strengthened by the so-called "Hitler's wave" of the early 1970s, they gained significant visibility. Initially the work of several marginalized individuals, their approach developed in the course of the 1970s into a recognizable standpoint on the margins of this extremely controversial and sensitive field.

2. THE LONG HAND OF THE STATE: DEFINING "REVISIONISTS"

Ironically, it was precisely the limited success of the new revisionists of the late 1970s and 1980s which put in motion a set of legal mechanisms against them, and has assigned to them the derogatory label of "revisionists." In fact the authors of revisionist literature regularly come into collision with the law. Maurice Bardéche himself was sentenced to a year in prison, although he never went to jail. However, with growing global sensitivity towards the crimes of the Second World War, enhanced through the second generation of Holocaust related trials (The Ulm trial, the Eichmann trial, the Frankfurt-Auschwitz trial and so on), new sentiments were powerfully augmented by controversies like the one over President Reagan's visit to the Bitburg cemetery, and the tables have turned against the revisionists. The shaken social consensus started calling for the legal protection of public memory, and there were tools available. Contrary to popular belief, freedom of speech in the public sphere is far from unlimited in functioning democracies. Many aspects of expression are, in one way or another, suppressed in public life. Certain ways of addressing the past are also illegal in a number of countries. This is particularly the case with the denial of mass atrocities, above all with Holocaust denial. A number of countries have criminalized Holocaust denial or other ways of contesting the existence of crimes against humanity. Expressed in formulations which differ significantly, Holocaust denial constitutes a crime in Austria, Belgium, the Czech Republic, France, Germany, Lithuania, Poland, Portugal, Romania, Slovakia, Spain, Switzerland and Israel. Where direct criminalization was absent, as in the United Kingdom, Canada, the United States and elsewhere, legislation concerning hate-speech and incitement to racial hatred also paved the way for a new wave of Second World War related trials, concerned with the aberrant memory or inadequate representation of those events.

However, the vigor with which these mechanisms are applied varies from jurisdiction to jurisdiction. Germany has a long tradition of legally combating revisionism, which might be seen as an insistence on discontinuity between the Federal Republic and the Third Reich, as well as the determination never again to allow the judicial system to become the mere bystander of a prospective *Machtergreifung*. Hence, such proceedings have become a matter of routine under article 185 of the Penal Code, which punishes behavior violating the honor of the complainant or under article 130 (3), which explicitly prohibits incitement to racial hatred. In addition, from the *Zionist Swindle* case (1977) onwards, the denial and minimization of the number of Jewish victims of the Nazi regime specifically constitutes a crime. In 1985, the law colloquially called *Gesetz gegen die "Auschwitz-Lüge"* (Law against the "Auschwitz Lie") was passed and has been upheld in trials like the *Deckert* case, in which the leader of the National Democratic Party, Günther Deckert, was found guilty of incitement to racial hatred and the *Holocaust Denial* case in which the German Supreme Court ruled, after a neo-Nazi rally, that the right to freedom of speech does not protect Holocaust deniers.[15]

Similar historical experience probably guided Austria in the same direction, with a zeal which shows no signs of withering six decades after the Second World War. On 20 February 2006, David Irving, a British self-styled revisionist historian, was sentenced to three years in prison for Holocaust denial, under Austria's 1947 law prohibiting the "public denial, belittling or justification of National Socialist crimes."[16] The law under which Irving was found guilty dated from 1945, but was severed in 1992 to combat the revival of the ideology of the NSDAP through explicit criminalization of the denial and minimization of National Socialist crimes. In the reasoning of the court, this is exactly what Irving was doing in the course of lectures he held in Austria in 1989.

A comparable practice developed somewhat later in France, as Henry Rousso labeled it, the "Vichy syndrome" was long dormant.[17] However, as one of the many after-effects of the 1968 rebellion, the issue of appropriate remembrance of the Second World War reappeared, strengthened by the burden of more recent instances of crimes committed in the course of decolonization. The anti-Jewish policy of the Vichy government became an issue of contention in a number of cases, beginning with the trial of Klaus Barbie in 1987. Barbie's skilled lawyer, Jacques Verges, based his defense on stretching the notion of crimes against humanity to the conduct of the French authorities in Indochina and Algeria, and in effect suggested a powerful alternative reading of the recent history of France.[18] In a subsequent wave of moral-revisiting of French history, the high profile of revisionists became an embarrassment to France, leading to a legislative reaction—in 1990 Parliament passed the so-called Gayssot law, which was furthering the 1972 Holocaust denial law and criminalized the contestation of crimes against humanity.[19] One of the first defendants under that law was Robert Faurisson, a professor of literature at the University of Lyon and the most vocal Holocaust denier in France, who unsuccessfully appealed against the verdict of the United Nation's Human Rights Committee. However, the Gayssot law does not necessarily concern only mavericks in scholarship, like Faurisson, Vincent Reynouard or Roger Garaudy, but also right-wing politicians like Jean-Marie Le Pen.

European countries are generally in the forefront of the criminalization of harmful interpretations of the past, which are deemed to be a means of spreading hate-speech and inciting racial and ethnic hatred. Their commitment to combating this phenomenon is apparent in a set of initiatives started recently by the Council of Europe through the *Additional Protocol to the Convention on cybercrime, concerning the criminalization of acts of a racist and xenophobic nature committed through computer systems.* Article 6 of this Protocol obliges the signatories to penalize "distributing or otherwise making available, through a computer system to the public, material which denies, grossly minimizes, approves, or justifies acts constituting genocide or crimes against humanity, as defined by international law and recognized as such by final and binding decisions of the International Military Tribunal, established by the London Charter of 8 August 1945, or of any other international court established by relevant international instruments and whose jurisdiction is recognized by that Party."[20] The intention is to regulate this realm as well, for the Internet has become one of the main battlefields for deniers and defenders of the memory of the Holocaust.

The involvement of the state in this debate had, and still has, many opponents in very different quarters. Revisionists are naturally very much against such laws, but such activities are disapproved of by many liberals too. Criticism is strong in countries with a long tradition of the constitutional protection of free speech, and particularly in common law countries—criminalization of the Holocaust denial has never been discussed seriously in the United States, and Great Britain has recently dropped the idea of introducing it. The exception in this respect is Canada, where a denier, Ernst Zündel, was put on trial. However, even his verdict was eventually quashed by the Supreme Court on the basis of protection of free speech.[21] One of the great controversies regarding revisionism was sparked off when Noam Chomsky's essay *Some Elementary Comments on the Rights of Freedom of Expression* prefaced Robert Faurisson's *Memoire en defense*. Chomsky's argument was that, although he does not concur with Faurisson's thesis, he feels the need to defend his right to express it.[22] Even the most vocal fighters against Holocaust denial, like Deborah Lipstadt, have many reservations about such laws: "As an American, I'm a staunch believer in free speech. I recognize, however, that the situation in Germany is different and that there might be room there for a law against Holocaust denial, but there is also a practical aspect to my general opposition to laws against Holocaust denial. When speech is restricted, it becomes 'forbidden fruit' and more interesting to people."[23] Other tactical issues are also at stake. The trials lend the revisionists, as noted by Ernst Zündel himself, a million dollars' worth of publicity, through which they can also count on some public sympathy, claiming to be persecuted thinkers and comparing themselves, as Robert Faurisson did, with Galilei: "Did Galileo Galilei have the facts right? Do we, the Revisionists, have the facts right? ... That is the question."[24]

Many public figures who otherwise do not think revisionists have the facts right are championing the retraction of such laws and showing concern about the tendency towards restrictive legislation in Europe.[25] Professional historians are particularly engaged in working for their revocation. A group of 19 historians in France has recently protested against all "historic laws."[26] The gist of their argument is captured by Timothy Garton Ash, who commented on the French Parliamentary 2005 law on colonialism: "No one can legislate historical truth. In so far as historical truth can be established at all, it must be found by unfettered historical research, with historians arguing over the evidence and the facts, testing and disputing each other's claims without fear of prosecution or persecution."[27] The other way of addressing the legitimacy of a certain interpretation of the past is available and advocated as a less harmful alternative. Holocaust denial could be sanctioned indirectly, through civil proceedings in which individuals or groups file complaints against the alleged offenders on the grounds of causing mental harm, or producing and distributing offensive publications. A *cause célèbre* in this respect in the United States was the 1981 *Mermelstein case* in which a Holocaust survivor, Mel Mermelstein, sued the Institute for Historical Review following their announcement of a reward to anyone who could prove that Jews were put to death by gassing in Auschwitz.[28] The Institute lost in a way which constituted a major juridical defeat for revisionists, for the Californian court admitted the Holocaust into evidence as judicial notice, proclaiming it an event so well-known and indisputable that it need not be proven in court.

The huge success in the *Mermelstein* case, which was both preceded and followed by similar ventures in both continental and common law, indicated that criminal law is not indispensable in combating denial. If criminal action aims at delegalizing many facets of revisionism, civil suits aim at delegitimizing them, frequently with equal success. "Once someone is labeled as a Holocaust denier that person becomes illegitimate, and rightly so," claims Jewish Professor Neil Gordon who recently won a suit against his colleague Steven Plaut, who alleged him to be "a fanatic anti-

Semite."[29] This aspect of libel defamation undoubtedly made litigation over revisionism develop in rather unexpected directions towards the end of the century, and showed that civil cases also have their weaknesses. Quarrelling scholars address the court to resolve their claims. This option is open to "revisionists" as well as to others, and is particularly utilized in their attempt to present themselves as credible revisionists, rather than contemptible deniers. Revisionist historian David Irving tried to play this card by suing Deborah Lipstadt in 1996 for calling him a Holocaust denier. Mainstream academia has also seen a number of similar initiatives. One of the legal after-effects of the Goldhagen debate was a libel threat by Daniel Goldhagen against Ruth Betinna Birn, whom he decided to sue unless she retracted her devastating review of his book *Hitler's Willing Executioners*. Writing about the Holocaust and writing about writing about the Holocaust, already subject to very different interpretations, have become a true intellectual minefield.[30]

3. THE COURT SPEAKS: OVER THE EDGE OF THE ACADEMIC DISCOURSE

Many revisionists have been prosecuted, and some of them have gone to jail. But does this have an impact on conventional historiography? It depends. Although cases regarding revisionists are sometimes conducted in an isolated courtroom context, their ability to influence scholarship should not be underestimated, as the following examples show. Whether the cases involve criminal or civil suits, there are a number of ways in which the proceedings can break out of the courtroom and directly or indirectly involve scholars. As the law invades their realm, tensions regarding authority arise. Are the courts in a position to judge history? Can they assess the work of historians? How should historians react in such situations? Scholars could attract the attention of the public prosecutor or civil claimants for their views and findings, which would not only put them in danger of punishment, but would put the judges in the strange position of rendering judgments over the quality of their historical interpretation, producing peculiar text in which legal form transmits the historiographical content.

In 1994, one of the best known American Orientalists, Bernard Lewis, stood trial in Paris for an interview in which he cast doubts on the appropriateness of the term "genocide" for the 1915 massacre of Armenians in the Ottoman Empire, which he referred to as "the Armenian version of this event."[31] He was indicted under the Gayssot law, but acquitted on the basis of the interpretation of the court, which defined crimes against humanity in accordance with the definition of the London Charter of 1945 and was hesitant to stretch the notion to prior events. However, Lewis was sued in a civil case in three separate suits by the French Forum of Armenian Associations. The French court claimed not to be interested in resolving either historical issues or historiographical method:

> The Court is not called upon to assess or to state whether the massacres of Armenians committed from 1915 to 1917 constitute or do not constitute the crime of genocide … in fact, as regards historical events, the courts do not have as their mission the duty to arbitrate or settle arguments or controversies these events may inspire and to decide how a particular episode of national or world history is to be represented or characterized… in principle, the historian enjoys, by hypothesis, complete freedom to relate, according to his own personal views, the facts, actions and attitudes of persons or groups of persons who took part in events the historian has made the subject of his research.[32]

However, in spite of those reservations, in order to assess whether Lewis had injured the Armenian community or was simply doing his job, legal scrutiny of his scholarly activity was necessary:

> Whereas, even if it is in no way established that he pursued a purpose alien to his mission as a historian, and even if it is not disputable that he may maintain an opinion on this question different from those of the petitioning associations, the fact remains that it was by concealing elements contrary to his thesis that the defendant was able to assert that there was no "serious proof" of the Armenian genocide; consequently, he failed in his duties of objectivity and prudence by expressing himself without qualification on such a sensitive subject; and his remarks, which could unfairly revive the pain of the Armenian community, are tortious and justify compensation under the terms set forth hereafter.[33]

Lewis lost one of the suits, and paid the sum of one franc as compensation for an offense towards the sentiments of the Armenian community. Clearly, the court was both in the position of rendering judgment over the appropriateness of his scholarship, and under obligation to do so.

The other type of interaction between academics was displayed in *R. vs. Ernst Zündel*, a 1985 criminal case in Canada in which a neo-Nazi publisher was accused of "spreading false news" after publishing an essay entitled *Did 6 Million Really Die?*[34] The prosecutor built his case on an attempt to prove that Zündel was purposefully spreading false news. He was bound to prove that Zündel was aware of the truth—that he knew about the Holocaust and maliciously misguided the public. As the judge declined to accept the existence of the Holocaust as a judicial notice, it became a necessity to prove that the Holocaust occurred and was to be believed in beyond reasonable doubt by an average person. In addition to the customary sorts of evidence, such as documents and eyewitness testimonies, the prosecution embarked on a less standard venture—bringing historians into court as expert witnesses. The expert witness for the prosecution was no other than Raul Hilberg, one of the best known Holocaust scholars. Zündel's lawyer, Dag Christi, set out to defend his client by relativizing the epistemological value of knowledge about the past. In order to convince the jury that "history is only an opinion," and that there are no firm criteria for preferring one opinion over the other, he dismissed historical expert testimonies as hearsay, and exposed Hilberg to highly abusive cross-examination.[35] However, he commissioned expert historical testimony for his own client from none other than Robert Faurisson.

Consequently, the trial offered the strange spectacle of a debate between the experts brought by the defense and those provided by the prosecution. The complex case dragged from the first hearing to the Supreme Court and back for a retrial. During the retrial, Hilberg's place was taken by another prominent expert on the period, Christopher Browning.[36] The defense also strengthened their ranks, bringing David Irving to the witness box. Needless to say, such skirmishes increased the fame of revisionists. Eventually, Zündel was found guilty. The case went to appeal and was sent for retrial owing to procedural faults. In a retrial, he was found guilty again, and this time the verdict was confirmed on appeal, but was eventually reversed by the Supreme Court on the grounds of protection of free speech. The ultimate failure unintentionally delivered the message that the Holocaust is a debatable event in scholarship, which did create many doubts about the feasibility of the venture.

However, a case in which the courtroom exposure of historians reached a peak, and which combined aspects of both the Lewis and the Zündel cases, was *David Irving versus Penguin Books Ltd. and Deborah Lipstadt*. The case was brought on the basis of a writ filed by David Irving in 1996, in which he claimed to have been defamed by Deborah Lipstadt, an American social scientist. Lipstadt labeled David Irving a Holocaust denier in her book *Denying the Holocaust*. He sued both her and her publishers, demanding compensation for his damaged reputation, and the trial began in 2000. According to British libel law, the burden of proof rests with the defendants, who were obliged to prove that the accusation was false. This meant that they had to prove that Irving was a Holocaust denier—a complex task. In order to convince the judge that Irving denied the Holocaust, the defendant had to show what the Holocaust was, prove that

Irving was familiar with the facts regarding the Holocaust, and that he had purposefully twisted or ignored crucial facts in order to deny it. As summarized by Irving himself, the defendants had to show "...first, that a particular thing happened or existed; second that I was aware of that particular thing as it happened or existed, at the time that I wrote about it from the records then before me; third, that I then willfully manipulated the text or mistranslated or distorted it for the purposes that they imply."[37] And that was exactly what the defense intended to do. In addition to the submission of an enormous amount of written evidence, one way was to call upon expert witnesses. The defense commissioned no less than five reports by prominent historians and social scientists (Richard Evans, Robert Van Pelt, Christopher Browning, Peter Longerich, Hajo Funke).[38] Irving also called upon historians such as John Keegan and Cameroon Watt to testify on his behalf. The outcome was "something new: a Holocaust trial without victims and without perpetrators... in which history is judged, as well as made."[39]

Irving was in fact fighting a battle to retain the title of respected, or at least relevant, revisionist historian. He objected to being labeled a Holocaust denier, claiming that at no time had he denied the mass murder of Jews by the Nazis, not resisting however the temptation to use the same strategy of globalizing the Holocaust as had been attempted by Verges in the Barbie trial—he stated that "the whole of World War II can be defined as a Holocaust."[40] To counter this, some of the expert reports of the prosecution were about the Holocaust; the others were about Irving, and his extreme right-wing politics and scholarship. Even more than in the Zündel case, historians were debating the appropriateness of an interpretation of the past. The quality of Irving's method was torn to pieces by Professor Richard Evans, who subjected Irving's entire opus to careful scrutiny and identified a number of factual errors, distortions, manipulations, and mystifications. He simply denied him the title of historian:

> It may seem an absurd semantic dispute to deny the appellation of "historian" to some one who has written two dozen books or more about historical subjects. But if we mean by historian someone who is concerned to discover the truth about the past, and to give as accurate a representation of it as possible, then Irving is not a historian ... Irving is essentially an ideologue who uses history for his own political purposes; he is not primarily concerned with discovering and interpreting what happened in the past, he is concerned merely to give a selective and tendentious account of it in order to further his own ideological ends in the present. The true historian's primary concern, however, is with the past. That is why, in the end, Irving is not a historian.[41]

As the attempts by Irving to refute Evans' findings in the course of cross-examination failed, his reputation as a scholar was badly damaged— nor was it salvaged by the unwilling and unenthusiastic testimonies of his own expert witnesses.

Interestingly enough, both of the otherwise bitterly opposed sides agreed on one thing: that the trial was not about history, but about the way Irving was interpreting it. Irving stated that "this trial is not really about what happened in the Holocaust." The defense attorney proclaimed that "this is obviously an important case, but that is not however because it is primarily concerned with whether or not the Holocaust took place or the degree of Hitler's responsibility for it." The judge also maintained that "this trial is not concerned with making findings of historical facts." He reemphasized this position in the opening of the judgment: "it is not for me to form, still less to express, a judgment about what happened. That is a task for historians."[42] However, as in the Lewis case, the judgment contained a strongly historicized verdict, worth quoting at some length, for it undoubtedly captures the moment in which a revisionist was transformed into a "revisionist" and the border of academic discourse was deemed to have been crossed:

> I have found that most of the Defendants' historiographical criticisms of Irving set out in section V of this judgement are justified. In the vast majority of those instances the effect of what Irving has written has been to portray Hitler in a favourable light and to divert blame from him onto others ... Mistakes and misconceptions such as these appear to me by their nature unlikely to have been innocent. They are more consistent with a willingness on Irving's part knowingly to misrepresent or manipulate or put a "spin" on the evidence so as to make it conform with his own preconceptions. In my judgment the nature of these misstatements and misjudgments by Irving is a further pointer towards the conclusion that he has deliberately skewed the evidence to bring it into line with his political beliefs ... The double standards which Irving adopts to some of the documents and to some of the witnesses appears to me to be further evidence that Irving is seeking to manipulate the evidence rather than approaching it as a dispassionate, if sometimes mistaken, historian ... In my view the Defendants have established that Irving has a political agenda. It is one which, it is legitimate to infer, disposes him, where he deems it necessary, to manipulate the historical record in order to make it conform with his political beliefs ... Irving has for his own ideological reasons persistently and deliberately misrepresented and manipulated historical evidence; that for the same reasons he has portrayed Hitler in an unwarrantedly favourable light, principally in relation to his attitude towards and responsibility for the treatment of the Jews; that he is an active Holocaust denier; that he is anti-Semitic and racist and that he associates with right-wing extremists who promote neo-Nazism.[43]

These long quotations are only excerpts from a devastating verdict over 300 pages long, which was clearly in favor of the defendants and disastrous for Irving's reputation. In the aftermath of the trial he spent some time recuperating as an academic outcast, desperately trying to retrieve some of his credentials, and radicalizing his standpoint in a way which eventually brought him to a Vienna prison cell, in which he apparently wrote a book about his clashes with the law entitled *Irving's War*.[44] Since the end of 2006, Irving has been free, but it seems that his career as a scholar has come to an end.

The Irving–Lipstadt case attracted considerable media attention. Much of it focused on the phenomenon of legal limitations on historical interpretations.[45] Numerous comments showed unease over the courtroom demarcation between legitimate and illegitimate revision. David Robson noted that "a libel court is somewhere to fight battles, score points and collect damages. But for seekers of light, understanding and historical truth, it is very often not the place to look." Neal Ascherson observed that in a trial "fragments of history are snatched out of context, dried, treated and used as firelighters to scorch an adversary … for establishing what really happened in history, English libel court is the worst place in the world." Daniel Jonah Goldhagen wrote that "the ruling of a court has no bearing on historical fact: the court is a place where legal issues are adjudicated according to the particular standards of a given country, not where historical issues are decided according to the different and well-established standards of historical scholarship."[46]

Richard Evans expressed a different, more optimistic view, enumerating the reasons why the court seemed an appropriate place to fight this methodological battle. He argued that during legal proceedings the participants are not subject to constraints of time and space, as is frequently the case in academic debates. Further, he claimed that in court, unlike in scholarly debate, it is not so easy to evade the debated questions. Finally, he pointed out that the rules of evidence in court, at least in civil cases, are not so unlike the historical rules of evidence.[47] This view is however, countered by a short remark by Simone Veil, warning that "one cannot impose a historical truth by law." Can one? The cases summarized above show that one can. But should it happen? The question remains open for discussion. It would surely be tempting to assess the best ways to combat revisionism, or to work out whether trials are the proper way to do so. However, this issue is beyond the scope of this paper, for it is likely to remain, in the words of Michael Marrus, a "serious question, upon which the people of goodwill seriously disagree."[48] It is worth mentioning though, that 2007 has started with precisely such disagreements, following the German initiative for the criminalization of the Holocaust denial at the level of the European Union and the Resolution of the United Nations General Assembly calling upon member states to suppress Holocaust denial.

CONCLUSION

As Napoleon once said, "history is the version of the past events that people have decided to agree upon." It would be professional blindness to maintain that the people in question are necessarily historians. They might easily be jurists or politicians. And they reach agreement in accordance with their own disciplinary requirements. The complexities of the cases described above demonstrate that the legal delineation between legitimate and illegitimate interpretations of the past is a global venture which takes very different shapes in particular local contexts. Hence generalized conclusions would most likely fail to honor the complexity of the entanglement between history and the law. They would also lack sensitivity towards the circumstances in which particular cases appear and would not give substantial information on the influence court activity actually has on communities of historians. However, outlining some general trends and posing a question or two might provide avenues for more structured discussion.

It is fairly obvious that criminal prosecution of Holocaust denial is more likely to happen within the realm of continental legal traditions. Although one of the most interesting such cases took place in Canada, the problems it encountered and the eventual extradition of Zündel to Germany, where he was promptly locked away and now awaits a verdict, support this conclusion. Similarly, the legal entanglements of David Irving, who served as an expert witness in the Zündel case, lost a libel suit, his money, and his reputation in Great Britain, but remained a free man until his arrest in Austria in November 2005, strongly indicate that leniency towards revisionism is more likely to be found in common law countries. How is this so? Several possible interpretations might be put forward for discussion. It is hard to neglect the fact that the borders of Hitler's Fortress Europe largely corresponded to the borders of continental Europe, whereas the classic common law countries, such as Great Britain and the United States, remained out of his grasp. Might it be that the countries which had more immediate experience of Nazi occupation and domestic collaboration have a particular take on the issues of the revision of that part of their past, whereas the more remote position of the non-continental jurisdictions allows them a more relaxed approach? That argument, however, could also be historically turned around into the research question: why was the German conquest so successful precisely in the realm of continental law?

Further inspection of the legal context of the cases brings us closer to the relevance of the trials for historiography. Why do some of the trials roll on in silence, whereas others constitute public events? In this respect, the difference between adversarial and inquisitorial legal procedure is revealing. In an inquisitorial proceeding, generally typical of continental law (with the notable exception of France), the role of the judge in the process is immense. The judge is not only the arbiter of the case, but also a very active fact-finder, as the underlying philosophy of the inquisitorial trial is a common quest for the truth, upon which a certain law is to be applied. In contrast, the typical adversarial, common-law based trial presupposes the detachment of the judge, who is primarily supposed to observe that the rules and procedures are properly observed by the contesting parties. In such cases, the truth is supposed to evolve from frequently disparate accounts given by the parties. The consequences of these differences are important. In an inquisitorial trial considerable segments of the case are handled in written form, frequently *in camera*, whereas the adversarial case is usually characterized by a public demonstration of the evidence and has a theatrical aspect to it. Hence cases handled in the inquisitorial legal system are not likely to turn the courtroom into a history classroom. The adversarial system has that potential, displayed both in criminal and civil cases, as demonstrated in the Zündel and Irving cases.

Juridical activity in the delineation of proper scholarship is an important reminder of a simple fact too easily neglected by contemporary epistemological debates. Historiography does not operate in isolation from the rest of society. It represents a social practice which is entangled, harmonized or contrasted, and finally, accountable to the other powerful factors which shape our reality. Wrestling with the problem of the proper interpretation of the past, the courts could not allow themselves abstract detachment. By and large, they had to resort to a strikingly plain criterion. What was necessary was to assess the intentions of the accused. If he was committing factual mistakes or errors in judgment in good faith, mere carelessness would not make him a denier. Bad intentions and deliberately deluding the public would. This differentiation between benevolent and malevolent writing, which bravely ignores Roland Barthes' dictum on the death of the author, is in fact not as unsophisticated as it may seem. It rests on a minimalist, yet effective epistemological presupposition that in a given system one might not necessarily have to know the truth to be able to recognize a lie. Such a demarcation line was drawn in distinguishing revisionists from "revisionists." At the same time, this line represents the edge of the credible academic position.

NOTES

1 Contributions by the participants of that conference are published in the collective volume: Saul Friedlander, ed., *Probing the Limits of Representation: Nazism and the "Final Solution"* (Cambridge, Mass: Harvard University Press, 1992). The link between postmodernism and Holocaust denial was further tackled and refuted by Robert Eaglestone, *Postmodernism and Holocaust Denial* (Cambridge: Icon Book, 2001).

2 The dilemmas of distinguishing the narrow and wider understanding of historiographical revisionism are exposed in Brigitte Bailer-Galanda, *"Revisionism" in Germany and Austria: the Evolution of a Doctrine,* www.doew.at/information/mitarbeiter/ beitraege/revisionism.html, (25 September, 2006). The sort of revisionism scrutinized in this article is increasingly being labeled as "revisionism" (in the USA) or negationism (in France). For a detailed account on negationism see Valérie Igounet, *Histoire du négationnisme en France* [History of negationism in France] (Paris: Seuil, 2000).

3 Mark Weber, *Freedom for Europe's Prisoners of Conscience! Irving Zundel, Rudolf Still in Prison* (16 November, 2006), www.ihr.org/news/061112_prisoners_of_conscience. shtml (22 October, 2006).

4 Article 231 and related parts of the Versailles treaty were based on the findings of the international "Commission on the Responsibility of the Authors of the War and on Enforcement of Penalities," *American Journal of International Law*, Vol. 14, No. 1 (January–April, 1920): 95–154.

5 For more about the impact of this debate, see Anthony D'Agostino, "The Revisionist Tradition in European Diplomatic History," *The Journal of The Historical Society*, Vol 4, No. 2 (2004): 255–287. The complex web of interdependency between such scholarly attempts and predominant political moods is revealed in contributions by Holger H. Herwig, Herman Witthens, Ellen L. Evans and Joseph O. Bazlen, collected in: Keith Wilson, ed., *Forging the Collective Memory. Government and International Historians through Two World Wars* (Providence, Oxford: Bergham Books, 1996), pp. 87–177.

6 Comparative overviews of the postwar retribution in Europe: Claudia Kuretsidis-Haider and Winfried R Garscha, eds., *Keine "Abrechnung." NS-Verbrechen, Justiz und Gesellschaft in Europa nach 1945* [No "Settlement." NS crimes, justice and society in Europe after 1945] (Leipzig, Wien: Akademische Verlagsanstalt, 1998); Klaus-Dietmar Henke, et al., *Politische Säuberung in Europa* [Political cleansing in Europe] (Munich: München Verlag 1991); István Deák, Jan T. Gross, and Tony Judt, eds., *The Politics of Retribution in Europe: World War II and its aftermath* (Princeton, NJ: Princeton University Press, 2000).

7 Quoted in Robert E. Connot, *Justice at Nuremberg* (New York: Carroll & Graf, 1988), p. xiii.

8 Lawrence Douglas, *The Memory of Judgement. Making Law and History in the Trials of the Holocaust* (New Heaven, London: Yale University Press, 2001), p. 2.

9 A.J.P. Taylor, *The Origins of the Second World War* (Middlesex: Penguin Books, 1961), pp. 68–72.

10 Mark Osiel, *Mass Atrocity, Collective Memory, and the Law* (New Brunswick, London: Transaction Publishers, 2000). Michael Marrus, "History and the Holocaust in the Courtroom" in: Ronald Smelser, ed., *Lessons and Legacies V. Holocaust and Justice* (Evanston, Illinois: Northwestern University Press, 2002), p. 235.

11 Maurice Bardéche's entrance into the limelight is analyzed by Igounet, *Histoire du négationnisme en France*, pp. 37–60. He is singled out as the forerunner of contemporary revisionists both by Deborah Lipstadt, *Denying the Holocaust: The Growing Assault on Truth and Memory* (New York: Free Press, 1992), p. 50, and by Bailer-Galanda, *"Revisionism" in Germany and Austria*.

12 Revisionists did find a foothold in this approach, whose last word is David Irving's *Nuremberg: The Last Battle* (London: Focal Point, 1996). This book delivered sharp blows both to the legality and the legitimacy of the Nuremberg proceedings, and is in dire need of factual scrutiny as many aspects of the book were criticized by the established scholar on Nuremberg, Ann Tusa, *Guilty on Falsifying History*, www.nizkor.org/ftp.cgi/people/i/irving.david/press/Electric_Telegraph.961109 (20 October, 2006).

13 Both authors attempted to systematize the typical strategies of denial: Pierre Vidal-Naquet, *Assassins of Memory. Essays on the Denial of the Holocaust* (New York: Columbia University Press, 1992), pp. 18–24; Deborah Lipstadt, *Denying the Holocaust*, pp. 21–27.

14 IHR, *A Few Facts About the Institute for Historical Review*, www.ihr.org/main/about.shtml (5 October, 2006)

15 About the legal fight against revisionism in Germany via criminal law, see Robert A. Kahn, *The Holocaust Denial and the Law* (New York: Palgrave, 2004), pp. 65–84. About the role of the "Auschwitz lie" in revisionist discourse, see Brigitte Bailer-Galinda, Wolfgang Benz, Wolfgang Neugebauer, eds., *Die Auschwitzleugner: revisionistische Geschichtslüge und historische Wahrheit* [Layers about Auschwitz: revisionist historical lies and the historical truth] (Berlin: Elefanten Press, 1996). The law against the "Auschwitz lie" is commented on and debated in Eric Stein, "History Against Free Speech: The New German Law Against the 'Auschwitz' and Other 'Lies'," *Michigan Law Review*, Vol. no. 85 (1986); "On the 'Auschwitz Lie'," *Michigan Law Review*, Vol. 87, No. 5 (April, 1989): 1026–1032.

16 More about the juridical dealing with the Nazi past in Austria in several contributions in Claudia Kuretsidis-Haider, Winfrid R. Garscha, eds., *Keine "Abrechnung,"* pp. 16–128.

17 Henry Rousso maintains that the postwar purge of Nazi collaborators and Vichy loyalists was followed by widespread public oblivion regarding the issues of the Second World War, which in turn reappeared with particular forcefulness after 1968, and again in the late 1980s. The main phases of this development are outlined in his *The Vichy Syndrome* (Cambridge, Mass: Harvard University Press, 1991), pp. 220–227.

18 Verges's strategy is analyzed in Douglas, *The Memory of Judgement*, pp. 207–9. Among the examples of such reactions in juridical terms, French General Paul Aussaresses, veteran of the Algerian war, was convicted in 2002 for justifying the implementation of torture during his operations in Algeria in his memoirs. The grounds for

his conviction were found in a 1881 law on the media. The case is analyzed by Stiina Löytömäki, "Legalization of the Memory of the Algerian War in France," *Journal of the History of International Law* Vol. 7, (2005): 157–179.

19 Legifrance, *Loi Gayssot*, www.legifrance.gouv.fr/WAspad/UnTexteDeJorf?numjo= JUSX9010223L (20 October, 2006). Gayssot Law is commented on and its application is described in: R. Kahn, *The Holocaust Denial and the Law*, pp. 94–117. The circumstances under which it was passed are described in Igounet, *Histoire du négationnisme en France,* pp. 444–446. The text of the law: Legifrance, *Loi Gayssot* www.legifrance. gouv.fr/WAspad/UnTexteDeJorf?numjo=JUSX9010223L (20 October, 2006).

20 Council of Europe, *Treaties*, (29 January, 2003) http://conventions.coe.int/Treaty/ en/Treaties/Html/189.htm (20 October, 2006).

21 The Zündel judgment and related material are available at: The Nizkor Project, Supreme Court of Canada, *1992 Zündel Judgement*, www.nizkor.org/hweb/people/z/ zundel-ernst/supreme-court/1992-preliminary-version.html, (20 October, 2006).

22 For more about Chomsky's involvement, see P. Vidal-Naquet, *Assassins of Memory,* pp. 65–73.

23 Jerusalem Centre for Public Affairs, *Denial of the Holocaust and Moral Equivalence. An Interview with Deborah Lipstadt* (1 August, 2003) www.jcpa.org/phas/phas-11.htm (20 October, 2006).

24 Robert Faurisson, *Letter to Christopher Hitchens*, October 5, 1994, www.vho.org/ aaargh/engl/FaurisArch/RF941005.html (20 October, 2006).

25 For a recent critical overview see Gerard Alexander, "Illiberal Europe," *Weekly Standard* Vol. 11, issue 28, (10 April, 2006), www.weeklystandard.com/Content/Public/ Articles/000/000/012/055sbhvq.asp (20 October, 2006).

26 Several such initiatives are mentioned in Christopher Caldwell, "Historical Truth Speaks for Itself," *Financial Times* (19 February, 2006) www.christusrex.org/ www1/news/ft-2-20-06a.html (20 October, 2006).

27 Timothy Garton Ash, "This is the Moment for Europe to dismantle taboos, not to erect them," *The Guardian* (19 October, 2006).

28 About the case: R. Kahn, *The Holocaust Denial and the Law*, pp. 22–31.

29 Ira Moskowitz, "U.S.-born Professor Guilty of Libeling Colleague," *Haaretz* (9 June, 2006).

30 The variety of approaches to Nazism is masterfully analyzed in Ian Kershaw, *The Nazi Dictatorship. Problems and Perspectives of Interpretation* (New York: Oxford University Press, 2000).

31 The case of Bernard Lewis became an important tool in on-going Turkish and Armenian wars of memory. Consequently, Internet information on the event shows considerable bias. Noteworthy exception: *The Bernard Lewis Trial*, www.ids.net/ ~gregan/lewis.html (20 October, 2006).

32 The Bernard Lewis Trial, "Judgment Rendered 21 June, 1995," p. 12, www.ids.net/ ~gregan/dec_eng.html (20 October, 2006).

33 Ibid., p. 14.

34 About the case: R. Kahn, *The Holocaust Denial and the Law*, pp. 85–94; Deborah Lipstadt, *Denying the Holocaust,* pp. 157–177.

35 Excerpts from Hilberg's cross-examination appear in Lawrence Douglas, *The Memory of Judgement*, pp. 230–238.

36 Christopher Browning talks about his experience in the witness box in *Holocaust Denial in the Courtroom: The Historian as Expert Witness*, www.plu.edu/~lutecast/2004/20041014-lemkin.html.

37 Abundant material on the case is available at Holocaust Denial on Trial, Transcripts, Day 01, *Opening Statements by Richard Rampton and David Irving*, p. 34, www.hdot.org/ieindex.html.

38 All the reports are accessible on Holocaust Denial on Trial, *Evidence*, (Richard J. Evans, *David Irving, Hitler and the Holocaust Denial*; Hajo Funke, *David Irving, Holocaust Denial, and his Connections to Right Wing Extremists and Neo-National Socialism in Germany*; Christopher Browning, *Evidence for the Implementation of the Final Solution*; Peter Longerich, *Hitler's Role in the Persecution of the Jews by the Nazi Regime* and *The Systematic Character of the National Socialist Policy for the Extermination of the Jews*; *The Van Pelt Report*) www.hdot.org/ieindex.html (20 October, 2006).

39 D.D. Guttenplan, *The Holocaust on Trial* (New York: W.W. Norton, 2001), p. 16.

40 Quoted in Richard Evans, *Lying about Hitler* (New York: Basic Books, 2002), p. 110.

41 Holocaust Denial on Trial, Richard Evans, David Irving, *Hitler and Holocaust Denial*, 6.21 www.holocaustdenialontrial.org/evidence/evans006.asp (20 October, 2006).

42 Quotes from D.D. Guttenplan, *The Holocaust on Trial*, pp. 29, 34, 30, 274. Irving's mistakes during the trial are analyzed by Yale F. Edeiken, *Irving's War*, www.holocaust-history.org/irvings-war/ (20 October, 2006).

43 Holocaust Denial on Trial, *Judgment*, XIII, Findings on Justification 13141, 13.144. 13.151, 13.162, 13.167, www.hdot.org/ieindex.html (20 October, 2006).

44 David Irving, *Vienna Imprisonment*, www.codoh.com/irving/irvvienna.html (20 October, 2006).

45 Media coverage of the trial was a subject of a survey: Dan Yurman, "The News media and Holocaust Denial," *Idea*, Vol. 5, No. 9, (24 May, 2000), www.ideajournal.com/articles.php?id=23 (20 October, 2006).

46 These critical approaches are assembled in Richard Evans, *Lying about Hitler*, pp. 186–187.

47 Ibid., pp. 188–191.

48 Michael Marrus, "History and the Holocaust in the Courtroom," p. 227.

"The Holocaustizing of the Transfer-Discourse"

Historical Revisionism or Old Wine in New Bottles?

EVA HAHN AND HANS HENNING HAHN

"My views are quite explicitly stated: the Holocaust was the most extreme atrocity in human history, and we lose our humanity if we are even willing to enter the arena of debate with those who seek to deny or underplay Nazi crimes."[1] Noam Chomsky's 1992 assertion would not be challenged openly in Germany today. However, even though the uniqueness of the Holocaust remains undisputed, comparisons between Nazi crimes and supposedly similar crimes allegedly committed by the Allies after World War II are also widely accepted in current German rhetoric. During the last couple of years the media have repeatedly claimed that debating the *Vertreibung* (expulsion) has been taboo until now, and that German "victims" of the Allies' policies should be commemorated in the same way as the victims of Nazi war crimes. Calls for a "new" form of collective memory are common, and many Germans believe that changes are necessary in order to "normalize" German historical consciousness. These attempts to revise the popular understanding of World War II and its aftermath are not openly presented as a debate about National Socialism, but as a debate about the resettlement of the German population from Eastern Europe during and after the war. In particular, this debate focuses on the *Vertreibung* of Germans from areas which had belonged to *Großdeutsches Reich*, the Nazi-enlarged German Reich, during the war and to Poland and Czechoslovakia afterwards.

These recent debates about the *Vertreibung* represent a more significant issue than another mere discussion about the past. Most Germans would agree with this statement, as voices suggesting that the *Vertreibung* is a European issue are heard regularly, and many Germans assert that the *Vertreibung* should be commemorated as a "European tragedy" in a "European manner."[2] The driving political force behind the new trend is the *Bund der Vertriebenen,*[3] an organization that is generally regarded as the political representation of the expellees. However, this kind of "Europeanization" of the *Vertreibung* has been called for from all sides of the present political spectrum in Germany. The term "European" might be more often spoken about than thought of in Germany, but there are good reasons why these debates do indeed appear significant for the whole of Europe.

Poland and the Czech Republic are directly connected with the recent debates about the *Vertreibung* because the popular views of Polish history stand together with those of Czech history in the focus of all these debates. Moreover, the major role played by the United States, Great Britain and the Soviet Union in those events indicates that the histories of these three states also belong to the issue. The discussion indicates that there is a close connection between popular ways of remembering the *Vertreibung* on the one hand, and remembering the Holocaust on the other.[4] The present development of collective memory in Germany will therefore have direct repercussions on the future understanding of the nature of the Holocaust and its historical interpretation. This concerns not only Europeans, but also Jews in general, and the state of Israel in particular. Moreover, the United Nations declared in 2005 that 27 January should become "International Day of Commemoration in Memory of the Victims of the Holocaust," and therefore the question of how the Holocaust is remembered naturally does matter for both the historical consciousness and the political future of all of Europe and beyond.

The issue of the *Vertreibung* is considered in Germany as an issue of national identity. In 1999, the *Bund der Vertriebenen* demanded that a national memorial should be created in Berlin to commemorate the *Vertreibung* so that this part of collective memory would become one of the pillars of German national identity. This proposal aroused new interest in the topic of the *Vertreibung* and calls for a "new" form of collective memory. In 2002, the German parliament expressed support for the idea that a new memorial to the *Vertreibung* should be created, even though the politicians disagreed over what the memorial should look like.[5] This decision of the *Bundestag* inspired wide-ranging discussion, but the main controversy involved only the two major political parties, the Christian–Democratic Union and its Bavarian section, the Christian–Social Union (CDU/CSU), and the Social Democratic Party of Germany (SPD); each side favored a different project. The CDU/CSU endorsed the plan for a *Zentrum gegen Vertreibungen*[6] (Center against Expulsions) proposed by the national organization of expellees. The SPD endorsed Markus Meckel's 2003 proposal that a *Europäisches Zentrum gegen Vertreibungen, Zwangsaussiedlungen und Deportationen* (European Center against

Expulsions, Forced Resettlements and Deportations) should be created.[7] However, both projects are based on the common understanding that the *Vertreibung* was a crime of "ethnic cleansing," committed by the Allies in 1945 and inspired by the same ideas which had led the Nazi regime to the Holocaust, and that about 15 million Germans are to be remembered as victims of the *Vertreibung*.

The "new" way of remembering the *Vertreibung* was obviously inspired by discussions about the Holocaust Memorial, which was erected in Berlin in 2005, but had been a subject for debate among the German public throughout the 1990s. With respect to the commemoration of the *Vertreibung* in a new way, the public expressed a wide range of opinions and attitudes, from the extreme right to the extreme left. However, this fact has not been reflected in the major media, which focus on politically significant issues rather than on the arguments presented. Voices critical of both projects for a state-funded memorial have been widely excluded from the media, and their arguments seldom heard in public. Not even the international petition *For a Critical and Enlightened Debate about the Past*, signed in 2003 by 116 scholars and intellectuals from 12 countries,[8] has been brought to the attention of the public. Consequently, the reasons for wide-spread criticism of this new development are not understood by many Germans. The stereotype that only "the Poles" and "the Czechs" raise objections has become popular, even though the major daily, *Frankfurter Allgemeine Zeitung,* accused critics from "East Central Europe" collectively of just copying "West German left wing intellectuals."[9] The new German government, a coalition of the two major parties mentioned above, announced in 2005 that the national memorial commemorating the *Vertreibung* should be created in Berlin during its term of office. It should become an expression of "new" ways of remembering the *Vertreibung* in Germany, and therefore, the study of this issue from the point of view of historical revisionism has become an issue of major importance both for Germany and for the international community.

***

A brief overview of the historical events labeled in Germany as *Vertreibung* might be helpful for an understanding of the subject of this essay.[10] The word *Vertreibung* is a designation which sums up the results of four major steps towards the resettlement of German minorities in Eastern Europe in the years 1939–1949. In 1949, there were about 11 million Germans in Germany, who had lived in areas east of the new German–Polish borders before World War II, and about 3.5 million Germans remained in their homes.[11] The resettlement took place in the following four stages:

- Between 1939 and 1944, the Nazi Regime resettled around one million Germans from the Baltic States, the Soviet Union, Hungary, Romania and Yugoslavia. These people were moved from their homes primarily to German-occupied territories in Poland, but also to occupied Czechoslovakia and Austria.
- Between August 1944, and 8 May 1945, around six million Germans, mostly women, children, and sick and old people (including the previously resettled Germans) were subjected to the Evacuation Orders of the German authorities in the areas east of the Oder–Neiße-Line, as the plans of the Allied governments for the future German frontiers became known to Nazi officials (on 1 January 1945, Hitler informed the German public of this in his New Year's Order[12]).
- In the first postwar months, the liberated western areas of Poland and northern Czechoslovakia were in a lawless state after the German authorities retreated. During this period, about one million Germans from Poland (partly the evacuees) and approximately 730,000 from Czechoslovakia became victims of arbitrary expulsions. At the same time, millions of previously evacuated German civilians found themselves homeless and their future status unclear.
- At the Potsdam Conference in 1945, the United States, Great Britain, and the Soviet Union declared their intention to resettle the remaining parts of the German population from Poland, Czechoslovakia and Hungary. By the provisions of these three occupying powers, 1.9 million people were resettled from Poland in 1946; 500,000 in 1947; and 76,000 in 1948/49.[13] 2.2 million Germans were transferred from Czechoslovakia in 1946.[14] 120,000 Germans left Hungary in 1946, and another 50,000 in the following two years.[15] 160,000 Germans left Austria during 1946.[16]

All these events have been blurred by the common German usage of the word *Vertreibung*, creating a major obstacle to a factual and analytic approach to the topic. To understand the German debates on the *Vertreibung* the following two points must be kept in mind. First, the *Vertriebene*, the expellees, were partly removed from their homes in Eastern Europe by the German authorities before the end of World War II and partly by the Allies after the end of the war. Second, the three occupying powers authorized the transfer of German populations from Poland, Czechoslovakia and Hungary, the vast majority of whom—in fact all except about 200,000 Germans from Hungary—had been citizens of the *Großdeutsches Reich*, the Nazi-enlarged German Reich. The decision taken by the Allies was not part of an attempt to apply any universally comprehended principles of ethnic homogeneity, but a strictly limited decision as part of their postwar policies towards Germany.

***

In Germany, the word *Vertreibung* does not designate these events which took place between 1939 and 1949 or distinguish between the various ways in which the expellees arrived in postwar Germany. The *Vertreibung* has traditionally been remembered in Germany as an event from the end of World War II and the postwar period only.[17] The numbers of "victims" of the *Vertreibung* used in the media and specialized literature vary between 5 and 20 million, and it is often claimed that 2.5 million German civilians lost their lives during the *Vertreibung.* The historical narrative is usually based on three images representing the *Vertreibung*. It begins by mentioning the flight and plight of German civilians from the Soviet occupied territories between late 1944 and early 1945, focusing on the atrocities committed by Soviet soldiers. Secondly, the term "wild expulsions" is used to characterize the fate of German civilians between May 1945 and late summer 1945, when atrocities committed by Polish and Czechoslovak citizens are in focus. Thirdly, the transfers supervised by the USA, Great Britain, and the Soviet Union from 1946 to 1949 are considered as the next stage of the *Vertreibung*, but they are not usually paid much attention in the traditional narrative. In addition to this, the German term expellees has been also used to designate people who moved voluntarily from Eastern Europe to the Federal Republic of Germany between 1949 and 1993.

The *Vertreibung* has been one of the central topics of collective memory in the FRG since the state was founded in 1949. Besides National Socialism, there is hardly any historical issue which has been discussed and reflected upon so often. There are places of commemoration in nearly every German town, scholarly research on this topic has been widespread from the very beginning, as has its reflection in literature and public discussion. The recent discussions on the *Vertreibung* can be traced back to a revived interest in Germany after the fall of the communist regime. During the 1990s, German politicians, media and the organizations of expellees exported their ideas into neighboring countries in Central Europe. Their principle targets were Poland and the Czech Republic, where over

90 percent of the expellees came from. In these countries, the topic aroused great interest and inspired controversies as well as numerous research projects and publications throughout the 1990s. In other European countries, interest did not develop to the same extent.

The ways in which the *Vertreibung* is commemorated in Germany have always been subjected to criticism. To understand the controversies accompanying the public discourse on the *Vertreibung*, we have to distinguish between two aspects: first, the history and the political demands directed by the German state at Poland and Czechoslovakia since 1949; and second, the history of the public understanding, interpretations and forms of commemoration in the FRG between 1949 and 1989. These two aspects are closely interconnected.

In the German Democratic Republic, the decisions taken by the Allied powers in 1945 were never questioned, but governments of the Federal Republic since 1949 have maintained a different position with respect to the interpretation of the *Vertreibung.* They claim that the expulsion of the German population from Poland and Czechoslovakia was illegal, that it constitutes a crime against humanity, and that it should be revised. The term *Vertreibung* is often used together with the words *Vernichtung* or *Völkermord* (extermination or genocide). A large majority of German politicians have striven since 1949 for the restitution of (or at least compensation for) lost territories, citizens' rights, and property from Poland and the Czech Republic. In particular, the Federal Republic adopted revisionist policies towards the German–Polish border as established *de facto* in 1945. As the British historian Elizabeth Wiskemann observed in 1956, it was not easy for many Germans to understand the situation in Germany after World War II:

> In the "smash-and-grab" land game which has gone on between Poles and Germans through the ages, and whose present phase may be regarded as dating from the partitions of Poland at the end of the 18th century, the Germans had now lost two rounds: the Second World War had deprived them of far more land—one measure of national power—than the first, and drawn a frontier *de facto* which (certainly in terms of earlier conceptions) had a greater air of finality.[18]

The political efforts to achieve a revision of the Potsdam Treaty were more rhetorical exercises than real political actions, and a number of these efforts were supported by various sections of the population between 1949 and 1989. The fall of the communist regimes led to a revival of expectations during the 1990s. The German–Polish border was accepted finally in 1990/91, but demands for the restitution of property owned by German citizens before the end of World War II appeared reasonable to major parts of the German public up to 2004, when the government of Gerhard Schröder distanced itself from the issue. Most other politicians joined Schröder and stopped calling for material restitutions and compensation even though the state still gives financial and political support to organizations which continue to pursue such claims. Germany has not succeeded in pressing Poland or the Czech Republic into any concessions. The position of these two states concerning the legality of the decision endorsed in Potsdam in summer 1945 has been confirmed by all three powers, as indicated by, for example, the official statement of the US Information Service of 14 February, 1996: "The decisions made at Potsdam by the governments of the United States, the United Kingdom, and the Soviet Union in July and August, 1945 were soundly based in international law... The conclusions of the Potsdam Conference are historical fact and the United States is confident that no country wishes to call them into question."[19] However, the traditionally common interpretations of the *Vertreibung* in Germany have been part of the unsuccessful attempts to reverse the postwar decisions of the Allies.

The second aspect of the recent debates on the *Vertreibung* in Germany concerns the emergence of the so-called "new" historical interpretations of the *Vertreibung*. Because of the political experience summarized above, all public discussion in this field has always been highly politicized. Since the fall of the communist regimes, the topic of the *Vertreibung* has aroused great interest in Poland and in the Czech Republic, and international cooperation among German, Polish and Czech historians has led to numerous new studies. In spite of the lively research and discussion on the topic throughout the 1990s, the so-called "new" ways of collective memory in Germany emerged after 1999 and it is this way of collective remembrance which has provoked considerable criticism in Germany, as well as in Poland and, to a lesser degree, in the Czech Republic. Criticism was leveled against this development because it is perceived as a dangerous process of reinterpretation of 20th-century German and European history. Many critics argue that we are confronted with historical revisionism in the sense of a politically motivated approach that downgrades or denies essential historical facts concerning the Nazi regime and its crimes.

In Germany, the reasons why commentators have raised the idea of revisionism have generally not been understood. However, the notion of rewriting history, *Revision der Geschichte*, has become a topic that appears regularly in the media. Its significance today is indicated, for example, by the speech given by President Horst Köhler on 2 September 2006. Speaking to some 1,000 representatives of 21 expellee organizations on the main commemoration day in Germany devoted to the *Vertreibung,* the so-called *Tag der Heimat* (The Day of the Homeland), Köhler said: "We have to make clear in a patient way that there is no political force which should be taken seriously that would strive to rewrite history."[20] According to this and numerous other statements, we should not look for any form of historical revisionism in present-day Germany.

Such statements are surprising because since 1999, the German media and many German commentators have stressed that a change in German historical consciousness has taken place, that Germans are "at last free" to speak about German suffering during and after World War II. Who should have prevented "the Germans" from speaking about their sufferings in the free and democratic FRG has never been clarified, but even the famous German weekly magazine *Spiegel* demonstrates how popular this idea has become: in 2003, the magazine announced that "a new climate" had emerged in Germany, because it had now become possible to speak about topics which had been previously taboo.[21] These two topics were "the Germans as victims" and "the Bombing of Germany," and two series of articles were published: the first devoted to the *Vertreibung*, and the second to the air raids during World War II. No new information was presented by the magazine, but comparisons between the Nazi regime and the Allies were made in a more explicit way than in earlier times.

This new fashion aroused attention around the world. Even *Wikipedia* brought the new developments on the topic of expulsion to the attention of the international public, describing them as follows:

In the early 1990s, the Cold War ended and the occupying powers withdrew from Germany. The issue of the treatment of Germans after World War II began to be re-examined, having previously been overshadowed by Nazi Germany's war crimes. The primary motivation for this change was the collapse of the Soviet Union, which allowed for issues previously marginalized, such as the crimes committed by the Soviet Army during the World War II, to be raised.

In November and December 1993, an exhibit on Ethnic Cleansing 1944–1948 was held at the Stuart Centre of De Paul University, in Chicago, where it was called an unknown holocaust, which had been forgotten about. Reports have surfaced of both Czech nationalist as well as Soviet massacres of German civilians (see the book *A Terrible Revenge*). Also, some of the former German concentration camps were used as temporary camps for German civilians.[22]

This passage, and many other texts,[23] indicate that some kind of rewriting of history is in progress in spite of all attempts to deny any "revisionism." What exactly is new, on what sources the so called "new" information is based, and towards what kind of changes in our understanding of European history the "new" way of writing that history is leading us, are all questions which deserve our attention. The major media in Germany have not discussed such questions. Among academic observers, the commentators belong either to the supporters of the new trend, or to its critics, but few attempts have been made to look at the "new" German historiography from a historical point of view.

***

Traditionally, numerous authors in Germany focus their interpretation of the *Vertreibung* on the crimes committed against German civilians by the Soviet Army and by Czech and Polish perpetrators during the last months of the War and its aftermath. They base their understanding of the *Vertreibung* on the idea that 15 million Germans from numerous countries in Eastern and Central Europe were victims of criminal acts committed by the Allies in general, but in particular by the Poles and the Czechs. In their view, these two nations bear the main responsibility for the *Vertreibung*, partly shared by the three powers. These authors do not attempt to explore and describe the events which brought the expellees from their original homes in Eastern Europe to postwar Germany or to explain why the Allies took their decisions; they concentrate rather on presenting the evidence of crimes, used as *pars in toto* evidence. Several popular symbolic representations of such crimes—place-names such as Nemmersdorf, Lamsdorf, Aussig and Brünn—accompany the common narrative without being placed in their real historical context.

In contrast, the protagonists of the "new" interpretation of the *Vertreibung* emphasize what they consider to be its "European" character. This kind of "Europeanization" of the expulsion is presented as the new understanding of history, maintaining that the *Vertreibung* was not just an event concerning the German population or nation, but rather that it has to be seen as the result of a *europäischer Irrweg* (European deviation).[24] All Europeans should remember the European history of the 20th century as a "deviation," and the Holocaust and the *Vertreibung* as two consequences of this "European deviation." Today, most German historians, politicians, and commentators advocate this so-called European way of looking at the expulsion, and they believe that European institutions should be created to guarantee the proper commemoration the *Vertreibung* as a European tragedy and to teach Europeans about it as much as about the Holocaust.

These attempts to "correct" the common understanding of European history by declaring that Europe was on a "wrong" path throughout the 20th century—on the path of "European deviation"—have not yet been successful anywhere outside Germany. In the European Union, politicians have not paid any attention to the topic of the *Vertreibung*, there are few historians working in this field, and the public has not shown much interest. In 2002, the European Parliament rejected German demands concerning the "Beneš Decrees," that is the attempt to reverse the Czechoslovak legal provision on the basis of which German nationals lost Czechoslovak citizenship and their property in 1945. In 2005 the German-initiated "European Network for Studying and Commemorating the *Vertreibung*" was founded in Warsaw, but apart from Poland, Hungary and Slovakia, no other country has joined. All this might be taken to suggest that the new trend in Germany should not have provoked serious controversy, as it does not seem likely to become popular anywhere outside Germany.

What kind of controversies has the "new" interpretation of the past caused, and why? None of the critics of the "new" trend in remembering the expulsion deny that many German civilians suffered greatly during and after World War II, and no one has denied the right of Germany to commemorate the victims and the sufferings of millions of its citizens. The controversies concern the ways in which the *Vertreibung* is being historically conceptualized. When we try to assess the major issues at stake, we find two positions:

1. The representatives of the "new" interpretations use the term ethnic cleansing and believe that the expulsion of Germans was motivated by an idea which was generally accepted in Europe from the 19th century onwards and which maintained that modern national states should be ethnically homogenous. They argue that this was the reason why Armenians were mistreated in the Ottoman Empire during World War I, or why the 1923 Convention of Lausanne authorized the exchange of populations between Turkey and Greece. They contend that the Nazi regime discriminated against and killed the Jews for the same reason, and that for the same reason, the Allies in Potsdam, in 1945, made the decision to transfer the German populations from Poland, Czechoslovakia and Hungary. The Yugoslavian civil war of the 1990s is represented as having been caused by the same "mistaken" idea. All these events are labeled with the same term "ethnic cleansing," declared to be crimes against humanity and

genocide, and looked upon as major events in European history, which should be commemorated in a German national museum labeled a "Centre against Expulsions"[25] in order to "heal" Europe and prevent ethnic cleansing in the future.

2. The opponents of this concept stress the significance of the historical context of each of these events. In the case of the *Vertreibung,* they point out the unique nature of World War II as a defensive war against the brutal tyranny of the National Socialist regime and the Nazi policy of instrumentalizing the German minorities in Poland and in Czechoslovakia. Citing diplomatic documents concerning the decision-making, they stress that there is nothing to indicate that the governments of the United States, Great Britain and the Soviet Union were concerned about the ethnic homogeneity of modern European states. There is nothing to show that they would have believed in or attempted to create a new European state order based on ethnic homogeneity, or punished Germany by their decision to move the German population from the three named countries. The critics argue that the *Vertreibung* was not an example of any kind of "European deviation," but rather the consequence of Hitler's expansionistic war as well as an attempt to solve the question of the eastern border of the modern German national state. They contend that the three powers wanted to prevent any repetition of the situation in the 1930s when Germany destabilized neighboring countries and began a war in the name of German minorities in Poland and Czechoslovakia.

Among the general public in Germany, the controversy is perceived as a conflict between two popular images. First, the well-known historian and protagonist of the "new" interpretation of the expulsion, Götz Aly, entitled one of his articles *Europas Selbstzerstörung* (European self-destruction).[26] He argues that Europe was destroying itself throughout the 20th century because "ethnic cleansing" had become a fashion and had made the 20th century into a "Century of Expulsions". Therefore, we should overcome the popular understanding of National Socialism as an exceptional historical phenomenon, and place Nazi crimes, including the Holocaust, together with the *Vertreibung* in the context of general European attempts to achieve the ethnic homogeneity of modern states. Unlike Aly, former Minister for Foreign Affairs Joschka Fischer looks upon the *Vertreibung* as the result of the *Deutsche Selbstzerstörung* (German self-destruction) under National Socialism. Fischer alludes to the German

crimes against other Europeans as well as at the crimes committed by the
Nazi regime against the German population and its culture, and considers
these to be the cause of the *Vertreibung*.[27]

One could argue that such controversy about the interpretation of an
event is normal; one might wonder why it raises the issue of historical
revisionism at all. Is not every historical study a kind of revision and is
not every interpretation of an historical event controversial? Present developments in Germany indicate *prima facie* that the issue at stake is not
"new" information and a "new" assessment thereof—as indeed many
authors in Germany stress by arguing that the present writings on the *Vertreibung* are not "new" interpretations based on new discoveries, but by a
"new" way of understanding and remembering the *Vertreibung*. No one
has suggested that the "new" way of looking at the *Vertreibung* offers new
insights into past events thanks to historians who have provided us with
some new factual information and improved our knowledge of the past.
The major German media agree, and numerous historians have reiterated,
that it is the way in which this event has been recalled by the German
public during the last few years that is "new," and that therefore the topic
should be awarded a "new" status in the national identity of the German
people. In this respect, the "new" writings on the expulsion are not a legitimate reexamination of a historical narrative. Why is it that the German
president and most of the commentators in the media assert at the same
time that history is not being rewritten in Germany?

Examining the "new" writings carefully, it becomes obvious that the
recent interest in the topic of the *Vertreibung* has not been accompanied
by an interest in the event itself. Numerous new books on the *Vertreibung*
have been published in recent years in Germany, but they are not based on
new information, on new research into the experience of the expellees, or
new documents about the decision-making. Moreover, the research conducted in Czech, Polish, and other public archives since the fall of Communism has gone unnoticed, and most recent studies based on newly accessible archives have not been translated into German. When new information appears, it receives little attention in the media. Consequently, no
new questions have been asked and no contradictions have been resolved.
As a result, the public are still ignorant even of basic information about
how many Germans were expelled, by whom, and when.[28] One example
exemplifies the carelessness in dealing with even the most fundamental
information: at the Berlin commemoration of the 60th anniversary of the
end of World War II, on 8 May 2005, the head of the German Catholic
Church, Cardinal Karl Lehmann spoke of five million expellees,[29] but

when his speech was reproduced in the *Sudetendeutsche Zeitung* one week later, that number was increased to 15 million.[30]

In fact, the "new" way of writing about the *Vertreibung* indicates remarkable continuities with the traditional ways of interpreting the expulsion in the FRG. It is being said today, as it always was before, that the expulsions took place beginning in late 1944, but no difference is made between those Germans from Eastern Europe who were moved by the Nazi authorities, and those moved by the Allies after the end of the war. Little information is available to the public about the differences between the resettlement-practices of the Nazi regime and those of the Allies; consequently, the people who were resettled by the Nazi regime between 1939 and 1944 are considered *Vertriebene* (expellees), even though it is not clear who expelled them. Neither the numbers of people who were victims of crimes committed by the Nazi regime, nor of those who became victims of crimes after the end of the war has been established. Blurring all these differences leads to blurring the differences between the Nazi regime and the policies and practices of the Allies. This also belongs to the traditional ways of remembering the *Vertreibung*, but today it seems that the issue at stake in the controversies regarding expulsion in Germany is not the expulsion of the Germans but rather National Socialism. In discussing expulsion, the German public concentrates nowadays more on the interpretations of National Socialism than on the *Vertreibung* itself. The "new" writing on the expulsions represents a new approach to writing about National Socialism.

Until recently, the consensus in Germany was to consider the Nazi chapter of German history a unique phenomenon. Today, this has changed, as we have seen: the protagonists of the "new" interpretation of the expulsion stress that the German crimes committed against the Jews were unique, but they believe that the Holocaust was just one extreme consequence of the general "European deviation," that is the alleged common acceptance in 20th-century Europe of the idea that a modern state should be ethnically cleansed in order to become ethnically homogenous. Accordingly, the Nazi form of anti-Semitism is reinterpreted by the protagonists of the "new" trend as an ethnically based form of anti-Semitism, as if Jews in Germany did not belong to German ethnicity. "The Expulsion of Jews in Germany from 1933 Onwards: The Start of the Holocaust" has become a popular image today, enabling authors to suggest that the Holocaust was a part of "The National Socialists' Germanization Policy."[31] Most politicians and commentators favor this approach because, in their eyes, it offers a "European" way of looking at National Socialism. And indeed, it does offer a "new" scenario of modern European history in which National Socialism is not looked upon as a specific chapter of German history, but as the "normal" ideology and practice of a mistaken development in Europe.

With the Nazi regime interpreted as a part of "normal" European practice and the Holocaust as a brutal variation of "accepted" European criminal practices, the expulsions represent a consequence of the same ideas and practice as the Holocaust. Thus the similarities between the expulsions and the Holocaust have become the central theme of the "new" writing about the expulsions. As a result, a new term has emerged among critics of this development, "The Holocaustizing of the Transfer-Discourse."[32] Andreas F. Kelletat reminded his readers of a line from the British Daily Telegraph: "Germany breaks the Hitler taboo," and explained to what extent this observation had been justified. His essay is a most informative survey of German public imagery from the point of view of an author who would agree with Noam Chomsky about the unique nature of the Nazi crimes, but whose understanding of the *Vertreibung* certainly does not represent the common view in contemporary Germany. From this perspective, it is hardly surprising that the planned national memorial in Berlin exhibits aspects of the Holocaust Memorials in Yad Vashem and in Washington, as if Germany was determined to challenge the traditional understanding of the Holocaust as a unique atrocity against innocent people. Similarly, the "Expulsion of the Sudeten Germans" was commemorated in 2006 with the slogan *Vertreibung ist Völkermord* (Expulsion is Genocide).[33] In addition, historians such as Götz Aly call for a "new" historiography which combines the study of the *Vertreibung* and the Holocaust[34] as if they were offering academic legitimization for the "new" trend.

***

This new development is not based on new information and new ideas. In fact, the notion that the Holocaust and the *Vertreibung* are similar crimes goes back to the postwar era. Alfred Rosenberg, the famous administrator of the German-occupied territories in Eastern Europe, became the first author to propose this connection. In his memoirs, written in the prison of Nürnberg before his execution in 1946, he argued that the criminal acts committed by the Germans against the Jews should be balanced by the crimes of *Vertreibung* committed by the Allies.[35] In 1950 Eugen Lemberg, another well-known German expert in interpreting the *Vertreibung*, wrote in a similar vein: "What the Germans did to the Jews, the Poles and the Czechs did to Germans."[36] The pre-1945 Nazi historian Gotthold Rhode also proposed the idea that both the Nazi crimes and the *Vertreibung* should be viewed in the context of so-called "group migration" in Eastern Europe. His book *Völker auf dem Wege* (Nations Underway)[37] became popular in Germany in the early 1990s, and was used uncritically by Götz Aly, who recommended Rhode's book to the public for further reading in 1993.[38] In turn, Götz Aly's work has been used uncritically by many other historians, not only in Germany, but world-wide. In fact, one of the world's best known protagonists of the "new" way of remembering the *Vertreibung* has been the US historian, Norman M. Naimark. His much-translated book *Fires of Hatred: Ethnic Cleansing in Twentieth-Century Europe,*[39] played a crucial role in internationalizing the postwar German concept of "The Holocaustizing of the Transfer-Discourse." Naimark based his book on German publications, and moreover, he revived the traditional forms of German anti-Slavism with his essay "Die *Killing Fields* des Ostens" (The Killing Fields of the East).[40] In this essay he argues that the traditional history of World War II in Eastern Europe should be rewritten using images of a kind of *international killing* in Eastern Europe, in which the Nazi crimes are to be represented as just one kind of "killing" among many others since all East European nations were killing each other[41]; similarly, Götz Aly proposed that the Holocaust should be studied in the context of "European nationality wars."[42]

These observations indicate that the concept of *Vertreibung* as "ethnic cleansing" is based on ideas already popular half a century ago in post-war Germany. But these ideas have not been a popular way of remembering National Socialism and World War II until recently, and Götz Aly himself mentions that "European nations and historians have little willingness to discuss these matters."[43] Nevertheless, this perception has not inspired him to reexamine the reasons for it or the arguments of his critics; instead, Götz Aly believes that his efforts will need more "relaxation and exercise in the whole of Europe."[44] This attitude indicates that Aly is attempting to replace concepts rather than to become involved in the discussion of existing questions. To a reader well-acquainted with the historiography of the *Vertreibung* in Germany, the seemingly "new" development indicates cultural continuities with the postwar era, but at the same time also an attempt to replace the sofar common consensus concerning the interpretation of National Socialism by promoting one of the postwar concepts which have been marginalized until now. In this light, the "new" discourse on the *Vertreibung* and the Holocaust could be looked upon merely as an internal shift of balance within the history of German collective memory. Why then, should we use the term "revisionism"?

The use of the term *historical revisionism* to describe this "new" fashion is appropriate for the following reason. The "new" fashion is new because of its implications for the remembrance of National Socialism. Until now, the mainstream discourse in Germany has been based on the understanding of German responsibility for the Nazi regime. National Socialism has been considered a specific phenomenon of German history, so that a narrative which situates the *Vertreibung* as well as National Socialism in the context of so called "European historical deviation" tends to cut off National Socialism from its roots in Germany. The construction of the "new" narrative of European history in the "new" discourse on transfer suggests that the Nazi regime and the Allies are responsible for the same kind of crimes. Placing the names "Hitler, Stalin, Beneš and Churchill" next to each other and accusing them all of "ethnic cleansing" as a crime against humanity indicates that the knowledge of the history of World War II and the ability to understand the differences between democracies, the Nazi regime and Communism is still not common even among well-known German historians—such as for example Hans Lemberg, who wrote in 2001:

> The lack of understanding, indeed, the repugnance, the horror are not just directed against the many individual perpetrators, but also against those who set the population transfer—what a cold bureaucratic term for such a brutal action—in motion, whether their names were Hitler or Stalin, Beneš or Churchill.[45]

This emotional way of writing about the *Vertreibung* and lack of understanding about the historical differences between major political figures in 20th-century European history is not new in the German discourse on the *Vertreibung*, yet it is a new phenomenon in that it has been accepted by the general public in Germany and is about to become a part of German national identity.

If the term *historical revisionism* is understood as a stigmatized term, and used as a description of suspect historical works dealing with the Holocaust and the Third Reich, then the "new" writing on the *Vertreibung* surely does constitute a part of this kind of *historical revisionism*. It does not deny the Holocaust or make any direct attempt to use neo-Nazi images of the Third Reich, calling for a rehabilitation of that regime. This would be a false understanding of the problem raised by the "new" trends in the transfer discourse. The protagonists of the new trend are more outspoken about distancing themselves from the Nazi regime than their predecessors, and they emphasize the uniqueness of the Holocaust. However, by arguing that the Allies committed similar crimes based on the same idea, by presenting Nazism as a normal phenomenon within European history, and by claiming the innocence of the victims of the *Vertreibung* as they do, the protagonists of the "new" historiography are achieving the same goals as the classic narratives for which the neo-Nazi revisionists strive: a rewriting of twentieth-century European history as most Europeans have understood it from World War II to the present.

To sum up, we can conclude that the recent debates about the expulsions in Germany are not merely academic debates intended to improve our knowledge of the past. These politicized debates about a major component of the national identity of one of the largest and most powerful European nations have implications that will be felt in the future far beyond Germany. It is impossible to overestimate the significance of the question: To which images of World War II and its aftermath—that is, of the Nazi regime and the *Vertreibung*—does the German state subscribe? Thus the current debates about the *Vertreibung* are also debates about the future ways of remembering National Socialism with all its implications for the history of all European nations, and for our understanding of European history in general. The words Nazism, Fascism or Munich 1938 are used all over the world as important terms of reference in political disputes, while names like Winston Churchill or Adolf Hitler are significant pillars of moral orientation. It is therefore a matter of major importance whether we agree or disagree with the assessment of Noam Chomsky: that the Holocaust was the most extreme atrocity in human history and that we lose our humanity if we are willing to enter the arena of debate with those who seek to deny or underplay Nazi crimes. No one in present-day Germany denies the Nazi crimes, but the issue at stake concerns the problem of "underplaying" them, by linking the images of the Holocaust and the *Vertreibung* as two kinds of "ethnic cleansing." Current developments in Germany indicate that the "new" ways of remembering the *Vertreibung* are in fact a return to postwar images based on the equation "what the Germans did to the Jews, the Poles and the Czechs did to Germans."[46] The concept of "ethnic cleansing" has provided an only seemingly new framework. This might be the reason why it has won such popularity within a short period of time in Germany and why some foreign scholars have taken it up too, while at the same time it has not been able to find wider acceptance outside Europe. In view of this development, Noam Chomsky's warning should be subjected to careful rethinking. A debate with those who seek to underplay Nazi crimes seems inevitable. It is also desirable, if we want to preserve our humanity and our orientation in the European history of the 20th century.

NOTES

1 Noam Chomsky: "Historical Revisionism," March 31, 1992, in www.chomsky.info/letters/19920331.htm (21 November 2006).

2 Anja Kruke, ed., *Zwangsmigration und Vertreibung—Europa im 20. Jahrhundert* [Forced Migration and Expulsion - Europe in the 20th century] (Bonn: J.H.W. Dietz Nachg., 2006).

3 BdV - Bund der Vertriebenen, www.bund-der-vertriebenen.de (18 December 2006).

4 E. Hahn and H.H. Hahn, "The Resettlement of the German Population from Eastern Europe in Retrospect: On the New Interpretation of 'Expulsion' as 'Ethnic Cleansing'," *DAPIM Studies on the Shoa* 19 (2005): 197–217 (In Hebrew with English Abstract).

5 Beschluss des Deutschen Bundestages vom 4. Juli [Resolution of the German Bundestag] 2002 (Drucksache 14/9033 i.V.m. 14/9661), see also www.bohemistik.de/beschluss.html (18 December 2006).

6 Zentrum gegen Vertreibungen [Centre against Expulsions] www.z-g-v.de/index1.html (21 November 2006).

7 Markus Meckel www.markusmeckel.de (21 November 2006).

8 Für einen kritischen und aufgeklärten Vergangenheitsdiskurs [For a critical and enlightened debate about the past] Vertreibungszentrum [Centre of the Expulsions] www.vertreibungszentrum.de (18 December 2006).

9 S. Dittrich "Unfähig zur Versöhnung" [Incapable of reconciliation] in *Frankfurter Allgemeine Zeitung* (7 September 2006), 1.

10 For a brief overview of the basic facts see W. Benz, "Fremde in der Heimat: Flucht—Vertreibung—Integration" [The strangers in the homeland: Flight—Expulsion—Integration] in Klaus J. Bade, ed., *Deutsche im Ausland—Fremde in Deutschland. Migration in Geschichte und Gegenwart* (Munich: C.H. Beck, 1992), pp. 373–386; and W. Benz, ed., *Die Vertreibung der Deutschen aus dem Osten. Ursachen, Ereignisse, Folgen* [The expulsion of the Germans from the East. Causes, events, consequences] (Frankfurt am Main: Fischer Taschenbuch, 1985; 2nd ed. 1992).

11 Münz Rainer and Ohliger Rainer, "Vergessene Deutsche—erinnerte Deutsche. Flüchtlinge, Vertriebene, Aussiedler" [The forgotten Germans—the remembered Germans. Refugees, expellees, resettlers], in *Transit. Europäische Revue* No. 15 (1998): 141–157, here 145f.

12 *Völkischer Beobachter*, 2 January 1945.

13 Bernadette Nitschke, *Vertreibung und Aussiedlung der deutschen Bevölkerung aus Polen 1945 bis 1949* [Expulsion and evacuation of the German population from Poland 1945 until 1949] (Munich: Oldenbourg, 2003), p. 275.

14 Tomáš Staněk, "Vertreibung und Aussiedlung der Deutschen aus der Tschechoslowakei 1945–1948" [Expulsion and evacuation of the Germans from Czechoslovakia 1945–1948], in Der Weg in die Katastrophe. Deutsch-tschechoslowakische Beziehungen 1938–1947, Detlef Brandes and Václav Kural, eds., (Essen: Klartext, 1994): 165–186, here 182f.

15 Ágnes Tóth, *Migrationen in Ungarn 1945–1948: Vertreibung der Ungarndeutschen, Binnenwanderungen und slowakisch-ungarischer Bevölkerungsaustausch* [Migration in Hungary 1945–1948: Expulsion of the Hungarian-Germans, internal migration and the Slovak–Hungarian exchange of population] (Munich: Oldenbourg, 2001), p. 217. "The Holocaustizing of the Transfer-Discourse" 57

16 Brunhilde Scheuringer, *30 Jahre danach. Die Eingliederung der volksdeutschen Flüchtlinge und Vertriebenen in Österreich* [30 years after: The integration of the ethnic Germans and expellees in Austria] (Wien: Braumüller, 1983), p. 24.

17 Hans Henning Hahn and Eva Hahn, "Mythos 'Vertreibung'" [Myth 'Expulsion'], in *Politische Mythen im 19. und 20. Jahrhundert in Mittel- und Osteuropa*, Heidi Hein-Kircher and Hans Henning Hahn, eds., (Marburg: Verlag Herder-Institut, 2006), pp. 167–188.

18 Elizabeth Wiskemann. *Germany's Eastern Neighbours: Problems Relating to the Oder-Neisse Line and the Czech Frontiers Region* (London et al.: Oxford University Press, 1956), p. 120.

19 Official Statement. US Information Service, Embassy of the United States of America, Washington (14 February 1996) cited according the copy in the archive of Eva and Hans Henning Hahn, Augustfehn.

20 VERTRIEBENEN-TREFFEN: Köhler warnt vor Umschreiben der Geschichte [Expellees-Convention; Köhler warns against rewriting of history], in www.spiegel. de/politik/deutschland/0,1518,druck-434851,00.html (07.09.2006).

21 *Der Spiegel* (February 2003), S. 5.

22 Flight and expulsion of Germans during and after WWII, in Wikipedia's entry: "Expulsions" http://en.wikipedia.org/wiki/German_expulsions#Reexamination_of_the_ expulsions_in_the_1990s (07 September 2006); the book cited above is by Alfred-Maurice de Zayas, *A Terrible Revenge: The Ethnic Cleansing of the East European Germans* (New York: St. Martin's Press, 1994).

23 For more about the way in which Norman M. Naimark uses earlier German interpretations of the Vertreibung, see Eva Hahn and Hans Henning Hahn, "Alte Legenden und neue Besuche des 'Ostens'. Über Norman M. Naimarks Geschichtsbilder" [Old Legends and New Visits in the 'East'], in *Zeitschrift für Geschichtswissenschaft* Vol. 54, No. 7/8 (2006): 687–700.

24 Mathias Beer, ed., *Umsiedlung, Flucht und Vertreibung der Deutschen als internationales Problem. Zur Geschichte eines europäischen Irrwegs* [Resettlement, flight and expulsion of the Germans as an international problem. History of a European deviation] (Stuttgart: Haus der Heimat, 2002).

25 The exhibition *Forced Migration: Flight and Expulsion in Twentieth-Century Europe,* shown in Berlin in 2006 offers a good example of this position; see the catalogue of the exhibition Forced Migration: Flight and Expulsion in Twentieth-Century Europe. *An Exhibition by the Centre against Expulsions Foundation* (Berlin: 2006).

26 Götz Aly, "Europas Selbstzerstörung. Zum geplanten 'Zentrum gegen Vertreibungen'" [Europe's self-destruction. About the planned Centre against Expulsions], in *Süddeutsche Zeitung* (24 July 2003).

27 Joschka Fischer, "Was haben wir uns angetan" [What have we done to ourselves], in *Die Zeit* (28 August 2003), p. 6.

28 See e.g., Ingo Haar, "Hochgerechnetes Unglück. Die Zahl der deutschen Opfer nach dem Zweiten Weltkrieg wird übertrieben" [Calculated disaster. The figures of German victims after WW 2 are exaggerated], in *Süddeutsche Zeitung* (14 November 2006), p. 13 and the reaction by the leading politician in this field, Erika Steinbach, in www.bund-dervertriebenen.de/presse/index.php3?id=496&druck=1 (19 November 2006).

29 Deutsche Bischofskonferenz [German Bishops-Conference] www.dbk.de (21 September 2005).

30 *Sudetendeutsche Zeitung* (13 May 2005).

31 *Forced Migration: Flight and Expulsion in Twentieth-Century Europe. An Exhibition by the Centre against Expulsions Foundation* (Berlin, 2006).

32 Andreas F. Kelletat, "Von der Täter—zur Opfernation? Die Rückkehr des Themas 'Flucht und Vertreibung' in den deutschen Vergangenheitsdiskurs bei Grass und anderen" [From the nation of perpetrators to the nation of victims? The return of the topic 'Flight and expulsion' in the German discourse about the past in the works of Grass and others], in *Triangulum. Germanistisches Jahrbuch für Estland, Lettland und Litauen* 2003/2004 (Riga: 2006), pp. 132–147.

33 *Sudetendeutsche Zeitung* (2 June 2006).

34 Eva Hahn and Hans Henning Hahn, "The Resettlement of the German Population from Eastern Europe in Retrospect: On the New Interpretation of 'Expulsion' as 'Ethnic Cleansing,'" in: *DAPIM. Studies on the Shoa,* No. 19 (2005): 197–217 (In Hebrew with English Abstract).

35 Alfred Rosenberg, *Letzte Aufzeichnungen. Ideale und Idole der nationalsozialistischen Revolution* [Last notes. The ideals and icons of the national socialist revolution] (Göttingen: Plesse-Verlag, 1955), p. 291.

36 Eugen Lemberg, *Geschichte des Nationalismus in Europa* [History of nationalism in Europe] (Stuttgart: Schwab 1950), p. 11.

37 Gotthold Rhode, *Völker auf dem Wege...: Verschiebungen der Bevölkerung in Ostdeutschland und Osteuropa seit 1917* [Nations underway...: Dislocation of population in East Germany and Eastern Europe] (Kiel: Hirt, 1952).

38 Götz Aly, "Jahrhundert der Vertreibung" [The century of expulsion], in *Wochenpost* (29 April 1993).

39 Norman N. Naimark, *Fires of Hatred: Ethnic cleansing in twentieth-century Europe* (Cambridge, Mass.: Harvard University Press, 2001).

40 Norman M. Naimark, "Die Killing Fields des Ostens und Europas geteilte Erinnerung" [The Killing Fields of the East and the divided memory of Europe], in *Transit* Vol. 30 (2005/2006): 57–69.

41 Eva Hahn and Hans Henning 'Hahn, "Alte Legenden und neue Besuche des 'Ostens.' Über Norman M. Naimarks Geschichtsbilder" [Old legends and new visits in the 'East'], in *Zeitschrift für Geschichtswissenschaft* Vol. 54, No. 7/8 (2006): 687–700.

42 In the original: "mit den europäischen Nationalitätenkriegen verbunden," in Götz Aly, "Auschwitz und die Politik der Vertreibung" [Auschwitz and the policy of expulsion], in Zwangsmigration in *Europa. Zur wissenschaftlichen und politischen Auseinandersetzung um die Vertreibung der Deutschen aus dem Osten*, Bernd Faulenbach and Andreas Helle, eds. (Essen: Klartext, 2005), pp. 35–44, here 43.

43 In the original: "Die europäischen Nationen und die Historiker dort sind bisher sehr wenig bereit, über diese Dinge zu sprechen," ibid. p. 59.

44 In the original: "Das erfordert aber sehr viele Lokerungsübungen noch in ganz Europa," ibid., p. 59.

45 Hans Lemberg, "Mehr als eine Wanderung. Eine Einführung" [More than a walk: An introduction], in K. Erik Franzen. Die Vertriebenen. Hitlers letzte Opfer (Munich: Propyläen, 2001), pp. 12–33, here 12.

46 Eugen Lemberg, Geschichte des Nationalismus in Europa [History of nationalism in Europe] (Stuttgart: Schwab, 1950), p. 11.

The Anti-Fascist Myth of the German Democratic Republic and Its Decline after 1989

INGO LOOSE

INTRODUCTION: THE RISE OF ANTI-FASCIST SELF-CONSCIOUSNESS IN THE GDR AFTER 1949

After the end of World War II the Allies and the Germans themselves had to solve the questions of how to safeguard freedom and democracy, and how to deal with the heritage and moral burden of National Socialism, the Holocaust, and an unbelievable scale of devastation throughout Europe. While the Western parts of Germany soon found encouraging support in their Western Allies, the Soviet occupied zone (SBZ) was in a much worse situation. The onset of the Cold War finally led to the foundation of two German states, based on very different political conceptions and on mutual aversion. Such foundations are usually accompanied by myths, used by political communities for the sake of self-presentation and for integration, both elements of national identity. The contents of political myths in modern history usually show very different patterns—between fairy tales and real events in history, which are interpreted in a mythical way. The main difference, however, between political myths and professional historiography is that myths often focus not on the events themselves but on their results and meaning in the (self-)perception of a country. Moreover, every myth presents itself as an authoritative, factual account. In contrast, historiography must always attempt to render its narratives plausible.

This paper aims to outline two aspects: 1. the main stages in the rise and decline of the anti-fascist myth in the GDR; and 2. the social and mental consequences of confronting GDR citizens with Nazi inclinations after 1989—something which had not been allowed for decades. All of this is, of course, deeply embedded in the process of transformation which the communist states in Central and Eastern Europe have gone through since then and which was accompanied by historically shaped conflicts on almost all levels of social, economic and political life. However, the case of the GDR is a peculiar one, predominantly with regard to two aspects:

1. In contrast to other countries of Eastern Central Europe, the GDR as
   an independent state ceased to exist with German unification in
   1990. Dealing with the time period from this point on we have to
   speak of "the former GDR" or of "the five new federal states" *(die
   fünf neuen Bundesländer)* or simply of East Germany. This is not
   only a simple *façon de parler* but gives a double perspective on the
   topic (a German and an East German one)—a different perspective
   from those of countries that continued their existence, although under new political circumstances.[1]
2. The example of historical revision (and I do not speak of "revisionism" now) directly concerns the role of Germany and the Germans
   during World War II. The GDR as a member of the Soviet Bloc always played a unique role, and not only because of its geographic
   and strategic location, or because of the unsolved German question.
   In 1949, the construction of an anti-fascist state on German soil,
   which presented itself as a good friend of countries which had been
   victims of German Nazism only a few years before, was for many
   people very far from convincing. Reading the relevant archival materials, one can see to what extent the so-called "eternal brother-
   hood" between, for instance, the GDR and Poland, was simply a
   hoax, and how unfriendly the countries remained to each other until
   the end in 1989.[2]

The basis for German anti-Fascism was the Comintern's definition of
Fascism in 1935, which went far beyond the classical characterization of
Italy and Nazi Germany as fascist states, and made it possible to stigma-
tize almost any non-communist political orientation as "fascist." On this
very meager theoretical basis Fascism, as the most radical form of imperi-
alistic monopoly capitalism, was—for the regime of the GDR, too—not
specifically a German phenomenon, but only one stage, albeit a terrible
one, in the march of history towards Communism. National Socialism was
therefore not typically *German*, but had at least a European dimension.
Fascism in Germany admittedly had been more brutal and aggressive than
in Spain and Italy, but only due to the fact that the class struggle between
the bourgeoisie and the proletariat had already achieved a higher level in
Germany. In fact, after 1945, for many Germans, who had more or less
passively benefited from the Nazi regime or at least definitely did not
belong to its victims, this was not an unwelcome interpretation of their
own role; it released them from responsibility for the period after 1933.[3]
In this way, the Nazis almost immediately and entirely disappeared right

after the war—first in the Soviet occupied zone and after 1949 in the GDR—and were to be found (according to the propaganda) only in the Federal Republic of Germany, where they often continued their careers without any regard to their "brown" past.[4]

Moreover, the Soviet occupied zone of Germany, as the puppet government itself put it, went through a so-called "anti-fascist democratic revolution" (*antifaschistisch-demokratische Umwälzung*[5]), which implied that full de-Nazification and democratization became realities only in the Soviet-controlled territories of Germany. In that respect, the end of the war was a sort of double disruption: a disruption in time, which drew an allegedly sharp line between National Socialism and the "purified" GDR; and a geographical one, which broadened the gap between the GDR and "fascist" West Germany and strengthened the former's self image as a democratic, anti-fascist, and therefore anti-imperialist state.[6] From this double break, which functioned as a combination of conspiracy threat and denial of guilt, the GDR gained a high degree of political legitimacy which lasted throughout its existence up to 1989, especially among the *intelligentsia*, although the GDR's search for its own national identity failed.[7] The myth of being anti-fascist, by defining Fascism, absolving the masses and identifying the new-old enemy in the West, convinced many people (and the regime itself) that the GDR and its population belonged to the victims of Fascism and at the same time to the winning side in history, but definitely not to the perpetrators of Nazi crimes or the losers of 20th-century history.[8] When the public discourse about Nazi victims was politicized, conflicts soon arose between the regime and the victims' organizations, which were forced to dissolve or to adapt themselves to the official interpretation of Nazism.[9]

This political strategy received backing from such prominent writers as Anna Seghers or the Buchenwald survivor Bruno Apitz, who cultivated the picture of a significant German communist resistance movement against National Socialism. No other state in Eastern Central Europe, then, drew so much legitimization from its foundation myths as the GDR did, and in no other state was the political legitimacy and the survival of the regime so dependent on them.[10] The case of postwar Austria, however, bears a certain potential for comparison, because the principle of whitewashing one's own history by "outsourcing the evil" ("Austria—the first victim of National Socialism") seems to be quite similar to those behind the processes in the SBZ and the early GDR.[11]

THE DECLINE OF THE ANTI-FASCIST MYTH

In the 1970s and 1980s, the population of the German Democratic Republic was kept well-informed about life and reality in Western Europe—by West German television. For the regime in East Berlin this was a structural threat that needed to be overcome, because the Western way of life, broadcast to almost every household, pitilessly exposed the growing gap between socialist theory and real life in the GDR and paved the way for the opposition movement of the 1980s.

The process of the decline of the anti-fascist myth, then, did not begin at the end of the 1980s, but much earlier.[12] There are good arguments, for instance, to support the interpretation of the erection of the so-called "anti-fascist security wall" (*antifaschistischer Schutzwall*) in August 1961, and the preceding flight of tens of thousands of skilled workers across the green border of Berlin, as proof of the weakness of the myth itself. The inevitable ruin of its legitimizing capability, however, was linked to the rise of activities which could properly be termed "opposition," at least from the end of the 1970s and the beginning of the 1980s onwards. This inevitable process of delegitimization depended also on the generational change in the 1970s and the appearance of a political elite with no personal experience of war or Nazism.

Nevertheless, the myth of the GDR's anti-fascist foundation in October 1949 was not easily overcome even after 1989. Undoubtedly, the very specific perception of the German Nazi rule was at that time deeply rooted in the GDR's self-definition (and partly self-deception) and therefore still played a decisive role in the legitimization of the regime and its adherents, but most probably also for the vast majority of the East Germans, who had long ago adopted anti-Fascism as part of their East German national identity. Therefore, anti-Fascism as part of one's self-definition does not automatically testify to lively support of the regime. The depth and thoroughness of the ideological breakdown of 1989 may be illustrated by a passage taken from Jana Hensel's extraordinarily successful essay (13 editions in the first two years) about the "Children of the Zone" (which means the GDR):

> There is only one item that we did not discuss before or after the fall of the Berlin Wall: during the history lessons of our youth, we were all anti-fascists. Our grandparents, parents, and neighbors—everybody was anti-fascist … The brochures of the pioneer movement were full of stories about the life of Ernst Thälmann, called Teddy, and of other workers' activists. Whenever I thought about the Second World War, we were all somehow members of the White Rose or used to meet clandestinely in the court-

yard and cellars to organize resistance and to print flyers. The war did not take place in our country. The world around me had begun in 1945, previously, however, nothing worth mentioning had happened.

...

Then, I became aware that we had never talked about those things. We did not know what our grandparents had done, whether they had been collaborators or in the resistance movement. We were born as a contemporary generation into a country of the past, which had extinguished questions and awful histories.[13]

Besides Hensel, who was born in Leipzig in 1976, several other authors have published books dealing with the psychological situation in which the Germans of the former GDR found themselves after 1989.[14] This cognitive distortion in thinking about National Socialism did not vanish automatically but turned out to be a long-term issue, which makes the topic relevant not only for historians, but for sociologists and teachers as well.

NEO-FASCISM AND ANTI-SEMITISM IN THE FORMER GDR AND IN UNITED GERMANY AFTER 1989

In fact, Fascism in Germany is by no means extinct; on the contrary it gained strength and spread wider after 1989 as neo-Fascism and anti-Semitism, especially in the territory of the former GDR. Discussing neo-Fascism in united Germany, I would like to raise the issue of possible links between the destruction of the myth on the one hand and the anti-democratic and anti-Semitic tendencies among the younger generation in the "five new states" in recent years on the other hand. Does historical revision—even if it is done by professional historians and based on methodological standards—commonly tend to be misused for more radical and far-right propaganda and ideology? Alternatively, is this phenomenon a peculiar heritage of the GDR's specific and one-sided way of dealing with history? Describing the myth as a historical phenomenon is one thing; the long-term consequences for the whole of German society and especially for the Eastern territories are another far more complicated issue.

It is striking in this context, that the word "revisionist," used in connection with history, has a very specific meaning in German. In scholarly historiography, revision carries the neutral meaning of disproving false theses, theories, and interpretations. Within the German political far right, however, the notion means the justification of National Socialism and its crimes and is, therefore, a fundamental part of extremist thinking: the *raison d'être*, so to speak, of the whole movement. This re-interpretation of history is carried out by comparing Nazi crimes with those of other regimes (especially those of the Soviet Union under Stalin), by questioning German responsibility for the outbreak of World War II and for the occupation regimes throughout Europe, and even, last but not least, by the wholesale denial of the Holocaust (the "Auschwitz lie"). In addition, extremist revisionism interprets even reunited Germany not as a legitimate state, but as the artificial construction of the Allied forces. Therefore, one of the main goals of the German neo-fascist movement is territorial revisionism, which means the renegotiation of the German borders with Poland, the Czech Republic, Austria, France and the Russian Federation.

After 1989, for the first time many East Germans had to face the fact that after the war elder Nazis had found their livelihood in the GDR, and also that anti-Semitism and neo-Fascism were not foreign to the "first socialist state on German soil," and that not a few of their grandparents were less "innocent" than they claimed to have been.[15] Moreover, scholarship revealed that parts of the "sacred" socialist myth, which had regularly exaggerated the importance of German communist resistance after 1933, had to be rewritten and that a number of former Nazi concentration camps, geographically situated in the GDR, had served as Soviet detention camps after 1945.[16] In that respect, in commemorating united Germany's geography there were, and still are, at least two very specific objects that held a double significance for history: Buchenwald[17] and Sachsenhausen, both former Nazi concentration camps and both Soviet special camps for higher and lower-ranking Nazis as well as for members of the anti-communist opposition between 1945 and 1950. A whole historiography (at least as far as it dealt with the 20th century), then, was almost entirely discredited after 1989—except for source publications and works often written by historians who already found themselves on the margins of official political approval. After 1989, critical evaluations of Party-controlled historiography were most often negative. At present, the communist or socialist way of explaining National Socialism has definitely no lobby, and there is no prospect of this changing.[18]

As in other countries of Eastern Central Europe, German scholarly and public revisionism since 1989 means to do far more than merely fill the gaps left by earlier official propaganda and historiography. Maybe the most serious "collateral damage" of the years following 1989 was the Germans' growing interest in their own contemporary history and identity, expressed in the widely accepted slogan: "What was not communist, Stalinist, or Soviet, cannot be so evil—not even National Socialism." The flight and expulsion of the Germans from the East during the last months of the war and the first postwar years stand now in the center of the Germans' interest in history. Günter Grass' novel *Im Krebsgang* (2002) in particular led to an unholy debate on whether guilt and suffering can be compared or even equated.[19] The belief that the Nazis had committed crimes on an incredible scale could be queried, especially in East Germany, as part of former communist propaganda, and thus hugely exaggerated or even untrue. If socialism and anti-Fascism were identical, then Fascism was automatically equal to criticism of socialism, which was blamed for all the problems of everyday life.[20] Sociologists may wonder to what extent teachers of history, freshly and hastily imported from the West, played their part in the failure of historical "reorientation" after 1989. The sharp and immediate caesura was regarded by many pupils as a deliberate paradigm shift on the whole issue. History as a topic was, then, part of the same "game" in life, in which the East Germans felt themselves once again subject to the "supervision" and propaganda of the historical winner. Having learnt a pragmatic approach to everyday life before 1989, many Germans retained it afterwards, regarding every political narrative, including historical narrative, as highly relative or even irrelevant. This approach became (and most probably remains) a good basis for the spread of right-wing and extremist ideas, especially among the disillusioned younger generation.

On the other hand, since 1989, the anti-fascist ideal has often been upheld by those who had been higher officials or politicians in the former GDR. This is why the problem of growing neo-Fascism did not seem to be so acute during the 1990s, because former party officials in power in the political structures of the Eastern states held on to their ideals and often ignored or downplayed warnings that harm could still be expected from the Nazi past. Moreover, with the growing temporal distance from 1989 many East Germans developed a certain nostalgic sentiment for the "good old socialist days" ("Eastalgia," in German "Ostalgie"), mainly based upon economic terms (e. g., specific foodstuffs and other products "Made in the GDR") and the conviction that the "real GDR" would definitely not return. With regard to these advocates of previous times (of course, not all "ostalgics" are adherents of the old regime), one may say that anti-Fascism now serves as a sort of exculpation strategy. Ostensibly, they agreed to serve the totalitarian regime in order to avoid something worse. Among their supporters there were also Western left-wing intellectuals who were upset by the loss of what they had had by promoting the positive aspects of the GDR in the West. Many writers and artists from the

GDR, too, now argue that their support and sympathy for the Eastern "democratic Germany" was part of their anti-fascist heritage, which had been summed up immediately after the War in the slogan: "Never again!" There is no reason to doubt that many Germans honestly tried to draw consequences from the past. However, the associations of Nazi victims in West Germany never gained a political voice but were mostly ignored, especially in the strictly conservative 1950s. It was the expellees who succeeded in promoting themselves at all levels of political representation. However, the great self-deception of the left in West Germany after the 1960s was that common anti-Fascism paved the way for sympathy for the GDR, or rather for a utopian picture of the GDR, which all too often had little in common with reality and underestimated the totalitarian character of the regime. Moreover, this seriously disturbed the activities organized by several groups of Nazi victims, who have been very often perceived as leftist or pro-communist.

One may argue, therefore, that the ideologically distorted way of talking and thinking about National Socialism in the GDR later hampered democratic traditions from taking root and flourishing among the right-wing subgroups of the East German population and thus prevented the consolidation of social stability throughout the country. For many politicians and for scholars of politics, too, the starting point of the fight against neo-Nazism is therefore the popular, but scarcely proven hypothesis, that it might be sufficient to tell the people the whole truth about Nazi crimes to turn them into convinced democrats and to condemn the right-wing parties to total insignificance. The thesis of a strong link between knowledge of the past and democracy is, of course, not intended to serve as a monocausal explanation for all the misfortunes of the East after the fall of the Berlin Wall. Nevertheless, the extreme right and neo-fascist movement undoubtedly gained strength because at least part of the population did not benefit economically from the unification process. The political parties from the West, hastily imported into the five new states, as well as the post-SED party named the Party of Democratic Socialism (PDS) did not provide proper answers to the uncertainties and conflicts after 1990. Many people then voted for the extreme right because everything that was not communist seemed to be a real alternative or, at least, offered an opportunity for protest.

It is undoubtedly very difficult to find empirically reliable proof of a link between social shortcomings, political orientations, and the need for simple historical narratives and idols. However, it can hardly be denied that such a link exists. The figures about the extremist evolution in East

Germany are far from ambiguous.[21] Since the second half of the 1990s, the center of the German neo-fascist movement has been located in East Germany, with a widening organizational structure and with ever-improving results in local and federal elections. Since then, the East Germans have been far more prone to vote for extremist parties than their Western co-nationals. Or to put it another way, the openly declared sympathy of the neo-fascists for the Nazi movement no longer scares people away from voting for such a party but has sometimes even become an additional reason.

All the transition problems mentioned turned out to be a "brown curse" in the new states. I would like to give only three examples:

1. Just before the inauguration of the FIFA World Cup in Germany in 2006, the former speaker of the German government, Uwe-Karsten Heye, published an announcement in which he advised foreign travelers not to enter so-called no-go areas in the states, for instance, of Brandenburg and Saxony in order to avoid being attacked or even killed. Although Heye's announcement was criticized by politicians as an exaggeration, he was only revealing an open secret, and it is no accident that similar warnings can already be found in American tourist guides.[22]

2. In Mecklenburg–West Pomerania (Mecklenburg-Vorpommern) in the local elections of 17 September 2006, the far-right National Democratic Party (NPD) won 7.3 percent and six seats in the local Schwerin parliament. In some districts, more than 10 or even 15 percent of the electorate voted for the NPD, which turned out to be a magnet for protest votes (it is also true that in the parliament of Saxony the NPD deputies turned out to be totally incompetent and prone to every sort of scandal).[23]

3. In the first eight months of 2006 the number of crimes (often involving violence) committed by neo-Nazis in Germany increased dramatically by more than 20 percent in comparison with 2005, reaching nearly 8,000 cases altogether. From 2004 to 2005 the number of neo-fascist crimes increased from 12,000 to almost 16,000, of which 958 cases (a rise of almost 25 percent) led to (sometimes severe) injuries.[24] Xenophobic, anti-Semitic and neo-fascist attacks have reached an openness and level of aggression which remind the president of the Central Council of Jews in Germany, Charlotte Knobloch, of the situation after 1933. Knobloch recently warned that these tendencies should be seen not as "regrettable single cases," but as a very frightening phenomenon.[25] True, in 2007 Ger-

many has spent 24 million euros on educational programs against neo-Fascism. However, one may wonder whether the successful defeat of neo-Nazism depends only on how much money the state pumps into such programs.

Analysts wonder whether the NPD has won most of its votes through its policy of historical purification, directed not only against the heritage of the GDR, but also against the anti-fascist consensus in the Federal Republic of Germany. Provocations such as open admiration for Adolf Hitler, his deputy Rudolf Hess, and other Nazi villains do not detract from, but, on the contrary, only add to the popularity of the NPD. There is most probably no other issue where the German tradition of acknowledging guilt and political and ethical liability can be hit so directly as by stirring up pseudo-historical discussions (for example the question of whether the Allied bombing of the city of Dresden in February 1945 can be called a "Bombing Holocaust" because of its lack of military necessity).

In targeting the political establishment, the neo-fascist groups are also targeting its historical conventions. If the establishment is unable to provide enough work, stability, and social security, its political and historical background is not worth mentioning either. For the far-right revisionists, history definitely has no meaning for its own sake, but serves only as a means for delegitimizing the enemy and winning the support of the discontented. No wonder, then, that all these groups are supported mostly by deeply dissatisfied and disorientated people. This tendency has turned into a self-fulfilling prophecy. The neo-Nazis frighten tourists as well as investors from abroad, who spend their money rather in Bavaria, for instance, than in Brandenburg or Mecklenburg, whose economies largely depend on tourism. The far-right parties' popularity stems from their simplistic answers to complex questions, and since they are not in power, they can promise whatever they want. Unemployment in the East, then, creates a new wave of voters for the NPD. To its strength may contribute the fact that their strategy for dealing with the Nazi past has more than one parallel with the GDR's—by blaming only a small group of criminals (capitalists after 1945, some Nazi super-villains like Himmler and Goebbels after 1989)—Himmler might have been a "bad guy," but in Germany at that time there was order and obedience, and Hitler at least initiated the building of the German *autobahns*.

CONCLUSIONS

As I have already pointed out, the case of the GDR is only one peculiar example of the transformation process which the Central European countries went through during the 1990s. In addition, anti-Fascism and its long-term echoes are only one topic within a whole transformation process that permeated and influenced almost every aspect of everyday life in the countries of the former Soviet bloc. The basic question is, to what extent concerns with the past adds anything to political legitimization and in which way revisions of tabooed historical issues affect this legitimization. However, this theoretical approach also has its limitations, for it is already a subject of lively discussion in Western democracies. How much legitimacy is needed for political systems to remain stable? The thesis, then, that the GDR's bankruptcy was closely linked to a total loss of legitimacy, definitely has much plausibility, but the problem of how to explain a population's behavior remains. The problem of how to overcome the historical myths that lay at the basis of state foundations in Eastern Europe after the end of World War II is a common one, not limited to the GDR. The fact is that this issue is not only an inspiring source of discussion among historians, but has long-term consequences and repercussions for the whole of German society and for that of the rest of Eastern Central Europe.

It is doubtful whether the specific concept of anti-Fascism, as it was used and understood in the GDR, can be an area for comparison with other countries of the former Soviet bloc, which suffered from Nazi occupation, while the GDR emerged from the "land of the perpetrators." The cleansing function that anti-Fascism had in Germany after the Second World War, was in other countries of the former Soviet bloc rather linked, if it came up at all, with the issue of collaboration, and therefore played a much smaller role than anti-Fascism in the GDR and in the whole of Germany.

Moreover, as we have seen, anti-Fascism was also employed in West Germany, both as a founding principle for the state and as a basis for ideological attacks on the "Nazi-like" totalitarian regime in the GDR. Anti-Fascism was available for use and misuse in both the FRG and the GDR; the difference lay in the way it was defined and also in the fact that in the FRG, where freedom of opinion and speech prevailed, the concept of anti-Fascism was open to change.

The extraordinarily large number of publications dealing with the history of the GDR may give the illusion that there is or might be something like a common historical perspective throughout reunited Germany about what happened before 1989 and what has happened since; and about the long-term heritage of the GDR, and its contribution, for instance, to a reunited Germany history. Was it the democratic unification of the two parts that had always belonged to each other, or the annexation of the weak East by the rich and arrogant West?[26] Despite the ever-improving factographical basis, the unified if not petrified vision of the past that the GDR historians have left us with remains part of today's discourse. The failure to create a single version of Fascism or anti-Fascism leads us to the question of the importance of anti-Fascism in post-1989 East Germany— on a long-term scale as well as in comparison with the whole transformation process, which contains much more difficult and painful problems to be solved. Blaming the former GDR for all the social and political short-comings that are still apparent, over 15 years after German unification, has become an exculpation strategy in politics. One may wonder, then, for how long neo-Fascism will continue to be explained by pre-1989 education and propaganda.

Thinking over the history of Nazism (the "Geschichtsaufarbeitung") in Germany had and still has a strong influence on views of history in general, although the aftermath of the GDR (for example, the ousting of former members of the *Staatssicherheit)*, touches more people, and more directly, than the aftermath of National Socialism did some decades ago. One of the main obstacles to building a new cohesive national identity has turned out to be the Holocaust. The former communist regime had severe problems, to say the least, in coming to terms with the increasingly central position of the Holocaust in the framework of a common European culture of commemoration.[27] Before 1989, for the East Germans there had actually not been any Holocaust, because the exterminated European Jews had been covered by the term "victims of Fascism." Now, after the fall of the Berlin Wall, the East Germans who were inclined to feel like victims of history have found themselves confronted by a competing group that undoubtedly went through a much more brutal experience than the Germans themselves. What is more, some commentators interpreted the GDR as the logical—and therefore justified—result of the Nazi crimes against mankind, as if the East Germans had to pay for the entire German nation. In that respect, one may argue, it is little wonder that anti-Semitism has spread rapidly throughout all sectors of society in the new states. Similar reactions, however, can be observed in the states of the "old" Federal Republic Germany, so this state of affairs is not entirely characteristic of the former GDR.

A compromise between independent historiography on the one hand, and some kind of enlightening historical education on the other is and will remain problematic. Historiography as a human science should always try to reduce ideological impetus to a minimum, but it is also clear that history will remain subject to political interpretation, if not instrumentalization. Anti-Fascism in the GDR and its repercussions may serve as a good example of how easily historiography can lose its last vestige of objectivity and become a self-service institution for every sort of political intention.

NOTES

1 For a broader context see Konrad Jarausch, *Die Umkehr. Deutsche Wandlungen 1945–1995* [Turning Back. German changes 1945–1995] (Munich: DVA, 2004), pp. 243–316.

2 See Burkhard Olschowsky, "Die staatlichen Beziehungen zwischen der DDR und Polen" [International relations between the GDR and Poland], in *Zwangsverordnete Freundschaft? Die Beziehungen zwischen der DDR und Polen 1949–1990* [Decreed friendship? Relations between the GDR and Poland, 1949–1990], Basil Kerski, Andrzej Kotula and Kazimierz Wóycicki, eds. (Osnabrück: Fibre, 2003), pp. 41–58; Mieczysław Tomala. "Eine Bilanz der offiziellen Beziehungen zwischen der DDR und Polen" [An account of official relations between the GDR and Poland], ibid., pp. 59–79.

3 Herfried Münkler, "Antifaschismus als Gründungsmythos der DDR. Abgrenzungsinstrument nach Westen und Herrschaftsmittel nach innen" [Anti-fascism as a founding myth of the GDR. Instrument of separation towards the West and instrument of power inside], in *Der missbrauchte Antifaschismus. DDR-Staatsdoktrin und Lebenslüge der deutschen Linken* [The abused anti-Fascism. State doctrine of the GDR and the existential lie of the German Left], Manfred Agethen, Eckhard Jesse and Ehrhart Neubert, eds., (Freiburg–Basel–Vienna: Herder, 2002), pp. 79–99, here 84.

4 See Ingo Loose, "'Blind wie die Schlafwandler war das deutsche Volk.' Die Debatte um die Schuld der Deutschen in der Korrespondenz zwischen Hermann Broch und Volkmar von Zühlsdorff 1945 bis 1949." ["As blind as sleepwalkers were the Germans." The debate on the Germans' guilt in the correspondence between Hermann Broch and Volkmar von Zühlsdorff 1945–1949], in *Zeitschrift für Germanistik* [new series] 15, No. 3 (2005): 592–609, especially 597, 602–604.

5 *Wörterbuch der Geschichte*, Vol. 1: A–K (Berlin [East]: Dietz, 1984): 43–46.

6 Münkler, "Antifaschismus als Gründungsmythos der DDR," pp. 91–92; Jeffrey Herf, *Zweierlei Erinnerung. Die NS-Vergangenheit im geteilten Deutschland* [Different memories. The Nazi past in divided Germany] (Berlin: Propyläen, 1998); Annette Leo, "Keine gemeinsame Erinnerung. Geschichtsbewusstsein in Ost und West," [No common memory. Sense of history in East and West] in *Aus Politik und Zeitgeschichte* No. B 0–41/2003 (29 September 2003): 27–32.

7 See Dietrich Orlow, "The GDR's failed search for a national identity, 1945–1989," in *German Studies Review* 29, Vol. 3 (2006): 537–558.

8 Raina Zimmering, *Mythen in der Politik der DDR. Ein Beitrag zur Erforschung politischer Mythen* [Myths in politics of the GDR. A contribution to research on political myths] (Opladen: Leske & Budrich, 2000).

9 Jürgen Danyel, "Die Opfer- und Verfolgtenperspektive als Gründungskonsens? Zum Umgang mit der Widerstandtradition und der Schuldfrage in der DDR" [The perspective of victims of persecution as a founding consensus? On dealing with resistance tradition and the question of guilt in the GDR], in *Die geteilte Vergangenheit. Zum Umgang mit Nationalsozialismus und Widerstand in beiden deutschen Staaten* [Divided past. Dealing with National Socialism and resistance in both German states], Jürgen Danyel, ed. (Berlin: Akademie, 1995), pp. 31–46.

10 Münkler, "Antifaschismus als Gründungsmythos der DDR," pp. 82–83; Sigrid Meuschel, *Legitimation und Parteiherrschaft in der DDR. Zum Paradox von Stabilität und Revolution in der DDR 1945–1989* [Legitimacy and party rule in the GDR. On the paradox of stability and revolution in the GDR 1945–1989] (Frankfurt/M.: Suhrkamp, 1992); Olaf Groehler, "Verfolgten- und Opfergruppen im Spannungsfeld der politischen Auseinandersetzungen in der Sowjetischen Besatzungszone und in der Deutschen Demokratischen Republik" [The victims' associations in the area of political conflicts in the Soviet Occupation Zone and the German Democratic Republic] in Jürgen Danyel, ed., *Die geteilte Vergangenheit*, pp. 17–30, especially 17–18.

11 See Hellmut Butterweck, *Verurteilt und begnadigt. Österreich und seine NS-Straftäter* [Sentenced and reprieved. Austria and its Nazi criminals] (Vienna: Czernin, 2003); Heinz P. Wassermann, *Naziland Österreich? Studien zu Antisemitismus, Nation und Nationalsozialismus im öffentlichen Meinungsbild* [Nazi land Austria? Studies on anti-Semitism, nation and National Socialism in public opinion] (Innsbruck: Studien-Verlag, 2002).

12 Annette Simon, "Antifaschismus als Loyalitätsfalle" [Anti-fascism as a trap for loyalty], in Manfred Agethen, Eckhard Jesse and Ehrhart Neubert, eds., *Der missbrauchte Antifaschismus,* pp. 145–154, here 150.

13 Jana Hensel, *Zonenkinder* [Children of the Zone] (Berlin: Rowohlt, 2003), pp. 108, 110–112. Translation by the author.

14 See Michael Tetzlaff, *Ostblöckchen. Neues aus der Zone* [Small Eastern Bloc. News from the zone] (Frankfurt/M.: Schöffling, 2004); Internationale Erich-Fromm-Gesellschaft, ed., *Die Charaktermauer. Zur Psychoanalyse des Gesellschafts-Charakters in Ost- und Westdeutschland* [The character wall. On the psychoanalysis of societal character in East and West Germany] (Göttingen: Vandenhoeck & Ruprecht, 1995); Brigitte Rauschenbach, ed., *Erinnern, Wiederholen, Durcharbeiten. Zur Psycho-Analyse deutscher Wenden* [Remembering, repeating, working through. On the psychoanalysis of German changes] (Berlin: Aufbau, 1992).

15 Heinrich Best and Axel Salheiser, "Shadows of the Past: National Socialist Backgrounds in East German Industrial Research," in *German Studies Review* 29, Vol. 3 (2006): 589–602.

16 Bodo Ritscher, "Die NKWD/MWD-'Speziallager' in Deutschland. Anmerkungen zu einem Forschungsgegenstand" [NKWD/MWD special camps in Germany. Some comments on a subject of research] in Jürgen Danyel, ed., *Die geteilte Vergangenheit*, pp. 163–179.

17 Manfred Overesch, *Buchenwald und die DDR oder die Suche nach Selbstlegitimation* [Buchenwald and the GDR or the search for self-legitimization] (Göttingen: Vanden-

hoeck & Ruprecht, 1995); Manfred Agethen, "Gedenkstätten und antifaschistische Erinnerungskultur in der DDR" [Memorials and anti-fascist commemoration culture in the
GDR] in Manfred Agethen, Eckhard Jesse and Ehrhart Neubert, eds., *Der missbrauchte
Antifaschismus*, pp. 128–144; Annette Leo, "'Stimme und Faust der Nation...'—
Thälmann-Kult kontra Antifaschismus" ['Voice and fist of the nation...'—the Thäl-
mann cult versus anti-Fascism], in Jürgen Danyel, ed., *Die geteilte Vergangenheit*, pp.
205–211, especially 208–209.

18 Wolfgang Küttler, "Auf den Inhalt kommt es an. Zum Verhältnis von Zeitgeschichts-
forschung und Geschichtsdiskurs im neuvereinigten Deutschland" [The content matters.
On the relationship between research on contemporary history and historical discourse
in reunited Germany], in Jürgen Danyel, ed., *Die geteilte Vergangenheit*, pp. 143–149,
here 147–148.

19 Hans Henning Hahn and Eva Hahn, "Mythos 'Vertreibung,'" pp. 167–188; see also Eva
Hahn's paper in this volume; Günter Grass, *Im Krebsgang* [Crab walk] (Göttingen:
Steidl, 2002); Hubert Orłowski, *Przemoc—tabu—trauma ofiar: Wokół najnowszej
powieści Güntera Grassa* [Violence—taboo—trauma of the victims: On the latest novel
of Günter Grass] (Poznań: Instytut Zachodni, 2002).

20 See Konrad Weiß, "Gefahr von Rechts" [Danger from the right], in *Freiheit und Öf-
fentlichkeit. Politischer Samisdat in der DDR 1985–1989* [Freedom and the public
sphere. Political samizdat in the GDR, 1985–1989], Ilko-Sascha Kowalczuk, ed., (Berlin: Robert-Havemann-Gesellschaft, 2002), pp. 356–357.

21 Richard Stöss, *Rechtsextremismus im Wandel* [Changing right-wing extremism] (Berlin: Friedrich-Ebert-Stiftung, 2005), pp. 109–123.

22 "Zu Gast bei Freunden?" [A time to make friends?], *Süddeutsche Zeitung* (May 20,
2006); Ludwig Greven, "Brandenburg meiden" [Avoiding Brandenburg], *Die Zeit
online* (http://zeus.zeit.de/text/online/2006/20/Nogoareas-Heye; accessed on 5 January
2007).

23 Sandra Pingel-Schliemann and Karl-Georg Ohse. "Der Wahlerfolg der NPD in Mecklenburg-Vorpommern" [Election success of the NPD in Mecklenburg–West Pomera-
nia], in *Deutschland Archiv* 39, No. 6 (June 2006): 968–972.

24 Federal Ministry of the Interior, ed., *Verfassungsschutzbericht 2005* (Berlin: 2006), pp.
33–40; see "Verfassungsschutzbericht heizt Debatte um 'No-Go-Areas' an" [Report of
the German Verfassungsschutz for 2005 heats the debate on no-go areas]
(www.world.de/popup/popup_printcontent/0,,2028520,00.htm, accessed on 5 January
2007).

25 "Rechtsextremismus. Knobloch sieht Parallelen zur Nazi-Zeit" [Right-wing extremism.
Knobloch sees parallels to the Nazi era] (www.focus.de/politik/deutschland/
rechtsextremismus_nid_37979.htm, accessed on 5 January 2007).

26 See Wolfgang Templin, "NRD i RFN. Aneksja zamiast zjednoczenia" [GDR and FRG.
Annexation instead of unification], *Gazeta Wyborcza* (4 October 2006), p. 22.

27 Bernd Kauffmann, and Basil Kerski, eds., *Antisemitismus und Erinnerungskulturen im
postkommunistischen Europa* [Anti-Semitism and cultures of commemoration in post-
communist Europe] (Osnabrück: Fibre, 2006); for Poland, see Michael C. Steinlauf,
Bondage to the Dead. Poland and the Memory of the Holocaust (Syracuse: Syracuse
University Press, 1997); Jonathan Huener, *Auschwitz. Poland and the Politics of Commemoration, 1945–1979* (Ohio: Ohio University Press, 2003).

In Search of "National Memory"

The Politics of History, Nostalgia and the Historiography of Communism in the Czech Republic and East Central Europe

MICHAL KOPEČEK

The complex process of transition from communist dictatorship to democracy in Central and Eastern Europe also involved the transformation of historiography which, during the communist dictatorship, served to a large extent as a means of legitimization of Communist Party rule. On the basis of strict Marxist-Leninist rules, historians were expected to interpret the socialist revolution and communist government as the highest and most progressive stage of historical development. This kind of historiography was to undergo far-reaching changes, from a centrally controlled and ideologically driven towards decentralized and pluralist academic discourse. Have the historians and academic managers in Czechia and other post-communist countries succeeded in this respect?

Only up to a point, I argue. Generally, the political changes of 1989 brought about an extraordinary expansion of research areas, especially in contemporary history, where a large number of taboos were broken. However, the introduction of new research topics did not necessarily mean the introduction of new problems or the elaboration of new methods. The development of Czech and other Central and East European historiographies was significantly determined by the rehabilitation of the nation-state in the political realm and the process of democracy building, with the obvious need to legitimize the existence of both.

The chapter starts by examining the role and achievements of the historical profession *vis-à-vis* the societal and political ways of dealing with the legacy of the communist dictatorship. Further it dwells on how this is linked to the redefinition of national identity and the concept of national history and how it relates to the internal restructuring and development of the historiography of recent history. The concluding sections turn to the debates around the so-called institutes of national memory or their possible establishment in East Central Europe. Concentrating mainly on Czech developments, it attempts to draw a broader picture and base the argument on comparisons with other countries in the region, primarily Poland.

DEMOCRACY BUILDING AND THE LEGACY OF COMMUNISM

Every new political order has to deal with the legacy of the *ancien régime*, since the legitimacy of the new one depends to a great extent on rejecting the old one and coming to terms with its legacy.[1] The new democracies in East Central Europe were surely not an exception. Hence, one of the principal questions for the new regimes has become how to deal with the communist past. To be sure, we can find the communist past and different memories of it playing an active role on all possible levels of political and social life, from the most comprehensive level of public political discourse down to the subjective level of personal memories. Every post-communist country in East Central Europe has witnessed spectacular political campaigns playing on the supposed or real collaboration of prominent public figures with the former communist secret services. More importantly, however, it was a politically generated picture depicting the whole postwar period in the black-and-white of totalitarian theory, which played a major role, especially during the first years after the fall of communist rule.

One of the most significant aspects of this kind of legitimization strategy was the relevant legislation, which was often regarded as the main tool in the politics of de-communization. In the Czech Republic—which in a certain sense took the lead among the former communist countries in their efforts to come to terms with the communist past by means of law—it has taken various forms, beginning with the total rehabilitation of political prisoners in 1990, through the 1991 Screening Act (*lustrace*) barring former communist functionaries and secret police agents from holding any public office in the new regime, through the 1993 Act on the Lawlessness of the Communist regime, to the restitution of private property confiscated after the February 1948 communist coup d'etat, and to several legal arrangements concerning the accessibility of archive records from the communist period.[2] The "exemplary" Czech case is, however, heavily relativized by the legal existence and successful political survival of the Communist Party of Bohemia and Moravia, the proud successor of the Communist Party of Czechoslovakia.

A similar, simultaneous process to that in the political realm was taking place in the symbolic organization of the public space. Regardless of how closely the ordinary people followed the debates of politicians or historians about screening procedures or the crimes of Stalinism, everybody noticed the obvious change of traditions with the renaming of countless streets, parks, squares, and public buildings, as well as the reconstruction or rebuilding of old statues and monuments.[3]

Understandably, the legitimacy of the new democratic order has been based on the rejection of the communist past as a whole. This picture—shared however in its entirety only by few—treats the communist period as an integral unit and depicts Communism in a grossly simplified way as a historical distortion, an interlude, an aberration from the supposed natural path of national history, an "Asiatic despotism" imported from the "East." The obvious advantage of this interlude theory is that depicting the whole period as the result of foreign interference somehow helps to exculpate both the ordinary citizen and the cultural and political elites from their responsibility for the communist dictatorship.[4]

Obviously, historians do not usually subscribe to this simplified version of history, but if we look closely at the results of recent historical research in the Czech Republic we can see how historians have in fact unwittingly contributed to this picture. So far, historical research on the communist period has been distinguished by a strong preponderance of political history with its emphasis on the main political events such as the February 1948 communist takeover, the communist reform movement of 1968, the formation of Charter 77 and democratic dissent, and finally the Velvet Revolution in 1989. This kind of historical research includes the decision-making of the communist party and analysis of political change; research on the apparatus of repression and the terrorist activities of the state against its citizens; studies on labor camps, political trials, the functioning of the secret police; the suppression of the resistance movement, democratic dissent and so forth.[5]

To be sure, these are all indispensable topics if we are to understand the nature of the communist dictatorship, and historians were quite right to focus on these areas. Moreover, there are still many forms of political and social repression still far from being satisfactorily researched and described by historians, such as, for instance, the abuse of psychiatry against political opponents and lesser-known dissenters during the 1970s and the 1980s.[6] But on the whole the emphasis on these topics makes the overall picture of the postwar period rather one-sided, depicting the communist dictatorship as a period of constant struggle, repression, and terrorist actions by the secret police and the arbitrary rule of the Communist Party, which invokes the totalitarian paradigms of Orwellian imagination and seemingly leaves no space for collective and individual memories that do not coincide with this image.

Nevertheless, even in the first few years after 1989 the picture of the recent past was never as dark as it may seem from the above description, and there are many reasons for this. To deal with some of them, I would first like to draw the reader's attention to the internal structure of historical scholarship devoted to the interpretation of the 1968 Prague Spring on the one hand, and the methodological innovation on the other hand. Second, there is a more general phenomenon that refers to an interplay—if not clash—between scholarly-produced and politically-supported historical knowledge, with a rich variety of historical memories reflecting the abundance of political, social and cultural identities in the democratizing society.

THE '68 GENERATION: THE RESISTANCE OF MEMORY

There is a peculiar generational constitution among Czech historians, which shows itself most clearly in the realm of recent history. To put it simply, after 1989 academic work in this field of historical research was conducted mainly by the generation born around 1930, whereas many of the younger generation beginning their work in the 1970s and the 1980s left academia after 1989. Historians from the youngest generation—born around 1970 and completing their education already under the democratic regime—have only recently started to publish their first books, leading to more frequent clashes of opinion between them and what is now the oldest generation of historians. The latter is largely identical with the "Generation of 1968" or the "Sixty-eighters": those who were active participants in or witnesses of the Prague Spring and who, after its suppression, went into exile or took an active part in the democratic opposition movement. In most historical writing after 1989 their memory and historical representation has visibly prevailed, for instance, over the memory of the representatives of the "third resistance movement" (active anti-communists) and the victims of the Stalinist purges.[7]

Theirs is a specific historical narrative, picturing Czechoslovak Communism as having been established with the help of the Soviets, albeit with significant domestic support, at the end of the 1940s; going through its first major political upheavals after the death of Stalin in 1953; attempting a peculiar reform in the name of "socialism with a human face" during the Prague Spring; and being fully discredited only after the Soviet-led military intervention in 1968 and the subsequent establishment of the "normalization" regime represented by the Brezhnevite Gustáv Husák from 1969 to 1989. The bone of contention is naturally the interpretation of the events of 1968. After its suppression, these authors strove to defend the Prague Spring both against the official Husákian communist interpretation, which depicted the reform as a counter-revolution supported by the imperialist West, and against those who were highly critical of the political project of "socialism with a human face" and castigate the exclusivity, insufficient democratization, and unrealistic expectations of the Dubček leadership. The "Sixty-eighters" usually emphasize the democratic nature of the movement and its resemblance to Gorbachev's later concepts of perestroika and glasnost; some of them defend the notion of the "third way" between capitalism and socialism. Regardless of political implications, these historians, former reform communists themselves, nevertheless managed to achieve a well-balanced representation of the political and social context of the Prague Spring, which hints at the complex dynamics of the historical development in 1968.[8]

Their own political interests notwithstanding, these witness-historians have been at pains to conceptualize the dynamic changes in the communist politics and to stress the differences between respective periods. Consequently, whereas the political rhetoric and legitimizing strategy of the nascent democratic order after 1989 spoke the dichotomous language of democracy versus totalitarianism, freedom versus oppression, the historiography strove to produce a more differentiated and nuanced analysis, free of direct links to current politics. It matters little to what extent it was the ethos of critical historical enquiry and to what extent it was their own political identity that made the generation of 1968 reluctant to accept the vocabulary of the traditional totalitarian theory that dominated the political discourse of the 1990s.[9] Hence, while the historiography of contemporary history was contributing to the de-legitimization of the communist regime through its overall research agenda, the individual historians' rhetorical stance was opposed to the mainstream historical legitimization strategy of the new political regime, which had an impact on the public cultural-historical discourse.[10] Nonetheless, the Sixty-eighters' historical narrative was hardly able to establish any historical consensus in Czech society and lately this interpretative framework has been called into question by a number of younger historians.

THE HISTORY OF THE NATION AS THE NORM

In recent years, there has been a certain shift towards subtler and less cen-
tralized facets of the recent past as Czech historians offer a gradually increasing number of works devoted to topics other than political history. In
social history, along with more traditional approaches focusing on major
institutions or social structures such as, for instance, the churches, new
works have appeared that try to deal with everyday life, consumer culture,
social mobility, and migration under state socialism. Similarly, there has
been a growing interest in the approaches of oral history, gender history,
or environmental history, written mainly by younger historians, historical
sociologists, cultural anthropologists and literary historians, usually educated abroad and inspired by French, German, or American historical
scholarship and methodological innovations. The contribution these approaches have made to academia lies in their having helped to create a
new space, where the prolific dialogue among various historical accounts,
perspectives, and theoretical positions can take place. The "mastering of"
or "coming to terms with" the recent past *(Vergangenheitsbewältigung)*
which prevailed at the beginning of the transition period might—along
with the stabilization of the democratic order—allow more space to less
directive and more conversation-like ways of dealing *(Vergangenheitsau-
farbeitung)* with this past.

Yet, so far, as much as the stability of the democratic order in the former communist countries could be questioned, the methodological and
theoretical innovations in these countries have come mainly from individual scholars, and instead of subtle, expert debate we are witnessing a renewed tendency to politicize recent history. Theoretically-based, method-
ologically-innovative research is still in a conspicuous minority in most
fields of historiography and surely marginal in the field of contemporary
history. Throughout the region there is an obvious shortage of autonomous research institutions that would support new methodologies inde-
pendently of the mainstream national research centers, and thus stir up
methodological discussion and carry out such theoretically-based historical research. "Transnational history" or "the history of concepts" still
sound to most of Czech historians more like a waste of time than a serious
historical undertaking. In general, the thematic expansion of Czech historical studies since 1989 has not been accompanied by innovations in
methodological reasoning; rather, the main driving force has been the
aspiration to fill in the "blank spaces," especially in the recent past. This
approach has strengthened political history at the expense of other fields.

Thus, the "liberalization" of historical studies after 1989 brought about the restoration of old conceptual models rather than the introduction of new ones.[11]

There is a clear lack of the kind of self-critical reflection about historiography's role and entanglement with the former communist state that would go beyond bitter *ad hominem* controversies and lead the way towards badly needed theoretical self-examination of the discipline. Marxist historical materialism has been quite thoroughly assessed by medieval and early-modern historical research, where the Marxist tradition was understood as a serious partner in the discussion. In contrast, in recent history the Marxist tradition has either been totally ignored or one-sidedly dismissed as mere "ideology."[12] Owing to the insufficient examination of the legacy of Marxism, new theoretical approaches coming from the new cultural and social history are often suspected of representing a disguised return of Marxism, and, thus a "violation of history." These works potentially challenging the one-sided picture of the totalitarian past are sometimes charged with whitewashing the communist dictatorship and are thus understood as "revisionist" in the negative sense of the term. The belief in value-free research and the possibility of separating "lies" from "the truth" is constitutive of most Czech historiography, a phenomenon present in many other post-communist countries. This has resulted, particularly in the case of contemporary history, in descriptive, event-oriented history writing, whose explanatory modes are often derived unconsciously from a simplified form of the theory of totalitarianism.

The lack of reflection on historiography's past has made the continuity of certain explanatory models and concepts of thought possible. Adapted to the new conditions prevailing after 1989, some interpretative patterns beyond the explicitly ideological have proved to be unexpectedly durable. In 1988, Eva Hahn pointed out a certain similarity between official Marxist-Leninist and unofficial dissent historiography. Both were indebted to the nation-centered narrative, the monistic and teleological notion of history, and involved an extremely polarized representation of the past.[13] With a tradition reaching back to the 19th-century nationalist movements and enhanced by the return of nation-state-centered politics, for many fellow historians—consciously or not—the old national history paradigm became the only way out of the ideological abyss after the collapse of the communist dictatorship.

The reconstruction of national history and the rehabilitation of partly suppressed, partly distorted aspects of national history and traditions were urgent tasks in all Central and East European countries after 1989. The difficulties of historical scholarship were greatly increased by the complex post-communist political-economic reform that in a way subordinated the reconstruction of historical cultures to state- and (in some cases) nation-building processes. The "reconstruction of the national historical sovereignty"—to use R. Jaworski's term—became an obvious priority for historians in Central and Eastern Europe. Liberation from the Marxist-Leninist strait jacket did not lead to a critical assessment of the persistent national historical narratives or recognition of an essential diversity of historical experiences under the surface of seemingly unified national histories.[14]

This trend takes various forms among historians, beginning with a concerted effort to cultivate a "national historical consciousness," promote the "positive conception" of national history and solidify national identity in the context of European enlargement, and ending with the unconscious but no less problematic approach of historical analysis that takes the nation-state, if not the ethno-culturally defined national community, as its natural, unquestioned point of departure.

Few historians of recent history (in the Czech context usually defined as the period after 1938) would subscribe to the militant nation-defending position, but the second case, the unproblematized acceptance of the nation-centered paradigm of history, is very common among them. An example is the lack of supranational perspective in the historical research agenda. There are almost no comparative research projects other than the numerous bilateral or multilateral conferences where representatives of the various countries present their own "national cases." This is even more striking in the history of Czechoslovakia, where Czech historians very often put aside the Slovak part of the story with the justification that this should be the concern of their Slovak colleagues. Similarly, the Slovak experts are engaged with the Slovak part of the Czechoslovak history, and as far as the "Czechoslovak" context is concerned they effectively confine themselves to references to the Czech historical production.

COMPETING NOSTALGIAS

The "absolutist" rule of the national history paradigm is unequivocal. At the same time, it coincides with the lively and growing "memorialism" of the late 20th and early 21st century, the world-wide "upsurge of memory," as Pierre Nora put it, and the concomitant democratization and autonomization of historical memory in modern society during the last twenty years.[15]

No doubt the democratizing effect of the numerous grass-root initiatives striving to give voice to the so-far silent witnesses of historical events is visible in Czechia and surrounding countries too, and this is true above all in the realm of recent history. The public political and cultural discourse reflects a variety of historical memories mirroring the relative plurality of political and social identities within Czech society, though not all these memories are equally represented. At any rate, the immense variety of memories present in society has often not corresponded with clear-cut and often politically driven historical narratives during the 1990s.[16]

This also constitutes the social background of the phenomenon of *Ostalgia*, or nostalgia for the former East, the lost security and seeming simplicity of life under the paternalistic regime of late socialism. The living memory of a relatively tranquil and predictable way of life contrasts sharply with the sometimes wild capitalist conditions that the neo-liberal free-market transformation has created since 1989 and, simultaneously, with the dark vision of the totalitarian hell of the Stalinist kind dominant in the public cultural discourse. Mere common sense, capacity for realistic assessment and agreeable photos in the family albums are enough to realize that life in the former state socialist country was more complex and less unpleasant than the imagined evil empire with secret agents hiding behind every corner.

Ostalgia originated in East Germany, the former German Democratic Republic, partly as a reaction to the identity crisis of the East German population after its unification with the Federal Republic of Germany. As a way to articulate the German–German difference it has been substantially enhanced by recent advances in communication technology, especially the Internet.[17] As a phenomenon of the turn of the century with its highest peaks represented by the 2002 bestseller *Zonenkinder* (Children of the Zone) by Jana Hensel and the 2003 hit movie *Good Bye, Lenin!* by Wolfgang Becker, the nostalgic view of the late socialist past with its ironic twist found plenty of enthusiastic fans in other former communist countries. As much as the political roots of *Ostalgia* are discernable in its various representations, however, it could hardly be interpreted as a "last stand of GDR (or, in fact, East European) anti-Western resistance," or a yearning for the return of socialism as it really existed.[18] Some of its analysts understand *Ostalgia,* especially outside the specific German context, rather as a manifestation of postmodern cultural mystification and harmless counter-culture provocation, even though it generally holds that literary texts, movies or other works of art as much as sophisticated web-museums or nostalgic e-shops could never fully untie themselves from political power and its language.[19]

From this point of view *Ostalgia* belongs to "reflective nostalgia," to use Svetlana Boym's term.[20] Wistful, ironic and playful by definition, reflective nostalgia does not follow direct political aims, but dwells on the ambivalence of human longing and belonging. By opening a multitude of historical potentialities it tries to mediate between history and the passage of time. Reflective nostalgia in contrast to "restorative nostalgia," Boym claims, does not shy away from the contradictions of modernity but casts doubt on the absolute truths of political and ideological programs. So *Ostalgia,* far from being a political program in any sense, does not follow a single plot and instead explores ways of inhabiting many places at once and imagining different time zones; it draws away from clear-cut political symbols and deliberately immerses itself in the details and material traces of the past. At its best, reflective nostalgia presents an ethical and creative challenge to mainstream cultural and/or political discourse.

The basically understanding, forbearing view of *Ostalgia* is not, however, shared by many political activists in the region. *Ostalgia's* successful international tour from the ex-GDR throughout East Central Europe, encouraged by the widespread revival of late socialist pop-culture kitsch, has aroused a counter-movement involving numerous former anti-communist activists and dissidents, and also many young intellectuals and politicians. They feel the need to oppose the "soft" version of the story of the communist rule, which stresses the majority's seemingly unproblematic way of life in the late socialist period and which—from the point of view of its critics—in fact covers up the complicity of a significant part of the population with the criminal regime. In the Czech case this feeling is considerably strengthened by the unprecedented persistence of the unreformed Communist Party, which for more than 15 years has won the majority of protest-votes in every general election. It is not only staunch anticommunists who are offended by their revisionist panegyrics about the beneficial effects of the paternalistic, state socialist welfare state, ignoring the political and social repression that took place, and by their direct vocal support for various present-day dictators.[21]

The political frustration caused by the existence of the political entities with more or less confessed roots in the totalitarian party-state leads to harsh criticism of the *Ostalgia* that allegedly obscures the watershed between then and now, and obliterates the deep moral failings of the former communist rule. From this point of view, *Ostalgia* constitutes an unacceptable form of relativization, no matter whether the motives are political in nature or rather feed on popular retro-fashion and counter-cultural incentives.[22]

In the last two or three years a new and urgent round of the debate about the politics of history has begun in East Central Europe that parallels, not by chance, the growing anti-communist political sentiments. Not surprisingly, the legacy of the 1989 Velvet Revolutions has always been an apple of discord between various political forces, and the images of the communist past which are drawn largely from the files of the communist secret police, have been a hotly contested issue since the reestablishment of democracy in the region.[23] After the formation of the Polish coalition government lead by Law and Justice in 2005, the politicization of the communist past has reached a new climax. The heated Polish controversies about the Third *Rzeczpospolita*, and the fervent rightist criticism of the 1989 round-table compromise between the old and new political elites, symbolize the rift in memories of the communist period and its political explosiveness.

The contest about the past in Poland is the most distinctive and illustrative in East Central Europe. Owing to the broad social background of the Solidarity movement and the role played by the Roman Catholic Church, various political formations lay sole claim to the legacy of the Polish anticommunist resistance. At the core of the discussions that are conducted at the intersection of various cultural fields such as historical scholarship, political education, the legitimacy of democratic political order, and, last but not least, the redefinition of national identity, there is the question of how far the state should intervene in the interpretation of history. One side, consisting mainly of right-leaning and conservative authors, argues that the state has to take the politics of history (*polityka historyczna*) seriously, and must make an effort to promote a positive historical interpretation with a clear moral view of the recent past in society. They claim that the lack of such a policy after 1989 and the skepticism of the political elites of the Third Republic towards collective historical memory and national identity effectively jeopardized the project of liberal modernization and the legitimacy of the democratic order. In contrast, the other side of the debate, composed mainly of historians and left-wing intellectuals concentrated around the daily *Gazeta Wyborcza*, warns against what they see as an instrumental understanding of the past, in which history is used predominantly as a tool in a collective identity-building project. They accuse the promoters of active politics of history of bringing back the 19th-century nationalist fantasies and criticize the concomitant moralization of historical discourse.[24]

Without going into details about the Polish debate, which is analyzed in the present volume by Rafał Stobiecki, my intention is to draw attention to the nostalgic rhetoric employed by the partisans of active state politics of history. They are convinced that both the self-understanding of Poles and their image abroad are distorted by the communist propaganda and the hitherto negligent political and cultural elites of the Third Republic. Consequently, they argue, the national historical heritage should be thoroughly reconstructed on the basis of a "true and correct understanding of history" and stripped of communist lies. They feel the need to defend the Polish romantic tradition, stress the traditional national allegiance to Roman Catholicism and the Church, and to promote the image of Poles as European freedom fighters (represented by the Home Army anticommunist resistance, post-1945 émigrés, democratic dissent, and Solidarity) against despotism and totalitarianism of both right and left.[25]

These motives and rhetorical figures, as well as the main intention of actively cultivating the national memory, testify to a powerful nostalgia for the supposed national golden age: a combination of pre-partition Poland and the interwar Second Republic. This kind of politics of history clearly corresponds to Svetlana Boym's other category of nostalgia: "restorative nostalgia," which attempts the transhistorical reconstruction of the lost home in the name of a return to the origins. In contrast to its reflective counterpart, restorative nostalgia regards itself not as nostalgia, but as truth and the reconstruction of the true tradition, a way of dealing with history that protects absolute truths against supposed misinterpretations. Weaving together two main strands, the return to origins and conspiracy theory, restorative nostalgia treats history as a simple modern story of conflict between good and evil, a narrative in which the ambivalence and complexity of history and the specificity of modern circumstances are omitted.[26] Some of the current Polish supporters of active state politics of history are conscious promoters of the interlude theory, which treats the communist period as an inorganic, foreign distortion of national history, which has to be rectified.

Such tendencies can be traced not only in Poland, where they are most apparent, but all over East Central Europe. The strong politically and culturally motivated anti-communist sentiments, merging with the unreflected national history paradigm and the upsurge of memorialism, result in the vague notion of national memory with clearly nationalist underpinnings, which is becoming an indispensable part of the public political discourse in the whole region. This is not to say that the concept of national memory has only just appeared; it clearly has a pedigree reaching back to the anti-communist dissident movements, where a significant part of the opposition regarded the cultivation of national memory as an important tool in opposing the amnesia of the official communist historical master-narrative and the unscrupulous political manipulation with historical research and education.[27] However, with the existence of the so-called institutes of national memory in Poland and Slovakia, and the expected establishment of a similar institution in the Czech Republic, the concept has gained a new dimension. In contrast to the period before 1989 when the strongly moralizing concept of "national memory" with distinctively conservative features has been raised as a banner in the struggle of the "powerless" dissidents against the despotic power, today it becomes a part of an organized, state-driven politics of history.

NATIONAL MEMORY *NEW STYLE*

The main aim of the institutes of national memory is to collect and process the almost unmanageable quantities of archival material produced by the secret police and other repressive institutions of the totalitarian state, which in Poland and Slovakia as well as in the Czech draft bill (after heated dispute) comprises not only the communist period, but also the Second World War. These institutions and their supporters find their model in the *Gauck-Behörde* in Germany, which was established in 1990 and nicknamed after the first Federal Commissioner for the Records of the National Security Service (the German acronym BStU) of the Former GDR, the pastor and civil rights activist Joachim Gauck. This specialized office organized and processed the records of the Stasi *(Staatssicherheitsdienst)*, the best-documented communist secret police force in the former Eastern bloc. Despite references to the German partner and the claims of the adherents of the new institutes that the notion "national memory" in the name of the institution is only a catchword with no significant meaning, the very name as well as the time and political context makes them quite different from the German model.

The BStU regards itself as a documentary and archival institution whose role is above all the elaboration of the history of the *Stasi,* the former communist secret police. As to its social and civic activity, it strives to play an important part in general political education, since by showing "the structure of dictatorships, how people live under a dictatorship and how they might also become perpetrators themselves is of considerable importance for the formation of democratic convictions and competencies."[28] The BStU is a governmental office with clear competencies which has no intention of adopting the role of historical research institution, still less of setting itself any kind of political or identity-building agenda. This however is hardly the case with the other East Central European institutes of national memory. The mission statement of the Polish Institute of National Memory (INM) in particular, as well as the Czech draft bill on such an institute, define their mission in terms of remembering—and in Poland prosecuting—"crimes against the nation," communist and Nazi crimes, war crimes and crimes against humanity and preserving the "patriotic tradition of the fighting against invaders, Nazism, and Communism."[29] The framing of this specific and, by any standards, necessary historical research into the emotionally charged nationalist rhetoric and black-and-white historical meta-narrative indicates the difference between these institutes and the BStU.

Nevertheless, easy as it might be, it would be quite misleading to dismiss the institutes of national memory in East Central Europe as just the latest nationalist inventions. Several aspects of the problem need to be distinguished in order to understand better both the aims and the impact of the institutes in recent political discourse and local historical cultures.

The goal of the supporters of the INM from the practical point of view is to gather, declassify, electronically process, and make accessible the archival resources from the archives of the communist or totalitarian repressive apparatus. The Czech supporters of the INM argue correctly that access to many of these materials (usually under the control of the key ministries) has been very difficult until now, often available only to a select few. They claim that the quantity and complexity of the materials call for a completely new organizational activity; thus a new institution with substantial financial support from the state ought to be established. Arguably, the work of the existing research institutions with their very limited financial and human resources has so far been very unsatisfactory in this respect, especially in the Czech and Slovak cases.[30]

There is also a moral and political motive that has been a guiding principle for Joachim Gauck and for the founder of the Slovak INM, the former dissident Ján Langoš. Namely the need to reverse the logic of the procedures followed hitherto, which stigmatized the victims of crimes against human and civic rights rather than the offenders: the officials of the secret police.[31] This should be possible only after a thorough electronic systematization of the files, which would enable partial reconstruction of the bulk of the files destroyed during the messy times of the bloodless revolutions in 1989. In the opinion of its supporters, the INM should create a clear statement about the criminal machinery of the communist state as well as the individual culprits, which would serve for future generations as a memento of the dictatorial times. The unbiased handling and opening up of the secret police archives is from this point of view understood as an indispensable part in the post-totalitarian democratic development, a process functionally resembling the South African Truth and Reconciliation Commissions after apartheid.[32] In Gauck's conception the effort to remember is a therapeutic endeavor that might lead to collective learning and education essential for civic democratic responsibility and the sense of society as moral community. Simultaneously, he stressed that opening up the files must not mean new anti-communist witch hunts and that by recovering individual stories of collaboration, betrayal, complicity or resistance, and courage it was not "the justice and the truth" that is being established, but merely a bit more justice and a bit more truth with regard to the recent past.[33]

There is also a social aspect of the whole situation that should not be neglected. A new generation of historians and researchers has grown up in recent years that has great difficulty finding jobs within the existing institutions. As is clearly demonstrated by the hundreds of new positions created by the INM in Poland for research into recent history, there are far more young university graduates than there are research and teaching jobs, which creates a natural generational conflict that sometimes takes the simplified form of young conservatives rising up against the allegedly complicit old (reform) communist academic officials who still hold positions with extensive decision-making powers.

And finally, there is a conceptual aspect, which is the main concern of this paper and which arouses criticism in the countries of interest. Why should the concept of national memory be connected with a basically archival institution concerned with a very specific, highly problematic, and from the general historical point of view only partly relevant source base, i.e., materials produced by the communist security services?

From the most general perspective, the concept of a centrally organized and state-sponsored institution bearing this name is highly problematic. Liberal political philosophers beginning with John Locke and Immanuel Kant were skeptical towards the concept of historical memory. Liberal democracy is a horizontal political order whose development and stability depends on a certain historical amnesia on the level of the *polis*.[34] Historical memory relates to identities and thus to basic values and norms. As a clearly vertical element historical memory could be represented and sustained in liberal democracy only by groups, political parties or movements, civic initiatives, families or individual citizens, but definitely not by the state or the nation as a whole. Thus a state-run institution whose main aim is to cultivate a national memory, whatever the source base might be, is a clear step towards a state-run cultural policy that potentially threatens to undermine the social positions and cultural background of groups and social or political strata who have no direct influence on the government.

This brings us to the other facet of the problem, namely the possible abuse of such an institution by the authorities. Despite the arguments of INM supporters about the basically research-oriented and archival aims of the institution and its political neutrality, the very existence of an institution with such financial and human resources (in Poland the INM has 1,400 full-time employees) necessarily creates the temptation to promote it to the role of true arbiter of the historical memory of the nation, and to misuse it for political purposes. In the discussions after the establishment of the Law and Justice coalition government in 2005, many left-wing and liberal Polish intellectuals claimed that this precisely was the case in contemporary Poland. The initially mainly research and educational institution with numerous academic credentials (e.g., in the Jedwabne cause) and considerable expert research and writing has recently been misused in the cultural struggle on behalf of the conservative national government. Moreover, on the basis of a new law made up by young conservative deputies and to the horror of its many employees, the INM became an examining institution of the new round of the lustrations (screening procedures), unprecedented in its scale and questionable in its legal status. The vulnerability of such an institution proves also the case of the Slovak INM. Due to a political deal in the government coalition, the post of the director has been engaged by the nationalist, anti-Hungarian Slovak National Party. The new director became a historian Ivan Petranský in his thirties whose previous efforts included a partial rehabilitation of the Slovak pro-Nazi war-time state and its President Jozef Tiso. His first commission at the INM announced in the second day in function is a project of documentation of the persecution and eviction of Slovak population by the Hungarian authorities after the so-called First Vienna Arbitrage in November 1938.

In contrast one might mention the Hungarian case, where recent history is as much a part of the current political struggle and ideological and political rhetoric as it is in Poland or the Czech Republic.[35] Besides, as the unrest in Budapest streets in fall 2006 showed, the political rivalry over dominance in historical discourse and patriotic credibility assumes considerable intensity at times. Nevertheless, the Historical Archives of Hungarian State Security, with no national memory agenda mentioned in either its name or mission statement, works as an institution entrusted with the inspection and mediation of the documents of the communist security apparatus. So far, the Historical Archives has served mainly professional and legal interests and has not been directly involved in heated cultural-political clashes.

Last but not least, there is the connection—deeply suspect from the scholarly point of view—of political and cultural anti-Communism, the recovered national history paradigm, and the vibrant culture of memorialization. The Czech draft bill about the Institute of National Memory[36] naturally refers to the 1993 Act about the lawlessness of the communist regime that symbolizes the basic legitimating strategy of the nascent Czech democracy towards the troublesome communist legacy in the early transition years. The diction of the draft bill itself, like many of its supporters' public statements, is closely related to the political legitimating discourse of the early 1990s. The avowed aim is to found a state institution "aware of the need to come to terms *(vyrovnat se)* with the communist regime" that would provide society with an exemplary historical master-narrative bearing "the memory of the immense number of victims, losses and injuries that the Czech nation and other nations on the territory of the Czech Republic suffered in the period of non-freedom *(nesvobody)*."[37] The document promulgating the draft bill, as well as the pronouncements of some INM supporters, draw on the dichotomous language typical of the simplified theory of totalitarianism and the mythical image of an integral, unified nation—the language of moral duty towards national community. Theirs are the moral-political concepts of crime, guilt, and suffering and, last but not least, the related conviction that it is possible to establish a real "historical truth." Quite significant also is the shift in the notion of "coming to terms" with the communist past, where the previous imperfective *"vyrovnávání se"* has been replaced by perfective *"vyrovnání se"* which implies the possibility of steering this process towards a final stage, i.e., a post-revolutionary purge of the historical and thus also the public political discourse of all vestiges of the communist past.[38] All this is evidence that the establishment of the Czech Institute of National Memory is above all a politically motivated project of specific collective remembering. Contrary to the claims of its supporters in academia, these projects are far from promoting the kind of detached, impartial and value-restrained historical analysis that strives to reconstruct and understand—though not to justify—past events, however disturbing they might be. The politics of memory is trying to replace serious historical scholarship, advancing a unified interpretation over sound arguments.

These initiatives cannot be dismissed as mere political, nationalist undertakings. Above all, it is clear that the memory of the suffering endured by numerous citizens and political, religious, and other groups needs to be better integrated into the historical picture of the communist period and thus become an integral part of political education. However, this cannot be done by constructing an official, state-sponsored national memory. "Only a pluralist interpretation of history may achieve a shared truth at best or reinforce divided memories at worst. History as an ongoing argument is still preferable to the myth-making of official collective memory."[39] Unfortunately as the analysis of the diction and conceptual background shows the Czech plan to establish a national memory institute, like its Polish counterpart, is heading precisely in this direction. In a way, it is a part of a broader phenomenon of the re-nationalization and legalization of history, which is appearing throughout Europe and beyond. As such, it is a small but noticeable step towards a society in which the pluralist, open-minded, and liberal historical culture formed within polemical academic discourse and the variety of historical memories in society might well be replaced by a normatively structured, sharp, majoritarian, and moralizing concept of this or that version of the so-called national memory.

NOTES

1 Cf. Dealing with the authoritarian and violent past as a world-wide phenomenon in e.g., A. Kenkmann, and H. Zimmer, eds., *Nach Kriegen und Diktaturen. Umgang mit Vergangenheit als internationales Problem* [After wars and dictatorships. Coping with the past as an international issue] (Essen: Klartext, 2005).

2 For an analysis of the legal handling of the communist past in the Czech republic and how this connects to the legal system and legitimacy of postmodern democracy, see the brilliant study by J. Přibáň, *Dissidents of Law: On the 1989 Revolutions, Legitimations, Fictions of Legality and Contemporary Version of the Social Contract* (Aldershot: Ashgate Publishing, 2002). Cf. also J. Rupnik, "Politika vyrovnávání s komunistickou minulostí. Česká zkušenost." [Politics of dealing with the communist past. The Czech experience], *Soudobé dějiny* 9, No. 1 (2002): 9–26.

3 Cf. Andrzej Paczkowski who deals with this question in the context of the Polish approach to the communist past, A. Paczkowski, "Was tun mit der kommunistischen Vergangenheit? Polen." [What to do with the communist past? The Polish case] *Transit,* No. 22, No. 1 (2002): 87–107.

4 Cf. R. Jaworski, "Geschichtsdenken im Umbruch. Osteuropäische Vergangenheitsdiskurse im Vergleich" [Historical Thinking at a Turning Point. East European Historical Discourses in Comparison] in *Umbruch im östlichen Europa. Die nationale Wende und das kollektive Gedächtnis* [Turning Point in Eastern Europe. The National Turn and

the Collective Consciousness] A. Cobrea-Hosie, R. Jaworski and M. Sommer, eds., (Innsbruck: Studienverlag, 2004), pp. 27–44.

5 See P. Kolář and M. Kopeček, "A Difficult Quest for New Paradigms: Czech Historiography after 1989," in *Narratives Unbound: Historical Studies in Post-Communist Eastern Europe,* S. Antohi, P. Apor and B. Trencsényi, eds., (Budapest: CEU Press, 2007), pp. 173–248.

6 Cf. J. Tesař, *Zamlčená diagnóza* [Withheld diagnosis] (Prague: Triada, 2003).

7 Cf. F. Mayer, "La prison pour passé, la résistance pour mémoire: La Confederation des anciens détenus politiques," [Prison as a past, resistance as a memory. The Confederation of the former political prisoners] in *Mémoires du communisme en Europe centrale.* (Prague: Cahiers du CEFRES, No. 26, 2001), pp. 121–158.

8 Cf. V. Kural, et al., *Československo roku 1968, I. Obrodný proces; II. Počátky normalizace* [Czechoslovakia in 1968. Vol. I, The Process of Regeneration; Vol. II, The Origins of Normalization] (Prague: Parta, 1993). For a more subjective and politically engaged view, see, for example, the recently published voluminous memoirs of one of the reform movement's leading politicians: Č. Císař, *Paměti: Nejen o zákulisí Pražského jara* [Memoirs: Not just about the backroom of the Prague Spring] (Prague: SinCon, 2005).

9 Even though I stressed the peculiarity of the Czech situation with respect to the historical reflection and elaboration of the Prague Spring, one can naturally find structurally similar phenomena in other former state socialist countries. Perhaps the closest in this respect is the Hungarian revolution of 1956 and its disputed legacy.

10 See the more elaborated version of the argument in J. Cuhra and M. Kopeček, "L'historiographie tchèque du communisme depuis 1989," [Czech historiography of communism after 1989] in *La Nouvelle Alternative*, No. 60/61 (2004): 199–214.

11 One of the few initiatives striving to change the situation in Czechia has been the establishment of the programmatically theoretical historical journal *Dějiny, teorie, kritika* [History, Theory, Criticism] published in Prague by the Institute of T. G. Masaryk and the Institute of Contemporary History since 2003.

12 Cf. P. Kolář and M. Kopeček, "A Difficult Quest for New Paradigms."

13 E. Schmidt-Hartmann, "Forty Years of Historiography under Socialism in Czechoslovakia. Continuity and Change in Patterns of Thought," *Bohemia*, Vol. 29, No. 2 (1988): 300–324.

14 R. Jaworski, "Geschichtsdenken im Umbruch." For a broader context of the redefinition of national identity in the early transition period see the cultural anthropologist L. Holý, *The Little Czech and the Great Czech Nation. National Identity and Post-Communist Social Transformation* (Cambridge: Press Syndicate of the University of Cambridge, 1996).

15 P. Nora, "Gedächtniskonjunkur," [The conjuncture of memory] in *Transit,* No. 22 (Winter 2001/2002): 18–31.

16 See F. Mayer, *Les Tchéques et leur communisme: Mémoire et identités politiques.* [Czechs and their communism. Memory and political identities.](Paris: Éditions de l'École des hautes études en sciences sociales, 2004).

17 See P. Cooke, "Surfing for Eastern Difference. *Ostalgie,* Identity and Cyberspace," *Seminar—A Journal for Germanic Studies,* Vol. 40, No. 3 (September 2004): 207–220; M. Blum, "Remaking the East German Past. *Ostalgie,* Identity and Material Culture," in *The Journal of Popular Culture* Vol. 34, No. 3, (Winter 2000): 229–253.

18 Cf. P. Betts, "The Twilights of the Idols. East German Memory and Material Culture," in *The Journal of Modern History*, Vol. 72, No. 3 (September 2000): 731–765.

19 For the Czech situation see M. Franc, "Ostalgie v Čechách" [Ostalgia in Bohemia] in A. Gjuričová and M. Kopeček, eds., *Kapitoly z dějin české demokracie po roce 1989* [Chapters from the history of Czech democracy after 1989] (Prague, Litomyšl: Paseka, 2007, forthcoming), pp. 189–212.

20 S. Boym, *The Future of Nostalgia* (New York: Basic Books, 2001).

21 See one of the most recent expressions of this line of criticism in Czechia, A. Drda and P. Dudek, *Kdo ve stínu čeká na moc. Čeští komunisté po listopadu 1989* [Waiting for power in the dark. Czech communists after November 1989] (Prague: Paseka, 2006).

22 See ibid., pp. 149–167. The authors stress the political dimension of the nostalgic cultural comeback that in the Czech circumstances plays into the hands of the existing communist party.

23 Cf. the brilliant study focusing on Hungary's symbolic politics both prior and after 1989, I. Rév, *Retroactive Justice. Prehistory of Post-Communism* (Stanford, CA: Stanford University Press, 2005).

24 See Rafal Stobiecki's chapter in the present volume and also works such as D. Gawin and P. Kowal, eds, *Polityka historyczna. Historycy—politycy—prasa* [Politics of history. Historians—politicians—press] (Warsaw: Muzeum Powstania Warszawskiego, 2005); R. Kostro and T. Merta, eds., *Pamięć i odpowiedzialność* [Memory and accountability] (Kraków-Wrocław: OPM, 2005); P. Kosiewski, ed., *Pamięć i polityka zagraniczna* [Memory and foreign policy] (Warsaw: Fundacja im. Stefana Batorego, 2006).

25 See the typical discussion at the Institute of National Memory in April 2006, particularly the pronouncements of the INM's representatives Janusz Kurtyka and Jan Żaryn and the historian and editor of the journal *Arcana* Andrzej Nowak in "Czy Polsce potrzebna jest polityka historyczna?" [Does Poland need the politics of history?] *Biuletyn IPN*, 5 (64) (May 2006): 3–33. For a critique, see the pronouncements of Arkadiusz Rybicki, ibid., or A. Romanowski, "Kłamstwo I banał polityki historycznej" [Lies and banalities of the politics of history], *Gazeta Wyborcza*, 15 July 2006, downloaded from the gazeta.pl website on 8 August 2006.

26 S. Boym, *The Future of Nostalgia*; cf. also the classic work on the modern use of traditions E. Hobsbawm and T. Ranger, *The Invention of Tradition* (Cambridge: Cambridge University Press, 1983).

27 In the Czechoslovak context the most famous example, which stirred up a long-lasting discussion was the Charter 77 document "The Right for History" from May 1984, in *Charta 77. 1977–1989. Od morální k demokratické revoluci* [Charter 77. 1977–1989 From moral towards democratic revolution], V. Prečan, ed., (Scheinfeld-Schwarzenberg, Bratislava: Archa, 1990), pp. 254–257. Generally the critique of the communist dictatorship and the Czechoslovak years of "normalization" in particular as a "regime of forgetting" has, of course, a long history, perhaps the best known example being Milan Kundera's famous novel of 1979: *The Book of Laughter and Forgetting*.

28 Cf. the official website www.bstu.bund.de/cln_042/DE/Home/homepage__node.html__nnn=true (downloaded on 7 December 2006).

29 Cf. www.ipn.gov.pl/index_eng.html, the Czech draft bill is on www.upn.cz/store/185.doc (both downloaded on Dec 7, 2006).

30 The webpages providing sections (far from complete) of the Czech public discussion are www.aktualne.usd.cas.cz/index.php, www.upn.cz/view.php?page=polemika.

31 See the last interview with Ján Lángoš before his tragic death: "Chceme se zaměřit na pachatele" [To bend on the perpetrator] in *A 2,* No. 24 (2006), downloaded electronically from www.tydenika2.cz, on 30 August 2006.

32 A comparison between the truth commissions and institutes of national memory is beyond the scope of the present paper. Without idealizing the impact of the truth commissions, however, it seems obvious that there is a basic difference between attempts to create new forms of social solidarity and sense of community by organized truth-telling and procedures based on the documentary vestiges of the repression apparatus. See R. L. Nytagodien and A. G. Neal, "Collective Trauma, Apologies, and the Politics of Memory," in *Journal of Human Rights*, Vol. 3, No. 4 (December 2004): 465–475.

33 J. Gauck, "Akten und Gerechtigkeit. Gedanken zum Umgang mit der Vergangenheit." [Files and justice. Considerations on coping with the past], in *Plädoyers für Gerechtigkeit* [Pleas for justice] (Rostock: University of Rostock, 1994), p. 17.

34 In the Central European context see, for example, M. Król, *Liberalizmus strachu a liberalizmus odvahy* [Liberalism of fear and liberalism of courage] (Bratislava: Kalligram, 1999), especially pp. 158–177.

35 Cf. András Mink's and Ferenc Laczó's chapters in this collection.

36 The article has been submitted in March 2007. Later during the year, the Czech Parliament passed the law envisaging the establishment of the institute in January 2008. There were several amendments in the law as a result of the concomitant public and political discussion. Many of the amendments concerned technical details sometimes of high relevance, such as the mechanisms of how the Institute's board of trustees should be elected. Another was a change in the name of the institution from the Institute of National Memory to the Institute for the Study of Totalitarian Regimes. Only slightly less problematic than the previous one, the final name clearly was a partial concession to the vocal criticism that the project of INM aroused among academic as well as political public. Nevertheless, apart from the name, the main arguments, fundamental diction, as well as the general justification in the preamble of the law remained the same. Thus, despite the above mentioned changes, the main arguments of the present study concerned with the general development of the historical discourse and its broader cultural and political context keep their validity.

37 See Preamble of the draft bill, www.upn.cz/store/185.doc (downloaded on 7 December 2006).

38 In all of these aspects the supporters of INM are quite far from Joachim Gauck's language, which, though morally and religiously based, is sophisticated and programmatically non-moralizing, allowing for the ambiguity and complexity of the historical reality and its representation.

39 H. Adam, "Divided Memories: Reckoning with a Criminal Regime" in *Justice and the Politics of Memory—Religion & Public Life,* Vol. 33, (2003): 8.

The Czechoslovak Legionary Tradition and the Battle Against the "Beneš Doctrine" in Czech Historiography

The Case of General Rudolf Medek (1890–1940)[1]

KATYA A. M. KOCOUREK

OVERVIEW

Despite the fact that almost 18 years have lapsed since the Changes in East Central Europe, several "white spaces" (Jan Křen) in contemporary Czech (and Czechoslovak) history are yet to be reassessed objectively by historians.[2] "Historical revisionism" has in many respects obscured understanding of several key events in 20th-century history (most notably concerning ethnic cleansing). However, when considering other significant historical periods in Czechoslovak national history specifically—most notably the so-called Second Republic and the period immediately prior to the communist coup of 1948—the tendency among some historians has not been to negate fact but rather to reinforce ideologically-motivated narratives (which I refer to here as the "Beneš doctrine") in an attempt to legitimize the moral standards of Czechoslovak political culture.[3] Labored efforts to overcome the Marxist historiographical heritage by underlining the founding myths of Czechoslovak history and defending the political traditions of the First Republic, evidenced most notably in the cult-like adulation of T.G. Masaryk and Edvard Beneš, has, in some cases, resulted in the "periodization" and conceptualization of history into "fascist" (center- to extreme-right) and "democratic" (center-left) sub-groups, thereby blurring the political motivations of particular individuals or groups, particularly those belonging to the conservative right wing. Revisiting "historical revisionism"—particularly the Czech brand of which Beneš is such an obvious part—need not necessarily lead to more fudging; it should in fact help clarify core detail and viewpoints obscured by existing "gray spaces." This chapter discusses three political narratives about Czechoslovak history in relation to Edvard Beneš's conception of the political tradition represented by the Czechoslovak legionaries during the 1920s. It begins with an introduction of the case study, General Rudolf Medek, and an appraisal of scholarship published since 1989 relating to the Czechoslovak political right; followed by a discussion of the institutionalization of the Beneš doctrine after the Second World War; and ending with a section about the political crisis of the mid-1920s, which is crucial for understanding the origins of Edvard Beneš's conception of "left" and "right" in Czechoslovak political ideology. Several legionary groups played a critical role in the interwar period in helping to consolidate the legitimacy of the political ideology of the Czechoslovak state;[4] and therefore, it is the contention of this paper that it is necessary to reassess the history of Czechoslovak legionary politics during the 1920s, and the role played by Edvard Beneš in the legionary sphere, in order to account for the multitude of political ideologies and viewpoints in interwar Czechoslovakia, particularly on the right of the political spectrum.

I. THE HISTORIOGRAPHICAL DEFICITS OF CZECH SCHOLARSHIP AFTER 1989: RUDOLF MEDEK AS CASE STUDY

Introducing Rudolf Medek (1890–1940)

Rudolf Medek's name is inextricably linked with the history of the Czechoslovak legions during the First World War. He was a legionary, a professional soldier, as well as a legionary poet and impassioned promoter of the legionary ideal after 1918. His military career on the Eastern Front, first as a volunteer in the Russian Imperial Army and then as a Czechoslovak legionary, was highly successful.[5] He rose rapidly through the ranks; his outstanding record in reconnaissance missions as well as key battles involving Czechs and Slovaks on the Eastern Front, for which he was decorated on numerous occasions, were matched by an impressive political and administrative career as a leading representative of Czechoslovak legionaries in Russia. Medek achieved high status within the Czechoslovak military leadership in Russia. He was promoted by Milan Rastislav Štefánik, the Czechoslovak minister for war, to the position of head of (Czechoslovak) military administration in January 1919 following Štefánik's two-month visit to Siberia. After Štefánik's departure, Medek was appointed, along with General Jan Syrový and fellow legionary and later Czechoslovak diplomat, Bohdan Pavlů, to a special three-man governing committee responsible for all matters relating to Czechoslovak soldiers in Russia, which included overseeing major reforms in the Russian–Czechoslovak branch of the evolving republican Czechoslovak army. Just shortly before his departure from Russia in the summer of 1919, Medek was honored with the Distinguished Service Order for his contribution to the organization of Czechoslovak forces in the country. Following his departure, an article by Jan Syrový (1888–1970) entitled "Rudolf Medek" appeared in *Československý voják*, a journal Medek had founded in September 1917. Syrový praised Medek for his journalistic work on the Eastern Front and particularly for the patriotic tone of his poetry (captured most notably in Medek's most celebrated poem, "Zborov" written in July 1917), which had helped consolidate the meaning of the "Czechoslovak idea" in the minds of fellow legionaries.[6] Medek joined the Czechoslovak Ministry of Defense on 8 January 1920, following his return to the new Republic, where he worked as the head of a complaints committee and oversaw the first critical reforms of the newly evolving Czechoslovak army, until he became Director of the Resistance Memorial Institute, *Památník odboje* (after 1929 it was re-named as the *Památník osvobození* or Liberation Memorial Institute), established in May 1920.

Rudolf Medek is much admired for his popularization of the political and social history of the Czechoslovak legions as well as for his portrayal of the idea of *vlast* (homeland) and nationhood more generally. He is rather less admired for his politicization of the role of the legions in the period during and after the Bolshevik Revolution. The fact that Medek envisaged a distinct political role for the legionaries in Russia between 1918 and 1921, after their return to the Czechoslovak Republic, should come as little surprise, and yet the politics of Medek's nationalist discourse remain gravely misunderstood. The fact that Medek attributed a civilizing mission to Czechoslovak "freedom fighters" (rank and file legionaries) in order to rid Russia of the degenerate Bolshevik ideology in 1918, for instance, arises directly from his conception of the Czechoslovak idea not simply as a cipher for the liberation of "Czechoslovak" national territories, but as a source of political values for the new citizenry of a future Czechoslovak state. Medek remained a firm Czechoslovakist throughout his life, and he represented a distinct legionary tradition of state ideology rooted in "national defense," "patriotism," and "male courage." Medek was in many respects a typical product of the Central European tradition of littérateur as nation-builder. He was a conservative nationalist who stood on the right of Czechoslovak politics. He became associated with the National Democratic Party led by the Czech politician Karel Kramář in the early 1920s through his friendship with party members including the poets J.S. Machar, Viktor Dyk and party secretary, František Hlaváček. Most significant of all, Medek wrote for the journal that became the repository of national democratic thinking in the late 1920s, *Fronta* (The Front) established by the journalist and littérateur, Karel Horký.

Medek's case provides a unique example of a distinguished serving army officer who was also fully engaged in Czechoslovak cultural life and, during three key periods (1923–26, 1933–34, and 1938–39), the political life of the Republic. He was a high-ranking member of a distinct interwar elite made up of former Czech and Slovak or Czechoslovak-Russian legionaries who occupied significant positions at the Ministry of Defense, the Castle,[7] and in the General Staff of the Czechoslovak Army.[8] Medek's cult-like status of "legionary Bard" and "leading Czechoslovak revolutionary" amongst right-wing legionaries intensified after his creation of the "Independent Union of Czechoslovak Legionaries" (*Nezávislá jednota československých legionářů* or NJČsL) in December 1925. Medek's "independent union" was a military organization established in opposition to the social-democratic and state-sponsored "Union of Czechoslovak Legionaries" (*Československá obec legionářska* or ČsOL).[9]

Medek was a polemicist whose writing was both revered and fiercely contested.[10] As an ardent anti-Bolshevik and anti-German, Medek was inevitably shunned by both the Nazis and the communists. Owing to a combination of ideology, history and folkloric-political hearsay, since 1939 Rudolf Medek has become, according to his émigré-publicist son, Ivan Medek, "one of the most sequestered figures of the First Czechoslovak Republic."[11] A gradual dissipation of historical memory is inevitable and natural in this instance because Medek was placed on the index of banned authors after the German Occupation in March 1939, and remained there until the autumn of 1989. However, there are other factors that explain this loss of historical memory. The period 1945–48 was decisive in determining the fate of those figures that had been deemed taboo at the end of the First Republic. The victory over the Germans, albeit with Soviet help, provided a new context for the partial intellectual rehabilitation of some whose ideas (most notably Viktor Dyk's ideology of patriotism) were deemed useful for reinforcing the mores of postwar Czechoslovak state and society. However, the Košice program (4 April 1945), which laid down the institutional framework of the postwar Czechoslovak political order and forbade the participation of right-wing parties in government, made it almost impossible for those figures from the 1930s generation to make a comeback, posthumously or otherwise.[12] Several right-wing figures from the pre-1939 period, such as the renegade legionary

Radola Gajda, sought official forgiveness for their previous political mis-demeanors committed before the Second World War. This was not Medek's case. However, unlike members of Gajda's family, who re-mained out of favor with elite circles at the end of the Second World War, Medek's son Ivan was granted a private audience with Czechoslovak president Edvard Beneš in September 1945.[13] However, Ivan's defense of his father as a "vehement, impulsive and subjective" man who found it difficult to comprehend the "complex prudent realism of Beneš's politics" did little to alter existing perceptions about those on the opposing side of the ideological barricade prior to the war, despite the fact that they had not collaborated with the Germans after 1939.

Historical Writing and Rudolf Medek

Rudolf Medek presents most historians with a quandary. He represented neither the extreme nor the traditional conservative right wing of interwar Czechoslovak politics. Medek has fallen into the ideological crack exist-ing between "extremism" and "conservatism." He was neither a clear-cut traitor to the Czechoslovak idea nor to the Czechoslovak Republic, like fellow legionary figures, Radola Gajda (1892–1948) and Emanuel Mo-ravec (1893–1945); nor was he conventionally loyal to the Castle Group *(Hrad)*. He disliked Edvard Beneš intensely, but was immensely fond of T.G. Masaryk.

There has been little discussion about the political and cultural signifi-cance of Medek's writing. The greater part of the memoirs published by leading First Republic political figures discuss only the political role of former legionaries who became close to Masaryk's Castle Group, such as General Stanislas Čeček (1886–1930), and seemingly exclude those unable or unwilling to negotiate and compromise with the Castle.[14] Historical judgements about Medek as a representative of the interwar Czechoslovak political right through his work as a prominent ex-legionary writer, and as Director of the Resistance Memorial Institute, have been clouded by the polemical controversies in which he became embroiled during the 1920s and 1930s, which supposedly confirmed Medek's pro-fascist leanings.[15]

Medek's political infamy was confirmed by his frequently expressed public criticism of Edvard Beneš, both as foreign minister and later as Czechoslovak president. Medek's relationship with Beneš became increas-ingly complicated over the issue of capitulation at the time of Munich, when he branded Beneš "public enemy number one." Medek's criticism of Beneš after Munich was brutally blunt: "Edvard Beneš suffers from a misguided doctrinaire attitude. Beneš has placed humanitarian democracy above reality, and there is nothing more real and valuable than the nation and the homeland … [Humanitarian democracy] equates with pacifism; this is an absurdity. We are not enemies of the peace, but we were always enemies of phraseology which converts the belief of the masses, a Christian ideal, into a single phrase."[16] The events of Munich constituted a tragic blow for the military establishment. For those who considered themselves the architects of a new Czechoslovak army after 1918, Munich was also a cruel humiliation. And therefore Medek's writings about both T.G. Masaryk and Edvard Beneš in the aftermath of Munich must be understood in the context of a brutalized sense of disappointment at being unable to defend a country the legionaries had helped create.

The most politically significant moment in Medek's life came when his military career was already over, following the dissolution by the government of the Czechoslovak Army, during the so-called Second Republic, when he delivered an impassioned panegyric, "Zemi milovanou…" (Beloved homeland), about the critical importance of the nationalist verse of Karel Hynek Mácha on the occasion of the reburial of Mácha's remains in the Vyšehrad cemetery on 7 May 1939. With this Medek firmly established himself primarily as a figurehead of the type of Czech nationalism that was later frowned upon after the war, and less as a symbol of the archetypal Czechoslovak patriot, the cult of political acceptability— paradoxically precisely the quality with which Medek had captured public imagination during the interwar years. Propagandist journalism published during the Second Republic exploited the controversial nature of Medek's First Republic persona, and it was after 1938 that Medek's reputation as a "fascist" or figure of the extreme Czechoslovak right wing was consolidated. Medek was seemingly exposed as a "collaborator"[17] only nine days after his death on 31 August 1940 in an article by Vladimír Břetenář published in a leading Protectorate newspaper, *Arijský boj,* "Básník pod Hradem—Židé na Hradě" (The poet beneath the Castle—Jews at the Castle), which discussed Medek's "hatred of Jews," his ostracism from the Castle, and most significant of all, his personal feud with Beneš arising from his rejection of the Beneš presidency as part of a wider "Judeo-Bolshevik" plot against the Republic resulting in Munich.[18]

Historians writing about Medek from a purely military perspective, such as Jiří Fidler, Petr Hofman and Jitka Zabloudilová, do not write in much detail about Medek during the Second Republic, and end their narrative in the autumn of 1938. The period from October 1938 to March

1939 remains a politically sensitive topic. A more likely reason, however, is that the attempt to write about Medek after 1938 would prove far too difficult because of the plethora of actions and journalism that supposedly contradicted his First Republic persona. Due to the risk of further damaging Medek's already misunderstood and blighted reputation as "national hero, given the incompatibility of Medek's First and Second Republic personae, this is a task that has not been undertaken in the Czech Republic despite the fall of Communism. Unlike other leading military figures from the First Republic, such as the Chief of Staff during the 1930s, General Ludvík Krejčí (1890–1972), Medek has not been adequately rehabilitated *in memoriam* since 1989, a fact poignantly illustrated by the lack of proper acknowledgement of Medek's foundation and directorship of the Liberation Memorial Institute in Žižkov in either the main building itself or in recent publications about its history.[19] Despite past failings, however, the Czechs appear to be experiencing something of a 'Medekian' revival at present: two exhibitions commemorating Rudolf Medek's wartime and peacetime exploits have been held in Prague since March of this year[20] and newspaper articles published in the Czech broadsheets for the first time since the Changes are beginning to discuss the political, not simply literary or cultural, significance of Medek's First Republic writings.[21] Furthermore, the Vojenský historický ústav [VHÚ] (Military Historical Institute), the seat of Medek's First Republic home, the old Liberation Memorial Institute (*Památník osvobození*), has created a special commemorative medal in Medek's honour (*Pamětní odznak generála Rudolfa Medka*). The first recipient of this distinction was Rudolf Medek's son, Ivan, on the occasion of the opening of an exhibition entitled 'Rudolf Medek – soldier' at the Military Historical Institute in Žižkov on 29 March 2007.[22] These recent developments will help combat the multifarious misunderstandings existing in the public and academic domain about Rudolf Medek the soldier, writer and political figure.[23]

In *Bílá místa v našich dějinách?* (1990) Jan Křen identifies the political right as one of many thematic white spaces in Czech history and historiography. The revision of history for political reasons is an obvious cause of such spaces. Indeed Rudolf Medek did not feature in the communists' reinvention of themselves as Czechoslovak patriots after 1945 because as a "fascist" (which at that time meant "anti-Bolshevik" and "pro-German," in line with Marxist-Leninist ideology) he combined all the worst qualities of a class enemy typical of his reactionary generation which included, most notably, Rudolf Beran, Jaroslav Preiss, Jan Černý, Jan Malypetr, Konrad Henlein, Andrej Hlinka and Jozef Tiso.[24] Any competing sources of nationalist legitimacy from First Republic life, other than that associated with T.G. Masaryk, were ruled out of the new, highly selective communist reading of Czechoslovak history. (T.G. Masaryk was only deemed "acceptable" in the immediate aftermath of the communist coup and during the period of ideological thaw in the 1960s, otherwise he too was consigned to history by the communist regime). In death, Medek's name erroneously became associated with the "Protectorate mentality" described by Bradley F. Abrams[25] and was thus washed up in the wave of retributions aimed at the political right on the pretext of Nazi collaboration, starting in 1946 with the trial and imprisonment of leading Second Republic figures, many of whom were legionaries that had held influential positions in the Czechoslovak Army prior to 1938. Such ideological condemnation, coupled with the jettisoning of the historical status of individuals of the political right, resulted in the confirmation, rather than the alteration, of pre-existing judgements about the "extreme wings" of Czechoslovak politics. Medek's last published work, following an abridged collection of verse published during the Protectorate in 1943,[26] appeared in 1947 in a nationalist collection of poems compiled and edited by Jaroslav Seifert, *Křik Koruny české*.[27] However in the "Afterward" written by Karel Cvejn, Medek is the only poet not mentioned directly by name, and therefore the authorship of the poem "Hradec studentům—mučedníkům" is left blank, an ironic twist given that Medek's poem was more virulently anti-German than any other poem included in the collection. (Medek did not fit the criteria, outlined by Cvejn, of a suppressed left-wing poet, mouthpiece of the humiliated yet proud nation, silenced both prior to and following Nazi occupation).[28] After 1950, with the complete communist clampdown on the Czechoslovak legionary tradition, Medek's poems were never again reprinted, not even in commemorative literature about the Great War battles of Zborov or Bahmač, which formed an integral part of Czechoslovak nationalist ideology. The legionary tradition as represented by Medek was confined to the past once and for all in June 1954 with the display of Klement Gottwald's embalmed body (and not the remains of T.G. Masaryk, as had originally been planned by Medek) in the mausoleum of the Liberation Memorial Institute.[29] Any lingering memory that remained of Rudolf Medek thereafter, depicted most notably by František Halas in his wartime memoirs, *Bez legend* (1955), was the entirely negative representation of an aggressively elitist Czechoslovak legionary with no respect for the views of the "masses" and utter contempt for any form of equality.[30]

Medek remains misunderstood as a figure of the political right due to perhaps the largest white or misunderstood space of Czechoslovak history not mentioned by Jan Křen—a period that lasted less than a decade between Munich and the communist ascendancy.[31] It is ironic that the legacy of the Second Republic has damaged Medek's historical status most of all. The fascist epithet dished up by the communists is misplaced. The following image illustrates the point. At the same time as Medek's body was laid to rest in the cemetery at Olšany on the afternoon of 28 August 1940, the new Nazi occupants of the Liberation Memorial Institute in Žižkov whitewashed over captions written by Medek accompanying a mosaic by the artist Max Švabinský for the "Chapel of Executed Legionaries" inside the mausoleum of the Memorial which was built specially for the commemoration of the founding of the Republic that never took place in October 1938. The entirety of Medek's Czechoslovak nationalist program was rooted in anti-Bolshevik and anti-German sentiment and therefore remained anathema.[32] It would be incorrect to say, therefore, that Medek has been straight-forwardly airbrushed out of history. If anything, he has fallen into a rather large grey historiographical space that has resulted in the imprecise understanding of his political views.

The literature published since 1989 shows that Rudolf Medek is a figure associated primarily with the Second Republic, the cultural politics of the authoritarian-national state, and Czech "Fascism" in general. Together with the Catholic writer, poet and journalist, Jaroslav Durych, Medek managed the National cultural committee *(Národní kulturní rada)*, the cultural wing of the National Unity Party *(Strana národní jednoty)*, created in November 1938 during the Second Republic. Jan Rataj is explicit about Medek's politics after 1938 and notes that Medek associated with or belonged to "fascist sub-groups," the "militant right," and "integral Catholics," that is, all those apprehensive of German aggression.[33] However, according to Rataj's analysis, in which "left" seems to be synonymous with "democrat" and "right" with "demagogue," in their attempts to re-fashion the concept of the national state, the intolerant intellectual wing of political Catholicism laid the groundwork for cooperation with the Germans.[34] Reinventing the status of those on the right as pseudo-collaborators because their thinking "corresponded" with Nazi ideology is a view that clearly requires revision, and yet in Medek's case the impression remains also partly because several legionary colleagues with whom he had been closely associated during the First World War—most notably Czechoslovak legionary and Nazi collaborator Emanuel Moravec (1893–1945)—did become collaborators, although certainly many did not. Medek was not and was unlikely ever to have become a collaborator.[35] Medek wrote for *Řád*, the journal of the "integral Catholic" intelligentsia led by Count Karel Schwarzenberg; however after November 1938 he also wrote for a range of right-wing newspapers and journals (both centrist and more extreme) including *Tak, Národní politika, Narodní listy, Venkov, Národní obnova, Cesta, Lumír* and *Národní myšlenka*, besides indulging in polemics with Ferdinand Peroutka on the pages of the left-liberal journal, *Přítomnost*. In an article for the Catholic journal *Obzory*, Stanislav Vejvar correctly emphasizes the multifaceted nature of conservatism in the Second Republic and identifies distinct Catholic-conservative, conservative-national, and radical-nationalist ideological currents.[36] Medek did not identify fully with any one of these, but dabbled in each, a polemical practice carried over from the First Republic. It is overlooked that Medek distanced himself from Fascism on several occasions including, most notably, several months before the Munich crisis when he denounced the concept of fascist dictatorship in several articles for *Národní politika*, whilst calling on the population to prepare themselves to defend their country in May 1938.

According to dissident literature of the 1970s and 1980s, which sought to revise stringent Marxist-Leninist interpretations by offering a more objective interpretation of the First Republic, part of the problem in assessing the Czech political right is due to the fact that the interwar Czechoslovak political spectrum lacked a clearly defined conservative tradition, thereby pushing right-of-center figures to the extreme fringes of politics.[37] However, the existing distinctions between different groups of "right-wing" in the Czechoslovak legionary camp were not accounted for and some Catholic writers including those authoring, most notably, *Češi v dějinách nové doby (1848–1939)* (Podiven), developed the image of Medek as a proto-fascist due to his close association with legionary radical Radola Gajda during the 1920s.[38]

The work of the late Antonín Klimek has highlighted new avenues of investigation into the tense relationship between the Castle and the "nationalist right" in the First Czechoslovak Republic. When writing about the crisis that beset the so-called "Gentlemen's Coalition" in the summer of 1926, with the ousting of Jiří Stříbrný from the National Socialist Party in July of that year, Klimek notes that Medek joined several others, including one other army officer, two academics, a journalist, the party secretary of the National Democratic Party, František Hlaváček, and Agrarian politician, Adolf Hrubý, at a meeting designed to create a political oppositional front to Edvard Beneš.[39] Medek was appointed to a short-lived governing committee known as "[The] movement for national purification" *(národní hnutí očistné)* established by Jiří Stříbrný in protest to the style of politics promoted by the Castle. The movement and its journal, "The Revivalist movement" *(Obrodné hnutí)*, which never materialized, were to form and maintain alliances with controversial leading figures of the political right including the controversial legionary hero, Radola Gajda. Jitka Zabloudilová and Petr Hofman have identified some interesting new material in Medek's private papers that would suggest that Beneš made unsuccessful conciliatory overtures to Medek in the autumn of 1929 in an attempt to remedy the latter's estrangement from the Castle. However, they do not explain why these efforts came to nothing and thus do not explore the nature of political opposition on the "military right" in interwar Czechoslovakia. In current Czech literature the precise political stance of individual members of the military establishment remains an under-researched topic. The result is that old historiographical assumptions about the First Republic reminiscent of the uncritical political history written in English during the 1970s have now been duplicated in more recent literature, and accordingly anything connected with the Castle is politically legitimate, whilst everything that stood beyond the purview of T.G. Masaryk and Edvard Beneš is politically suspect.[40]

According to historian Zdeněk Kárník, for instance, the state-sponsored legionary organization (ČsOL) had a decisive influence on Czechoslovak public mood during the First Republic over and above Medek's Independent Union of Czechoslovak Legionaries. Kárník also argues that the ČsOL was the main promoter, in conjunction with the Castle, of the idea of Czechoslovak statehood.[41] The significance of the legionary right, represented most notably by Medek's Independent Union of Czechoslovak Legionaries, has therefore been marginalized despite the fact that it was the widely-known Resistance Memorial Institute, the *de facto* seat of the NJČsL under Medek's direction, that produced major publications about Czechoslovak legionaries and other promotional material which shaped both political and popular conceptions of Czechoslovak state ideology during the interwar period.[42]

II. THE LEGACY OF THE SECOND REPUBLIC AND THE INSTITUTIONALIZATION OF THE "BENEŠ DOCTRINE," 1945-48

The immediate postwar period 1945–48 constituted one of the most dramatic phases of Czechoslovak life in the 20th century. This was a crucial time for several reasons, not least because it was an interval between two types of dictatorship, a transitional phase for coming to terms with the immediate past and the evolution of postwar political discourse. The period 1945–48 was one of retribution for political crimes committed by figures of the "right," which, coupled with the oppositionless National Front government or Peoples' Democracy, split Czechoslovak society into "democratic," and "anti-democratic" or "fascist" camps and reinforced political stereotyping about ideological distinctions between "left" and "right," building on the black and white political experiences of the Second Republic and the Nazi Protectorate of Bohemia and Moravia (1939–45). The national tribunals, conducted throughout 1946 and 1947, convicted several leading right-wing figures on the basis of wartime collaboration and the propagation of anti-Semitic views. Several of these were former legionary figures from the First Czechoslovak Republic, and specifically those who had served in the Russian army as Czechoslovak legionaries during the First World War. The trial of General Vladimír Vojtěch Klecanda (1888–1947), co-founder of the nucleus of the Czechoslovak army in Russia, the "Czech unit" *(Česká družina)*, is a case in point. In his defense speech before one tribunal in August 1946, Klecanda attempted to explain that as a "Czechoslovak patriot" from the First World War, collaboration with the Bolsheviks was as unlikely as with the Germans. Furthermore, he underlined the difference between the "aggressive nationalism" of the Nazis and the "patriotic" nationalism (or *národovectví*) of the legionary right wing, which was patriotically "Czechoslovak" and expressed through the military establishment and the Czechoslovak army during the First Republic.[43] Klecanda's comment raises a crucial point about the multiple strands of right-wing ideology within the Czechoslovak legionary movement in the interwar period yet to be properly accounted for by historians, beyond the epithet of "integral nationalist" for all members of the extreme right posited by Petr Pithart during the 1970s.[44] It is clear from the transcript of Klecanda's trial that he was brought to account on the basis of his acquaintance after Munich with Czech army officer Emanuel Moravec and, more significantly, with the deputy German representative in Prague, Karl Hermann Frank, who had summoned Klecanda to his office in the Černín Palace in the closing months of the Second World War. The culture of "trial by association," that is the discrediting of right-wing figures in the immediate postwar period as "Nazi collaborators," was directly connected to the political climate of the Second Republic rather than the daily realities of the Protectorate that followed. The postwar writings of the priest-collaborator and deputy chairman of the (Catholic) Czechoslovak Peoples' Party in and after 1948, Josef Plojhar (1902–81), reveal that the Second Republic posed a much greater strain on postwar Czechoslovak imagination than the war experience itself because it was a specifically Czech nationalist experience, rather than a Nazi import, and a Czech political design that had distinguished itself from the Masarykian First Republic by its association with Catholicism and Bohemian Catholic traditions. On the eve of the communist takeover Plojhar argued that Czech collaboration with the Nazis after March 1939 was precipitated by a "Fascism" specific to the Czech political culture of the Second Republic which had fused Catholicism with the worst elements of intolerant nationalism left over from First Republic life, pushing all legitimate peace-loving Czechoslovak democrats aside.[45] This political line—later exploited by the communists in justifying their use of repressive force against "enemies of the state" after 1948—was preceded by the work of the national tribunals between 1946 and 1947, which created a heady propagandist atmosphere in which any form of right-wing political culture (both extreme and conservative) was legitimately banished from the political landscape along with the symbolic remnants of political "collaboration" in the new Czechoslovak state. The actions and writings of Edvard Beneš in the period from 1946 to 1948 corresponded ideologically to the work of the national tribunals in justifying the need for the symbolic cleansing of any form of "right-wing" opposition after the war.

There were two defining themes of the "Beneš doctrine" in the immediate postwar period. The first relates to the fight against a rather nebulous concept of radical right-wing ideology or "Fascism." In a speech delivered to the "Czechoslovak anti-fascist society" (*Československá protifašistická společnost*) in March 1946, Beneš explains that

> the war against Fascism in Czechoslovakia has deep roots which can be traced back to the founding of the state during 1918 and 1919, to our legionary problem and the conflict with [Karel] Kramář about Czechoslovak military intervention in Russia [following the Bolshevik Revolution] … These represent the worst aspects of our political life in the First Republic. However this is now part of our political history, and it is now possible to identify precisely why and how our war with Fascism began, which predated the Occupation. Everything that occurred during the Occupation is logically rooted in the First Republic, and specifically in the period following our return [to Czechoslovakia] after the Paris Peace Conference [in 1919] … When taking account of these facts, the views and actions of many periods during and after Munich, and during the Occupation, become clear.[46]

For Beneš, therefore, the national tribunals heralded the "beginning of the end of all forms of Fascism and Nazism [and their arch-representatives] in a Czechoslovak context, and the return to a clean form of political ideology and a Masarykian conception of Czechoslovak democracy."[47] The second theme of the "Beneš doctrine" relates directly to the organization of Czechoslovak legionaries in postwar Czechoslovakia, and their role in securing social and national justice for the state. Beneš had always maintained a close working relationship with the state-sponsored Union of Czechoslovak Legionaries (*Československá obec legionářská* or ČsOL), in effect becoming its unofficial patron after its establishment in Prague in January 1921. In his address to the first postwar annual meeting of the ČsOL, which convened in St Wenceslas Square in July 1947, Beneš declared that the ČsOL was the only legionary organization to have continuously and faithfully represented the Masarykian Czechoslovak ideals of "freedom," "democracy" and "genuine humanitarianism" making it, according to Beneš, the only legionary tradition worth preserving.[48] As Jan Galandauer notes in his recent work about the "Battle of Zborov,"[49] the ČsOL was the only legionary organization recreated after the war, in 1946, which signalled the beginning of the gradual transformation of historical memory about Czechoslovak legionary culture as it had existed before 1938. The traditions associated with the legionary right-wing, particularly their commemoration of wartime, as well as their conception of the Czechoslovak national state and other military rituals, were gradually phased out of Czechoslovak national consciousness altogether, and indeed Beneš makes no reference to any other legionary organizations in his 1947 address. Beneš's depiction of the ČsOL as the only genuine, loyal and state-enforcing legionary organization devoted to the consolidation of the Czechoslovak state eclipsed the existence, and the work, of other legionary organizations in the interwar period. According to Beneš, the ČsOL represented an ideal combination of the best military traditions of both prewar and postwar Czechoslovakia. However Beneš's attitude towards the political role of the ČsOL changed after 1945 (his pre-Munich view about Czechoslovak legionaries will be discussed in the next section). In contrast to the interwar period, Beneš urged Czechoslovak legionaries within the ČsOL to remain firmly above politics, thus relieving the legionary superstructure of its role as a state-legitimizing entity. Whereas in the First Republic Czechoslovak legionaries felt directly responsible for the existence and defense of the state, given their dramatic experience of the First World War, postwar legionaries were to play quite a different role as defenders rather than promoters of the ideals of socioeconomic justice and Czechoslovak national state. In this way Beneš decreed that the ČsOL should take over the position occupied by Rudolf Medek's Independent Union of Czechoslovak Legionaries (NJČsL) as the leading promoter of the ideal of the Czechoslovak national state. In his 1947 speech Beneš further explains that the ČsOL constituted a repository of a new form of *Czechoslovakism* that equally and faithfully represented Czech and Slovak interests. This contrasted starkly with the reputation of the ČsOL during the interwar period as an overly "Czechophile" organization disinterested in Slovak affairs. However as of 1947, the traditions of the legionary right-wing were consigned to oblivion, which undoubtedly explains the lack of interest in Rudolf Medek's legionary organization in Czech scholarship today. The historian Ivan Šedivý is an exception in this respect.[50] The NJČsL was not simply, as Zdeněk Kárník has written, a fringe legionary organization or even the military wing of the National Democracy Party in the interwar period.[51] Medek managed the activities of the NJČsL under the auspices of the Resistance Memorial Institute in Žižkov, which was in effect the outpost of the Czechoslovak ministry of defense in interwar Czechoslovakia; and the position of director was considered a key political post by leading military figures.[52] Significantly, in one postwar pamphlet about the activities of the Liberation Memorial Institute, which became the "Military Historical Institute" *(Vojenský historický ústav)* in 1945 following the reorganization of a separate "Liberation Memorial Institute" and "Liberation Museum," Beneš insists that the role of the military institute had changed considerably since the First Republic.[53] In the postwar era, the Žižkov institute was reinvented as a purely academic, as opposed to political, organization, which gives some indication of the reputation of the institution, as well the level of notoriety surrounding Medek its director-general during the interwar period.

III. THE ORIGINS OF THE "BENEŠ DOCTRINE" OR THE "DEMOCRATIC-FASCIST" PARADIGM

Following T.G. Masaryk, Edvard Beneš conceived of Czechoslovak nationalism as an expression of "humanist" democratic principles, which formed the core of state ideology. For Beneš, patriotism had no distinct role to play in politics, for he considered this an obvious facet of nationalism. Beneš understood the ideology of the Czechoslovak state, *Czechoslovakism*, primarily as a social democratic ideal rooted in the social emancipation of the small Czech man *(malý český clověk)*.[54] Beneš's emphasis on the social aspects rather than the national-political meaning of the "Czechoslovak revolution" of 1914–18 (reflected most notably in his objection to Czechoslovak military intervention in Bolshevik Russia and his conception of a "democratic army" rooted in mutual respect between the rank-and-file and military leadership), brought him into conflict with right-wing legionaries and legionary organizations in the mid-1920s.[55] Even more damaging for Czechoslovak legionary politics in the long term was the furore surrounding the poor showing of center-left parties (particularly the National Socialists) at the parliamentary elections of November 1925, which precipitated a dramatic political crisis culminating in the summer and autumn of 1926 during which Beneš played a significant role in shaping perceptions about "left-" and "right-" wing politics. It is argued here that the "democratic-fascist" paradigm, propagated by Beneš after the Second World War, traces its origins to the political vacuum of the mid-1920s.[56]

The denunciation of the Czechoslovak political right by the center-left, which began in the autumn of 1925 in the run-up to the parliamentary elections, signaled the culmination of several years of tension between center-left and right-wing parties, most notably between the National Socialists and Social Democrats, on the one hand, and the National Democratic Party on the other. The chasm between left and right was also reflected in the increasingly politicized camp of Czechoslovak legionaries. Starting in the autumn of 1923, during the convening of the annual congress of the ČsOL in Bratislava, the first signs of a split between the left and right-wing leadership of the organization emerged, following Radola Gajda's accusation that the ČsOL had failed to properly represent the interests of all Czechoslovak legionaries—by which he meant a group of right-wing legionaries comprising himself, Rudolf Medek, and Vojtěch Holeček, which had evolved by 1923 into a separate political wing of the ČsOL combining both radical and conservative legionary viewpoints.[57] A volatile exchange of polemics between "left" and "right" wing legionary branches ensued. By the mid-1920s most leading Czechoslovak politicians, most notably Beneš, but also those who served as ministers of defense, had correctly gauged the potential value of using Czechoslovak legionaries as an unofficial tool of politics by engaging them as vessels of party-political interests. In this way organizations such as the ČsOL became gradually attached, albeit informally, to political parities. The increasing closeness between the ČsOL and the National Socialist Party through Edvard Beneš created an irreparable chasm between legionary left and right, and resulted in the departure of a significant group of right-wing legionaries, led by Rudolf Medek, from the ČsOL in the autumn of 1925. Although as a report from 1930, drawn up by a ČsOL member, Colonel Josef Vavroch, explains the right-wingers were dismissed from the ČsOL in 1925 on account of their refusal to terminate their association with the National Democratic Party.[58]

Coupled with the increasing dominance of former legionaries within the Czechoslovak military establishment, and the appointment of Agrarian František Udržal as defense minister (followed in early 1926 by the appointment of radical Jiří Stříbrný), the results of the 1925 parliamentary elections signified a short-lived political honeymoon for the conservative right in Czechoslovakia. Given that political circumstances favored the political right at the close of 1925, Rudolf Medek decided to establish a new legionary organization, the Independent Union of Czechoslovak Legionaries (NJČsL) with the full support of František Udržal,[59] which can be interpreted as a response to Beneš's active support of the ČsOL throughout the early 1920s. However, even the creation of the NJČsL was shrouded in controversy—journalists from the ČsOL speculated that the new legionary movement was created on the basis of the close collaboration between Medek and Gajda during 1923 and 1924.[60]

The new legionary organization did indeed fuel the suspicions of the Castle Group about the political agenda of the legionary right-wing. Beneš's reaction to the creation of the NJČsL is significant; immediately following its creation, Beneš branded the NJČsL the military arm of the National Democratic Party.[61] Beneš sensed that a more sinister plot was afoot and that Medek's legionary union was part of a broader "proto-fascist," anti-Castle bloc in the Republic. Furthermore, Medek's friendship with the poet and National Democratic politician Viktor Dyk throughout the 1920s did nothing to alleviate Beneš's concerns about the evolving legionary right wing.[62] The animosity between the legionary left and right remained, and this is illustrated by Medek's impassioned article published in Karel Horký's *Fronta* in May 1927 calling for a legionary organization that would remain "above-politics."[63]

The term "fascist" appeared intermittently in the daily press at the time of the split of the ČsOL and the creation of Medek's NJČsL in the autumn of 1925. However, it became an intrinsic part of Czechoslovak political discourse during the coalition crisis of the summer and autumn of 1926 as a result of Beneš's frequent use, and misuse, of the term in reaction to two political affairs at the time: the so-called "Stříbrný" and "Gajda" controversies. Beneš cleverly used these scandals (which related to two separate plots aiming to shift the balance of power away from the Masarykian Castle Group to the more right-wing elements in the Republic) as a pretext with which to discredit both the political (National Democratic) and legionary right-wing (led by Medek and Gajda) in Czechoslovakia.

During the inter-party coalition crisis that followed the split within the National Socialist Party in June 1926, the ČsOL publicly expressed their support for Beneš, in opposition to the factional intrigues led by party renegade Jiří Stříbrný who had endeavored to bring the National Socialist party under his control. In return for their support, Beneš actively promoted the ČsOL as the leading legionary organization in Czechoslovakia that best represented Czechoslovak military traditions and, crucially, Czechoslovak state nationalism. Given Beneš's support, the ČsOL was formally acknowledged as the official legionary guardian of Czechoslovak state legitimacy. Beneš delivered two significant speeches at two separate sessions of the ČsOL annual congress held in September 1926, the contents of which are discussed here.

In his main address to the congress, entitled "Bratřím legionářům" (To brother legionaries, later published by the ČsOL publishing house as a pamphlet entitled *Pro čistotu veřejného života* [In support of a clean public life], Prague, 1926), Beneš underlined the role of the ČsOL in the new state in maintaining a "clean public life"—this exposed Beneš's concern about the politicization of the military establishment during the 1920s, and particularly the impact of Radola Gajda's anti-state plotting on the political character of the Czechoslovak army:

> I am absolutely and always against any kind of politics in the army. In a democratic state the politicians deal with politics and the soldiers are obliged to fulfil their military obligations. The permeation of politics into the army signifies the disruption of the army. Similarly, I have always maintained that the minister of foreign affairs must stand above politics in our state, both left and right, and I have always attempted to do just that ... much like in the state itself, politics are to be found within the army ... however for the reasons I have explained, I have always opposed the political agitation of generals within the [Czechoslovak] army.[64]

Rudolf Medek's own peripheral involvement in Czechoslovak politics during the mid-1920s seemingly fits Beneš's evaluation of a "politicized army general," and indeed Medek, much like Gajda, was unpopular with Czechoslovak politicians as well as the General Chief of Staff because of his tendency to air his political views in public.[65] According to Beneš, a "clean public life" is ensured by maintaining both an apolitical army and apolitical representative veteran organizations such as the legionary unions. However, by addressing the ČsOL as minister of foreign affairs Beneš was making a clear political statement about the "correct" form of Czechoslovak nationalism:

> This [debate] is not about a left or right bloc ... Legionaries must be the guardians of a clean public life. They must be the bricks and mortar of the nation; they must be com-

mitted to integrity and to the truth ... This is about the battle for the future of the nation, and you [the legionaries] play a critical and steadfast role in this battle. This is your national calling and your mission. I am and will always remain, to the end of my life, a legionary in this sense of the word."[66]

Beneš's second address to another session of the congress on the following day, during which he also signed a formal letter endorsing the political ideology espoused by the ČsOL, revealed the extent of his obsession with the difference between legionary "left" and "right" wings. This speech signified a watershed in Czechoslovak political rhetoric because in it Beneš clearly provided a justification for the naming (and shaming) of the "right-wing" as "fascist" or "demagogue," and anything center-left or "left-wing" as "democratic" or "progressive." Beneš declared that by adopting the motto of "humanism," the ČsOL had categorically expressed its loyalty to the politics of the Castle represented by T.G. Masaryk and Beneš himself. "Humanism," explains Beneš:

> determines the character of nationalism ... The fascists attempt to justify their patriotism on the basis that they are the primary and genuine defenders of the nation. They [the fascists] lecture us about patriotism ... When discussing nationalism, we must be aware of the difference between the others and our definition of patriotism and the fascist definition. We [the ČsOL] harbour a different philosophical view of nationalism. We feel deeply national, however we explain our national consciousness differently to our leading nationalists, those swastika-bearing fascists. It is on account of our diverse psychological viewpoints, and our understanding of nationalism, that we advocate quite different political practices and tactics.[67]

Most significant here is Beneš's conviction that the ČsOL's respect for the cult of the *President-Osvoboditel* (President-Liberator) favorably distinguishes the "humanists" on the "center-left" of the political spectrum (ČsOL) from the "fascists" (NJČsL) on the right. In other words, it is only through absolute deference to T.G. Masaryk as the founding father of the Czechoslovak state that genuine Czechoslovak patriotism is expressed. According to this logic, "fascists" are conceived as primarily anti-Masarykian and thus illegitimate actors in the Czechoslovak political process. Much like T.G. Masaryk, Beneš failed to grasp the true significance and nature of Czechoslovak right-wing ideologies. However, Beneš went further than T.G. Masaryk in his insistence that:

> Fascism is an over-excitable nationalism which develops into aggressive forms, [nationalism is] a force which is in fact overwhelming for a small nation. ... We [the ČsOL and the National Socialist Party] stand for a reasonable and calm definition of

nationalism acceptable for all … the entire debate about nationalism represents a dis-
agreement over the nature of the national philosophy of state, which is rooted in principles of humanity. These unpatriotic, fascist demagogues exploit this distinction for
their own political purposes.[68]

Beneš's tirade against the "right" helped consolidate the prevailing
view in the press at that time, propagated by the leading newspaper of the
ČsOL, *Národní osvobození* (National Independence), that everything connected to the National Democratic party as a whole, irrespective of distinct wings of the party, was fascist.[69] In this respect Beneš's view was
close to that of T.G. Masaryk, who also equated practically everything on
the right with creeping Fascism, by which he meant the "political disorientation of the bourgeois members of the National Democratic party."[70]

Beneš's sweeping, almost facile categorization of the Czechoslovak
extreme right quickly achieved the status of legitimate political canon,
despite its ideological fluidity, and was further disseminated by left-
leaning legionary historians and journalists such as, most notably, Václav
Cháb, a ČsOL member.[71] It was with the same ideological brush that Rudolf Medek's legionary organization became tarnished. In a report compiled by one of Beneš's personal assistants about the Independent Union
of Czechoslovak Legionaries (dating from the autumn of 1926) it is noted,
albeit erroneously, that Rudolf Medek is "an anti-Masarykian figure" who
shaped the agenda of his organization according to the "need to fight the
[Czechoslovak] political center-ground represented by Masaryk and
Beneš."[72] Significantly, Medek's founding of the NJČsL in 1925 is described in the report as the first institutional manifestation of Fascism in
the Czechoslovak Republic, disregards the Union's commitment to Masarykian principles and the cult of President-Liberator. The formal declaration issued at the time of the founding of the NJČsL pledges that
Medek's union is a "non-political organization" devoted to the propagation of Masarykian principles, particularly "social justice" and "Czechoslovak national unity." However, Medek's organization distinguished
itself from the ČsOL by emphasizing the importance of a national, as opposed to social, program committed to increasing awareness about the
importance of national defense in the minds of all "Czechoslovak citizen-
soldiers."[73] The 1926 report originating in Beneš's office defines Fascism
as both "conservative" and "active nationalism," indicating that few
Czechoslovak politicians, not even Beneš himself, had a clear concept of
Fascism during the 1920s. However the conceptual flexibility afforded by
such indeterminate ideological fudging suited Beneš as a tool of coalition
party political intrigue, which he employed in his dealings with legionary

organizations during the 1920s, as described here; but the mislabelling of "Fascism" proved a costly political tool, for by becoming directly involved in legionary affairs Beneš helped politicize further, whether deliberately or inadvertently, the work of those legionary organizations that were supposed to remain above politics. The legionary groups remained forever split by the crisis of the mid-1920s and were unable to reach agreement on any issue until the Munich crisis of 1938.

IV. DEFINITIONS OF THE CZECHOSLOVAK POLITICAL "RIGHT"—NEW PERSPECTIVES

This chapter has argued that Edvard Beneš's sweeping characterization of political ideology, as well as his direct involvement in legionary politics during the mid-1920s, and again during the mid- to late-1940s, has hampered historical understanding of the diverse nature of right-wing political ideologies, and the political persuasions of their representatives (in this instance, Rudolf Medek) in interwar Czechoslovakia. Indeed, Beneš's writings influenced the perception of "Fascism" in interwar and postwar Czechoslovakia more than any other Czech political figure. Contrary to recent work about the history of Czechoslovak Fascism,[74] which stresses the marginality of extremists in the First Republic, this paper has demonstrated that "Fascism" was of great concern to Czechoslovak political society several years before the economic crisis of the early 1930s and that "Fascism" as perceived by Czechs, as opposed to Slovaks, evolved from the internal Czechoslovak political crises of the mid-1920s. A new approach to the "political right" is therefore required. Several historians have begun this task. In *Česká politická pravice mezi převratem a krizí*,[75] Jana Čechurová distinguishes between different branches of the "Right": the "Fascism" associated with the young generation of National Democracy enamored by Benito Mussolini's rise to power in 1922; the "Agrarian Conservatism" of Republican Party leader Antonín Švehla; and the "clerical right" represented by those such as the priest-politician Jan Šrámek. This approach largely builds on Václav Černý's earlier distinction between "patriots" (conservative nationalists) and "religious politicians" (clericals) in addressing the political right. Both the "clerical" and "conservative" members of the right led a political campaign against Beneš in the mid-1920s (in reaction to both foreign and domestic policy), however this did not mean that these groups were "fascist."

Zdeněk Kárník has recently pointed out the difficulties with the term "integral nationalist" coined by dissident writers in the 1970s, noting that it is rooted in a conception of a First Republic of two political extremes, the "extreme right" and the "democratic-center," thus fudging the different brands of Czechoslovak political right.[76] "Integral nationalist" is obviously too broad a term to accommodate all the ideological forms, "moderate," "conservative" and "extreme." More should be made, for instance, of the typology relating to the "genesis of Czech conservatism" devised by Miloš Havelka in the Catholic journal *Obzory* in 2005.[77] As is the case with all ideologies, conservatism is context-specific and instead of adopting the "fascist" epithet for all right-wing positions in the period between 1925 and 1948, Havelka underlines the analytical value of associated political concepts such as "populism," "traditionalism," "historicism" and "authoritarianism" (which help define the conceptual traits, components and characteristics of ideologies and their relationship to each other) when making the distinction between different types of "right-wing." This history of ideas approach is advocated by British political scientists such as Michael Freeden in their discussion of variant forms of nationalist ideology as being indicative of specific conservative traditions.[78] Adopting this approach, for instance, reveals that Medek's Independent Union of Czechoslovak Legionaries (NJČsL) aimed to preserve a particular legionary tradition rather than to radically alter it for some anarchic political purpose, which clearly distinguishes the organization from Radola Gajda's National Union of Fascists (*Národní obec fašistická* or NOF). Gajda's 1931 political pamphlet about the "Ideology of Czech Fascism" *(Ideologie Čsl. fašismu. Cyklus přednášek "O ideologii Českoslov. politických stran")* defines what is understood by "fascist" in a Czechoslovak context, beginning with the concept of the corporate state model alongside the institutionalization of political order through the rejection, by force, of coalition government. In his political pamphlet, *Poslední události a nezávislá jednota čsl. legionářů* (Recent events and the independent union of Czechoslovak legionaries) published in November 1926, Rudolf Medek attempted to deflate much of the speculation about his organization as a "fascist movement," explaining that the NJČsL is opposed to any form of "red guard" or fascist militia: "our state is strong enough to defend itself against all those who wish to create a new state other than that created by the legionaries." And indeed, following the Gajda affair in the summer of 1926, Medek distanced himself from Gajda altogether. In contrast to Gajda's NOF, the NJČsL, Medek explained further, was committed to the "creation of an active and responsible [Czechoslovak] patriot concerned more with order and stability than with political coup and national consciousness rather than corruption."[79] Legitimate legionary organizations, insists Medek, should retain and express their national orientation through their commitment to the "idea of Czechoslovak national unity proposed by T.G. Masaryk and Milan Rastislav Štefánik."[80] It is significant that Medek does not mention Beneš in relation to either Masaryk or Štefánik as state-builders. Unlike Gajda, Rudolf Medek was concerned about the importance of preserving legionary military norms and traditions for the creation of a new Czechoslovak army and a culture of national defense, perhaps even more so than the ideological significance of legionary culture for Czechoslovak politics.[81] The splintering impact of the Gajda affair of 1926 on the legionary political right cannot be underestimated—the affair signified the end of the short-lived partnership between "extreme" and "conservative" strands of the legionary right and their subsequent estrangement. In short, Medek's case necessitates a reevaluation of the role and significance of the "political right." I argue that the following analytical qualifications should be made when assessing the "right" and distinguishing between different right-wing viewpoints in Czechoslovak politics between the wars:

- Establishing the relationship between the (legionary) organization, individual or political party and the cult of President-Liberator; that is, the perception of T.G. Masaryk as representative of the Czechoslovak state and distinct from the ideas espoused by Edvard Beneš. The "Masaryk versus Beneš" distinction is critical when discussing political loyalty, legitimacy and authority in interwar Czechoslovakia.
- Assessing the nature of the perception of state legitimacy by an individual and group; that is, accounting for the multiple interpretations of Czechoslovak nationalism that existed in interwar Czechoslovakia.
- Accounting for the distinct experiences of groups and individuals during the First World War, resulting in diverse interpretations of "national history" and historical memory after 1918; that is, acknowledging the varied historical roots of Czechoslovak political legitimacy.

Organizations, individuals and political figures belonging to the political fringe, aside from the formal political arena (such as the legionaries, although they were unofficially connected to mainstream politics through political parties such as the National Socialists and Agrarian), considered themselves very much a part of state life. Consequently they conceived of political authority and state legitimacy differently—and the importance and function of the state and even the role of T.G. Masaryk as the founder of Czechoslovakia—from those occupying formal positions in government and state institutions. The ideological space between extreme and center-right politics must be accounted for in any assessment of Czechoslovak legionary traditions and the nature of political opposition in interwar Czechoslovakia. Those occupying the political right of the interwar political spectrum considered themselves loyal supporters of state ideology and as "Czechoslovakists." However many reinvented the cult of Masaryk President-Liberator to suit their military and nationalist agenda on the basis of their own legionary politics and the nature of their adjustment to Czechoslovak republican life after 1918. For those such as Rudolf Medek, allegiance to Czechoslovak state ideology was based on distinct precepts including, most notably, the cult of T.G. Masaryk as military leader and a commitment to a strong and unified national state.[82]

NOTES

1 I am most grateful for helpful comments received from Michal Kopeček & Adéla Gjuričová during the writing of this chapter.

2 J. Křen, *Bílá místa v našich dějinách* [White spaces in our history] (Prague: Lidové noviny, 1990).

3 For example, see most recently, E. Broklová, "Demokrat Edvard Beneš" in *Věře Olivové ad honorem. Sborník příspěvků k novodobým československým dějinám* [In honour of Věra Olivová: Volume of essays about contemporary Czechoslovak history] E. Broklová and M. L. Neudorflová, eds., (Prague: Masarykův ústav/T.G. Masaryk Institute, 2006), pp. 42–65.

4 For an introduction to this debate, see M. Zückert, "Memory of War and National State Integration: Czech and German Veterans in Czechoslovakia after 1918." *Central Europe* 4, No. 2 (November 2006): 111–21. Zückert does not, however, discuss in any great detail the impact of the creation of a Czechoslovak national memory after 1918 on the perceived legitimacy of the Czechoslovak state by key legionary figures both directly involved in, and external to, the political scene in the interwar period (although Rudolf Medek is not discussed at all).

5 Medek was conscripted into the Habsburg Army as an officer cadet at the beginning of the First World War. However, his military career began in earnest after he deserted to the Russians on the Eastern Front in a small town in eastern Galicia on the night of 25 December 1915, where he worked for a brief while as an interpreter for the General Staff of the 7th division of the Russian army. In June 1916 he joined the Czech *Družina* organization based in Kiev as a volunteer in the "Jan Hus First Czechoslovak Firing

Brigade" (1. Střelecký pluk Mistra Jana Husa). He was awarded a total of five medals on several occasions for his reconnaissance work, most notably for the successful mission he led in the town of Břežan in March 1917, which was mentioned in the official bulletin of the Russian High Command and in the world press, as well as for his participation in various battles, the most important of which took place near the village of Zborov in western Ukraine on 2 July 1917. He was promoted to the position of "flag bearer" (praporščik) in September 1916, then to "platoon commander" (poručík) of the 6th platoon of the Jan Hus Czechoslovak Firing Brigade in May 1917. In May 1917 Medek was elected to the "Organizational-financial commission" of the military branch of the Czechoslovak National Council in Russia. In this capacity he was sent by the National Council to officially welcome and brief T.G. Masaryk upon his arrival in Petrograd in the summer of 1917 following the battle of Zborov; he remained Masaryk's chaperone until the autumn of 1917. In December 1917 he was voted deputy chairman representing legionary-soldiers of the Czechoslovak National Council in Russia. Together with colonel Jiří Švec, he led the Czechoslovak legionary advance on Penza and Samara against the Bolsheviks in the spring of 1918, at which point he was reelected to the legionary assembly in Omsk as the head of the military branch of the Czechoslovak National Council.

6 J. Syrový, "Rudolf Medek," *Československý voják* [Czechoslovak soldier], No. 29 (Irkutsk: 20 November 1919): 1. Medek outlines the reasons for his departure from Siberia in his final article written for the legionary newspaper edited by Medek's colleague, Jaroslav Kuděla. See R. Medek, "Moje motivy" [My motives]. *Československý deník* [Czechoslovak daily], No. 137 (14 June 1919): 1.

7 The Castle Group was a powerful extra-parliamentary and extra-constitutional group of politicians, litterateur and intellectuals loyal to the Czechoslovak president, T.G. Masaryk, and his political views. Membership of the group was at Masaryk's discretion. Sessions of the "Castle," chaired by Masaryk himself, influenced thinking about Czechoslovak state and political ideology in the interwar period.

8 See M. Kučera, "Významní legionáři v roce 1938: Příspěvek k výzkumu společenských elit meziválečného Československa" [The significance of legionaries in 1938: A contribution towards research into social elites in interwar Czechoslovakia], in *Politické elity v Československu 1918–1948* [Political elites in Czechoslovakia], I. Koutská and F. Svátek, eds., (Prague: Ústav pro soudobé dějiny/Institute of Contemporary History, 1994), pp. 81–100; see also I. Šedivý, "Legionáři a československá armáda 1918–38" [Legionaries and the Czechoslovak army], in *České země a Československo v Evropě XIX. a XX. století. Sborník prací k 65. narozeninám prof. dr. Roberta Kvačka* [The Czech lands and Czechoslovakia in Europe during the 19th and 20th centuries: A volume of essays commemorating the 65th birthday of Professor Robert Kvaček], J. Dejmek and J. Hanzal, eds., (Prague: Historický ústav AV ČR, 1997), pp. 209–30.

9 The ČsOL was created with Medek's involvement in January 1921. The Independent Union of Czechoslovak Legionaries (NJČsL) increased its membership from 7,492 in 1926 to 13,000 in 1929. 1929 was its peak year in terms of membership, but this was dwarfed by the membership figures of the ČsOL. See also, Vojtěch Holeček, "Slavná rozvědka Medkova" [Medek's celebrated reconnaissance unit], *Legie* 2, No. 9 (20 March 1927): 1.

10 For instance, Medek's play *Plukovník Švec* (1929), about the suicide of the Czech legionary colonel Jiří Švec in May 1918, underlined the existing split in the Czechoslo-

vak legionary movement. Medek's pentalogy, *Legionářská epopeja* (1921–29), was praised by Matěj Čapek-Chod as a monumental work of national-political significance on par with the historical chronicles of Alois Jirásek.

11 V. Justl and I. Medek, eds., *Rudolf Medek. Odvrhnutý básník* [Rudolf Medek: Shunned poet] (Prague: Torst, 2002): 106.

12 Ivan Medek and Zdeněk Kalista had prepared a collection of Medek's verse during 1947 that was never published. An exception, as Robert Pynsent has pointed out, was the publication in May 1945 of Medek's volume of verse from his experiences during the First World War, *Lví srdce. Básně 1914–1918* [Heart of lions. Poems] (Irkutsk: 1918). "[Lví srdce] was published with an unnamed editor's preface stating that the work of the Great Legions in Russia had now been completed—without any indication of the fact that the editor had cut out the anti-Bolshevik poems and replaced them with poems from later collections." See R. B. Pynsent, "Resurrections of the Czech National Revival," *Central Europe* 1, No. 1 (May 2003): 76–95 (81).

13 Archív kanceláře presidenta republiky (KRP) [The archive of the office of the Czech president], Prague Castle, f. "Rudolf Medek," Ivan Medek letter to Edvard Beneš dated 20 July 1945.

14 See, for example, M. Hruban, *Z časů nedlouho zašlých* [From times recently past] (Rome-Los Angeles: Studium Křesťanská akademie, 1967), p. 214.

15 T. Pasák, *Český fašismus 1922–1945 a kolaborace 1939–1945* [Czech Fascism and collaboration] (Prague: Práh, 1999), pp. 148–164.

16 "Pražský večer" [Evening Prague] (28 November 1938), Rudolf Medek Collection, *Památník národního písemnictví* (PNP) [National Literature Memorial Institute], Strahov, Prague, "Newspaper clippings."

17 Medek never collaborated with the Nazis; after March 1939 the family doctor, and a close circle of friends, had gone to great lengths, following Medek's first admittance to hospital in January 1939, to keep him isolated from journalists working for Protectorate newspapers—author's interview with Ivan Medek, Letná, Prague, September 2004. See also I. Medek, *Děkuji, mám se výborně* [Thank you very much, I am keeping very well], Prague: Torst, 2005, p. 26. Ivan Medek notes that the efforts of Dr Otakar Janota to isolate Rudolf Medek from any visitors during 1939 saved him from both the Gestapo and the Czech journalist-collaborators.

18 The perception of Medek as an anti-Semite, a view largely borne of the Second Republic as described here, is to be found in some contemporary writing, which does not distinguish between Medek's popular nationalist literature such as that epitomized by his pentalogy, *Legionářská epopeja* (1921-28), and his more serious political writing – see most notably R. B. Pynsent, "The Literary Representations of the Czechoslovak 'Legions' in Russia", *Czechoslovakia in a Nationalist and Fascist Europe 1918-1948* ed. by M. Cornwall and R. J. W. Evans (Proceedings of The British Academy 140, Oxford University Press, 2007) pp. 63-89 (esp. pp, 80-82)..

19 See, for instance, A. Klimek, *Průvodce armádním muzeem* [A guide to military museums] (Prague: Historický ústav Armády České republiky/Historical institute of the Czech army, 1996), which fails to mention Medek's directorship of the Liberation Memorial.

20 On 29 March, an exhibition entitled 'Rudolf Medek – soldier' was opened at the Vojenský historický ústav (Military Historical Institute) in Žižkov; and on 21 June, an exhibition devised to complement that held at the VHU, 'Rudolf Medek –writer', was

opened at the Památník národního písemnictví (National Literature Memorial Institute) in Strahov, Prague.

21 See for example Š. Filípek, 'K čemu je generál, který vrací vyznamenání', *Mladá fronta Dnes*, 9 July 2007.

22 T. Jakl and Z. Polčák, "Výstava Rudolf Medek – voják" [Rudolf Medek – soldier] *Historie a vojenství*, No. 2, Vol. LVI, 2007 pp. 110-11. The mark of distinction bearing Medek's name was created in conjunction with the commemoration of the 90th anniversary of the First World War 'battle of Zborov.'

23 As an example of such viewpoints, see R. B. Pynsent, "The Literary Representations of the Czechoslovak 'Legions' in Russia" in Cornwall & Evans, *Czechoslovakia in a Nationalist and Fascist Europe 1918-1948* pp. 63-89.

24 V. Kopecký, *T. G. Masaryk a komunisté* [Masaryk and the communists] (Prague: 1950), p. 30.

25 See B. F. Abrams, *The Struggle for the Soul of the Nation: Czech Culture and the Rise of Communism* (New York & Oxford: Rowman and Littlefield Publishers, 2004), pp. 113–16.

26 In his memoirs, Václav Černý notes that *Křik Koruny české* [The Cry of the Czech Crown Lands], (1947) was a new edition of a collection of poems first published in Paris in 1940 under the title *Hlasy z domova* [Voices from home]. However, the original name for the collection suggested by František Halas in late 1939 was used for the 1947 edition. See V. Černý, *Křik Koruny české. Paměti, 1938–1945* [The Cry of the Czech Crown Lands: Memoirs], 3 vols, (Prague: Československý spisovatel, 1977), Vol. III, p. 102.

27 J. Seifert, ed., *Křik Koruny české* [The Cry of the Czech Crown Lands] (Prague: Klín, 1947), p. 39; see p. 44 for the description of Medek's poem.

28 D. Sayer, *The Coasts of Bohemia: A Czech History* (Princeton: Princeton University Press, 1998), pp. 256–75.

29 Letter from Max Švabinský to Eva Medková-Slavíčkova, (28 August 1940), Rudolf Medek Collection Památník národního písemnictví (PNP), Strahov, Prague, "Correspondence" file No. 2. Švabinský likened the Liberation Memorial Instituteto an "abandoned cemetery" following Medek's departure and the arrival of the Nazis in March 1939.

30 F. Halas, *Bez legend. "Sibířská anabase" ve vzpomínkách bývalého dělníka a rotního důvěrníka* [Without legend: The Siberian anabasis in the memoirs of a former laborer and sergeant major confidante] (Prague, 1955), pp. 56, 58–59, 69, 73.

31 Unlike the Second Republic, the Nazi Protectorate of Bohemia and Moravia after March 1939 nevertheless has been regularly discussed since the Changes as a prime example of a "white space" See, for instance, J. Loewy, 'Bílá místa 15. března 1939, *Lidové noviny*, 15 March 2000.

32 P. Tigrid, *Kapesní průvodce inteligetní ženy po vlastním osudu* [Pocket guide of an intelligent woman responsible for her own fate] (Toronto: Sixty-Eight Publishers, 1988), pp. 102–104.

33 J. Rataj, *O autoritativní národní stát. Ideologické proměny české politiky v druhé republice 1938–1938* [About an authoritarian national state: Ideological change in Czech politics during the Second Republic] (Prague: Karolinum, 1997), pp. 36, 65, 159, 36. Similar views are expressed by Miroslav Gregorovič, see M. Gregorovič, *Kapitoly o českém fašismu. Fašismus jako měřítko politické dezorientace* [Chapters about Czech

Fascism: Fascism as a gauge of political disorientation] (Prague: Lidové noviny, 1995). See also J. Gebhart and J. Kuklík, *Druhá republika 1938-1939. Svár demokracie a totality v politickém, společenském a kulturním životě.* [Second Republic 1938-1939. The struggle of democracy and totalitarianism in political, societal, and cultural life] (Praha-Litomyšl: Paseka, 2004) Gebhart and Kuklík note that ANO established itself as the "spiritual guide and heart of the consciousness of the nation," which attracted extreme right-wing elements particularly "anti-Semites and Germanophiles."

34 Rataj, *O autoritativní národní stát*, pp. 40–41, 74–48, 51–53, 61–63, 70–71 and especially 119–20.

35 Various pieces of "dis-information" about leading Czech nationalists circulated regularly during the Second Republic. For instance, the Cleveland-based newspaper, *Američan* [The American], carried a report in July 1939 of Medek's arrest by the Gestapo at the same time as the arrest of Agrarian leader Rudolf Beran.

36 S. Vejvar, "Český konzervatimus za druhé republiky" [Czech conservatism during the Second Republic], *Obzory*, Vol. 2 (February 2005): 62–73.

37 M. Havelka, "Zamyšlení nad genezí českého konzervatismu" [A thought about the genesis of Czech conservatism], *Obzory*, Vol. 2 (February 2005): 7–33.

38 Podiven [= Petr Příhoda, Petr Pithart, Milan Otáhal], *Češi v dějinách nové doby (1848–1939)* [Czechs in the history of the modern age] (Prague: Academia, 2003), pp. 494–95 and 566–67. Příhoda and colleagues develop the thinking of Count Karel Schwarzenberg on the non-existence of a Czech right-wing between 1918 and 1938. See K. Schwarzenberg, *Obrana svobod* (Prague: Československý spisovatel, 1991), p. 80.

39 A. Klimek, *Boj o Hrad 1918–1935* [The battle for the castle], 2 vols (Prague: Pan Evropa, 1996), Vol. II, *Kdo po Masarykovi? 1926–1935* [Who comes after Masaryk?], pp. 84–85; A. Klimek, *Velké dějiny zemí koruny české, svazek. XIII. 1918–1929* [Voluminous history of the Czech Crown Lands: Volume 13] (Prague: Paseka, 2000), p. 569. See also T.G. Masaryk Collection, "Fašismus" [Fascism file], Box 1, f. 3, letter from Karel Řežný to T.G. Masaryk, (30 July 1926), T.G. Masaryk Institute Archive, Prague. Řežný, a secretary at the Castle, had been instructed by the Castle to infiltrate the inner circles of this political clique around Adolf Hrubý and František Hlaváček.

40 See, for instance, the line adopted in V. S. Mamatey and R. Luža, eds., *A History of the Czechoslovak Republic 1918–1948* (Princeton: Princeton University Press, 1973).

41 See Z. Kárník, *České země v éře První republiky (1918–1938). Díl druhý. Československo a České země v krizi a ohrožení (1930–1935)* [The Czech Lands in the era of the First Republic. Volume two: Czechoslovakia and the Czech Lands in crisis and under threat] (Prague: Libri, 2002), pp. 336–37.

42 The 8,000 page, four-volume historical chronicle, *Za svobodu. Obrázková kronika československého revolučního hnutí na rusi, 1914–1920 (1925–1931)* [For (our) freedom: A picture chronicle of the Czechoslovak revolutionary movement in Russia], edited by Rudolf Medek and his NJČSL colleague, Vojtěch Holeček, is the most important of these.

43 "Obhajovací řeč generála V. Klecandy před Národním soudem dne 2. sprna 1946. Stenografický záznam M.V". [Defense speech of General V. Klecanda before the national tribunal, 2 August 1946. Stenographic record], Rudolf Medek Collection, Památník národního písemnictví (PNP), Strahov, Prague, f. 'Varia,' Box 23, p.3. Those convicted and imprisoned during 1946–47 included in the main, former legionaries, Jan Syrový, Radola Gajda, besides the Agrarian leader Rudolf Beran. Medek's former col-

league from the Liberation Memorial Institute, Otakar Husák, was imprisoned by the communists after a separate trial in 1950.

44 See P. Pithart, "První republika: jak ji viděla opozice" [The First Republic: as seen by the opposition] *Svědectví,* Vol. XVIII, No. 70/71 (1984): 271–314, see particularly pp. 274–80.

45 See for instance, J. Plojhar, *Vítězný únor 1948 a čs. strana lidová* [Victorious February and the Czechoslovak Peoples' Party] (Prague: 1948), pp. 8–9; see also J. Plojhar, "Poslání katolických kněží" [The mission of Catholic priests] in *Katolická církev v lidové demokracii* [The Catholic Church in the peoples' democracy] (Prague: 1951), pp. 18–19.

46 *E[dvard] B[eneš] národu. Z projevů presidenta republiky v letech 1945–46* [Edvard Beneš to the nation. Snippets from speeches delivered by the president of the republic between 1945 and 1946] (Prague: Jaroslav Jiránek, 1946), pp. 26–27 (27).

47 Ibid., p. 28. The same sentiments are expressed in Beneš's pamphlet, E. Beneš, *Nová slovanská politika* [The new Slav politics] (Prague: 1946): 39–40, 44, 46, 48–50.

48 E. Beneš, *President legionářům. Legionáři národu* [The president [speaks] to the legionaries. The legionaries to the nation] (Prague: Československá obec legionářská [ČSOL], 1947), p. 5. Beneš's speech was also published in Slovak as "Reč prezidenta-budovateľa dr. Ed. Beneša."

49 See J. Galandauer, *2.7.1917. Bitva u zborova. Česká legenda* [The battle of Zborov: Czech legend] (Prague: Havran, 2002).

50 See I. Šedivý, "Vznik Nezávislé jednoty československých legionářů" [The founding of the independent union of Czechoslovak legionaries], *Historie a vojenství* 6 (1996): 47–60.

51 See Kárník, *České země v éře První republiky,* pp. 2, 336–37.

52 See J. Pernes, *Až na dno zrady. Emanuel Moravec* [Emanuel Moravec: To the depths of traitorousness] (Prague: Themis, 1997), pp. 103–04.

53 E. Beneš, *Poslání vojenského historického ústavu* [The mission of the military historical institute] (Prague: Vojenský historický ústav, 1947), p. 5.

54 See E. Beneš, "Náš největší úkol národní" [Our greatest national task] in *Idea Československého státu* [The idea of the Czechoslovak state], 2 vols, J. F. Kapras Soukup and B. Němec eds., (Prague: Národní rada československá, 1936), pp. 2, 218–235 (218).

55 See E. Beneš, *Smysl čs. Revoluce* [The significance of the Czechoslovak revolution] (Prague: Památník odboje, 1924), pp. 16, 22, 55.

56 The significance of this period of vacuum has been discussed most recently by Jiří Kovtun in his excellent study. See J. Kovtun, *Republika v nebezpečném světě. Éra prezidenta Masaryka 1918–1935* [The republic in a dangerous world. The era of President Masaryk] (Prague: Torst, 2005), pp. 448–62.

57 It was at the same meeting that Gajda announced his intention to assume the leadership of the ČsOL. See V. Cháb, *Několik legionářských co a jak. Poznámky a polemiky* [Several legionary "what" and "how": Notes and polemics] (Prague: Československá obec legionářska, 1932), pp. 44–45.

58 Report about the founding of Medek's "Independent Union of Czechoslovak Legionaries" compiled by Colonel Josef Vavroch for Edvard Beneš (20 July 1930)—Archiv Ústavu T.G. Masaryka (T.G. Masaryk Archive), Edvard Beneš Collection [EB] I, box 62, "Legionáři, 1922–1937" (Legionaries file), Box 62, f. 165/3, p. 3.

59 *Vojenský archiv Vojenský historický ústav/VHÚ* [Military Archive, Military Historical Institute], Žižkov, Prague, Vojenská kancelář presidenta republiky [Military Office of the President of the Republic], f. 48, year 1937, "Response to article by Rudolf Medek published in Venkov" [by General Ludvík Krejčí, Chief of Staff], (1 January 1937), p. 2.

60 Cháb, *Několik legionářských co a jak*, p. 20.

61 See "Legie" [Legions] file on "Nezávislá jednota československých legionářů," Edvard Beneš Collection, T.G. Masaryk Archive, Box 62, f. 165/3 and "Gajda a blok pravice" [Gajda and the right-wing bloc], "Fašismus" [Fascism] file, Box 57, f. 168/3, pp. 1–3.

62 See Beneš's letter entitled "Gen. Medek" to Andrej Laurin (2 July 1934), Edvard Beneš Collection, Box 9, f. 197, Archiv Ústavu T.G. Masaryka [T.G. Masaryk Archive], Edvard Beneš Collection [EB] [unsorted material/external to catalogue]. Laurin's response to Beneš is also revealing (6 July). He states: "[Medek has gained the reputation of] an opponent of democracy. His political views are controversial and he is highly opinionated. However, he is an absolutely trustworthy and loyal person; he holds the president [T.G. Masaryk] in high regard; he spoke about the president with great fondness during the summer … [Medek] is a good man at heart."

63 R. Medek, "K situace v legionářstvu" [The situation amongst legionaries]. *Fronta* (6 May 1927): 4–6.

64 "Bartřím legionářům" [To brother legionaries], *Archiv Ústavu T.G. Masaryka* [T.G. Masaryk Archive], Edvard Beneš Collection [EB] I, Box 62, "Legionáři, 1922–1937" (legionaries file), f. 165/2–148, pp. 3–5.

65 See the report on Medek compiled by General Ludvík Krejčí, Chief of Staff in January 1937, later sent to the Military Office at Prague Castle—Vojenský archiv Vojenský historický ústav/VHÚ [Military Archive, Military Historical Institute], Žižkov, Prague, Vojenská kancelář presidenta republiky [Military Office of the President of the Republic], f. 48, year 1937, "Response to article by Rudolf Medek published in Venkov," (1 January 1937), pp. 1–4.

66 Ibid., p. 18.

67 "Reč dra Beneše" [Beneš's speech to the ČSOL congress], Archiv Ústavu T.G. Masaryka [T.G. Masaryk Archive], Edvard Beneš Collection [EB] I, Box 62, "Legionáři, 1922–1937" (Legionaries file), f. 165/2, p. 4.

68 Ibid., p. 5.

69 See "Legionáři a národní demokracie" [Legionaries and national democracy]. *Národní osvobození*, (23 October 1925): pp. 1–2.

70 F. Peroutka, *Muž přítomnosti* [Man of the present] (Zurich: Confrontation, 1985), p. 58; see also [T.G. Masaryk] *Cesta demokracie. Projevy, články, rozhovory, 1924–1928.* Svazek čtvrtý [Path of democracy: Speeches, articles and interviews. Volume four], Vols. 1–4, (Prague: Čin, 1938) Vol. IV, p.161.

71 See, for instance, V. Cháb, *Několik legionářských co a jak*, pp. 20, 26, 40, 42, 44, 45; and see also V. Cháb, *Spasí Radola Gajda a jeho fašismus náš lid?* (Will Radola Gajda and his Fascism redeem our people?) (Prague: 1932).

72 *Archiv Ústavu T.G. Masaryka* (T.G. Masaryk Archive), Edvard Beneš Collection "BA-Legie: Nezávislá jednota čs. Legionářů" (Legionaries: Independent union of Czechoslovak legionaries), Box 62, f. 165/3, (26 September 1926): 5; see also 'Gajda a blok pravice' (Gajda and the right-wing bloc) [23 April 1929], "BA-Legie: Fasišmus a národovci" (Legionaries: Fascism and patriots), Box 57, f. 168/3.

73 See F. Turek, "Prohlášení Nezávislá jednota československých legionářů" (Declaration of the independent union of Czechoslovak legionaries) (Prague: Památník odboje [osvobození], December 1925).

74 See in particular, M. Gregorovič, *Kapitoly o českém fašismu. Fašismus jako měřítko politické dezorientace* (Chapters about Czech Fascism: Fascism as a gauge of political disorientation) (Prague: Lidové noviny, 1995).

75 J. Čechurová, *Česká politická pravice mezi převratem a krizí* (The Czech right between revolution and crisis) (Prague: Dějin a součanosti, 2000).

76 Z. Karník, "Pravé a levé politické extrémy v Českých zemích a Československu především meziválečné doby, zvláště pak fašismus a komunismus" (Right and left political extremes in the Czech lands and Czechoslovakia, particularly in the interwar period and in relation to Fascism and Communism) in *Bolševismus, komunismus a radikální socialismus v Československu* (Bolshevism, Communism and radical socialism in Czechoslovakia), Z. Karník and M. Kopeček, eds., (Prague: USD/Dokořán, 2004), pp. 12–57 (37).

77 M. Havelka, "Zamyšlení nad genezí českého konzervatismu" (A thought about the genesis of Czech conservatism), *Obzory* 2 (February 2005): 7–25.

78 See, for instance, M. Freeden, *Ideology: A Very Short Introduction* (Oxford: Oxford University Press, 2003), pp. 50–52; see also M. Freeden, "Is Nationalism a Distinct Ideology?" *Political Studies* XLVI (1998): 748–65 (especially 755–51).

79 R. Medek, *Poslední události a nezávislá jednota čsl. Legionářů* (Recent events and the independent union of Czechoslovak legionaries) (Prague: Památník národního odboje [nakl.Legie], 1926), p. 15.

80 Ibid., p. 16.

81 Reflected most notably in the distinct approaches to the "legionary question" in Czechoslovakia adopted by Rudolf Medek and Radola Gajda—see R. Medek, *Pouť do Československa. Válečné paměti a vzpomínky z let 1914–1918* (Pilgrimage to Czechoslovakia: War memoirs and reminiscences from 1914 to 1918) (4 vols, Prague: 1929–32), Vol. 1: *V mundúru Rakousko-Uherska* (In the clutches of Austria-Hungary), p. 5; contrasted to Gajda's approach, R. Gajda, *Generál ruských legií R. Gajda, Moje paměti. Československá anabase. Zpět na Ural proti bolševikům. Admirál Kolčak* (General R. Gajda of the Russian legionaries: My memoirs. Czechoslovak anabasis. Back again to the Urals against the Bolsheviks. Admiral Kolchak) (Prague: 1920), pp. 177–78.

82 For the official military establishment view of T.G. Masaryk as "military leader and patron of all Czechoslovak legionaries" see, for instance, the introduction by General Jan Syrový in J. Dvorský, ed., *Naše vojsko a československý důjstoník v projevech T.G. Masaryka* (Our army and the Czechoslovak officer in the speeches of T.G. Masaryk) (Prague: 1931), pp. 9–12.

Begetting & Remembering

Creating a Slovak Collective Memory
in the Post-Communist World

OWEN V. JOHNSON

The archival reading room at Matica slovenská (the Slovak Cultural Organization) closed early 7 November 1973. Researchers were asked to leave so that Matica's employees could join the march to celebrate the anniversary of the Bolshevik Revolution. The employees were in a gay mood as they left, laughing and talking to one another. They were mandatory volunteers to celebrate an event that was said to have set off a wave of self-determination that extended into Slovakia. Throughout that day and into the next, the Czech and Slovak media reported with great fanfare similar marches across Czechoslovakia.

Thirty-two years later, only a handful of people in Bratislava came to pay homage to the anniversary of the 1988 candle commemoration, which under the east wind from Soviet Union, had manifested an expression of Slovak desire for freedom. No one was required to march. Journalists reported what happened because it was a planned event and their editors had sent them there. Coverage of the August 2005 commemoration in Bratislava of the Slovak National Uprising, attended by 300 people, was meager, the occasion having been overshadowed by demonstrations by *Slovenská pospolitosť*, a right-wing group.[1]

Even though history is not as consciously inserted into the Slovak and Czech public square as it once was, historians, politicians and journalists still keep returning to their histories and the traditions of their nations, trying to redesign the past and give it a new meaning. Politicians consciously try to shape the past to suit their work and their goals for the future. Historians, beneficiaries of the knowledge of what happened between the past and the present, probe both old and new evidence to give the past new meanings. As communicators of the present, journalists find the popular understandings of the past easier to employ than the complicated approaches of the historians. They also depend on politicians, other public figures, and historians to give them signals about how to understand the past. Throughout the 20th century the Czech and Slovak publics learned different histories, each history canceling out the previous one. "The historical consciousness of society had to be interpreted and reshaped according to the topical political themes," writes Elena Mannová.[2]

Historical periods pile up on each other, so that a reinterpretation of one historical period implicitly reinterprets other periods. This problem is not unique to Slovakia. The evaluation of the US war in Vietnam as a failure calls into question Americans' understanding of World War II as "the good war." When considering the Vietnam war in retrospect, US media have tended to focus on individual accounts of suffering, tragedy and success to present a "we-win-even-when-we-lose" description of the war.[3] Similarly, the end of the Cold War has brought reconsiderations of both its domestic and its international aspects.[4]

At the beginning of the 20th century, Slovak students in schools learned that they were beneficiaries of a thousand years of Hungarian glory while in their homes some of them were becoming increasingly aware of an alternative Slovak history. In the interwar Czechoslovak Republic they learned that Czechs and Slovaks had also had historical and cultural ties that led inevitably to the country's founding. During World War II, Slovaks were instructed about the apparently finally successful Slovak struggle for independence. After 1948 they learned that it was thanks to the continuing efforts of the Czech and Slovak working classes that Czechoslovakia (later the Czechoslovak Socialist Republic) had become a worker's paradise.

Since 1989 a public debate has raged back and forth about the meaning of Slovak history in general as well as about what individual portions of that history might signify. Former dissident and later Christian Democratic leader Ján Čarnogurský told me in a 1990 interview that the problem with Slovak history is that there were too few heroes, and that the color of Slovak history might well be gray. Slovaks agree on very few of their heroes. Only three are generally given broad positive ratings. One is Ľudovít Štúr, journalist and codifier of the modern Slovak language, who was at the head of the revolutionary Slovak movement in 1848. He died young. Another is Milan Štefánik, a general and astronomer, commonly considered one of the three founding fathers of Czechoslovakia. He died a year later in a plane crash in Bratislava. The third is Alexander Dubček, who was conceived in the United States, grew up in the Soviet Union, and became leader of the Communist Party of Slovakia in 1963, where he supported liberalization as well as Slovak national interests. To all intents and purposes his public career ended with the Soviet invasion in 1968, even though he returned as a post-1989 figurehead before dying in a mysterious automobile accident. Only these three Slovaks receive consistently good marks from a broad range of their compatriots.

It should be clear that what we are dealing with here is as much memory as it is history. Only for the communist period are we dealing with mass personal memory, although that also applies to people now at least 70 years of age who lived through World War II. But even those memories compete with the impact of communist power upon memory and national history. It is difficult to find the border between history and the present.

The first part of this chapter will discuss the role of journalists during the communist period in leading a reexamination of certain aspects of Slovak history. The second part will consider the role of the post-communist media as an institution in dealing or not dealing with difficult issues in Slovakia's modern history, the actions of the Slovak State during World War II regarding the country's Jews and the self-evaluation of the population's complicity during 40 years of communist rule.

During communist days it was said ironically that whoever controlled the past controlled the future. Limiting historical debate, it was thought, would guarantee that the media could teach the public historical lessons that would not be challenged by alternative stories about the past. Unsatisfactory events in that past would be forgotten. Public memory had to be approved. Under such conditions, private memory about certain events remained alive, ready to reemerge into public discourse when Communism fell. But this private memory sometimes reflected the public memory of past regimes, sometimes even of earlier incarnations of communist thinking.

What are we to make today of the Slovak past? Does it have a unity? Is there a distinctly Slovak experience? (I use Slovak here as an adjective for the geographical territory of Slovakia, not for the Slovak ethnic group). Stanislav Kirschbaum, taking a primordial approach, has never had any doubt about this, but rejoiced in a 2003 article that the rest of western scholarship, he thought, had finally recognized this perspective.[5]

From the days of the emergence of the Slovak national movement in the late 18th and early 19th centuries, its leaders sought to define a specific Slovak history that was above debate. History was assigned a supporting role in the nationalist cause. Intellectual debate and discussion about history was not encouraged. If anything, it was actively discouraged. Dissenters sometimes offered different story lines of the past that differed from the official line. Occasionally the official history that was put forward had not actually happened. History, like economic development, was planned. At its worst, history was falsified and myths were created out of nothing. Only since 1989 have professional historians (who had been few in number until the 1960s anyway) had the freedom to debate and discuss the past.

Costica Bradatan argues that the people who lived in the communist bloc have to face the past, but that they lack "a proper understanding of what the past is."[6] Yet this necessity of facing the past was mandated "to make moral judgments, establish responsibilities and accept/deny guilt..."[7]

Discussing the events of the communist period in Slovakia is particularly fraught with difficulty because many of the leaders of today's Slovakia participated in that earlier society. As one historian put it, these people and many others who are active in society do not want to address their own complicity in this system. "You know how it was," they say to each other.[8]

And we know to some degree how it was. The young Slovak communist leaders of the late 1940s who led the brutal political cleansings of the late 1940s and early 1950s, were themselves purged after they became leaders in "Socialism with a Human Face." A couple of incidents will help demonstrate this.

A so-called "Action Committee" was formed by the Union of Slovak Journalists on 27 February 1948, just two days after the communist seizure of power. It expelled 40 journalists from its ranks. One of those ousted was Karol Hušek, a Czech who had come to Slovakia before World War I and put himself at the service of Slovak journalism for more than 30 years. He had headed the Bratislava branch of the Union before World War II and was vice-chair of the organization after World War II. No matter. "The SUJ forbids you to do any kind of journalistic work, even as part-time employment," a letter from the action committee, chaired by Mieroslav Hysko, read. Hušek was ordered to return his membership card "in person or by mail" within two weeks. Without that card he could not work as a journalist.[9]

In May 1963, Hysko was the primary speaker at a conference of Slovak journalists that marked a frontal attack on the communist party authorities. The primary theme of the attack focused on the issue of national discrimination against Slovaks. Hysko even used the term "bourgeois Czechoslovakism," thus attacking the party leadership on two fronts: for not really being communists; and for being against equal rights for Slovaks. But an important supporting theme was the journalists' desire to recover Slovak history. Several speakers called for the rehabilitation of the Slovak understanding of the Slovak National Uprising of 1944, many of whose leaders had been condemned as nationalist and anti-communist.

What is important is that it was journalists, primarily those based in Bratislava since party control was too strong outside the capital, who started down that road. It was not the politicians or historians who led the reexamination, although the latter quickly joined the journalists' cause. In contrast to the Czech case, journalists as a group took on a more important leading role in this movement than did writers. (This can be explained partly by the fact that so many Slovak writers had been co-opted by the regime, and partly by the fact that those writers who more openly supported the regime, worked alongside journalists as what they called "publicists," something akin to the notion of public intellectuals serving the state.)

The printed press emerged as the center of this movement, with recent history as an important focus, most particularly the Slovak National Uprising of 1944 and the purges in the early days of Communism. Young historians crossed over into the media at times as publicists, including individuals such as L'ubomír Lipták, one of the two most important Slovak historians of the 20th century, and Samo Falt'an. Gustáv Husák, who had been purged and imprisoned as the leader of the Communist Party of Slovakia in the early 1950s, also weighed in with his own interpretation of the Uprising, which he had helped to lead.

The history of the Slovak State was not discussed during the reform communist period. To speak or write positively in any way about the Slovak State was taboo and not immediately relevant to journalists' or politicians' concerns. Historians began to look more closely at earlier periods of Slovak history, but journalists found them uninteresting.

In June 1969, members of the Communist Party of the College of Arts and Sciences (*Filozofická fakulta*) at Comenius University gathered to discuss the post-invasion situation. It was clear to most people at the meeting what way things were going. A crackdown was coming. The only question was when it would come and how hard it would be. Mieroslav Hysko was now on the faculty of the journalism department, which he had joined after the events of 1963. He raised his hand, asking to speak. He walked to the platform and pulled out of his jacket pocket a manuscript. The audience fell silent as it listened to a condemnation of the way things were going. We lived through lies before, Hysko said, and many of us were once accomplices in those lies. He would not be a part of that again.

He took out his party membership card and threw it on the table at the front of the room. He was leaving the party, he said.

After the invasion of Czechoslovakia by the Soviet Union and four other states, supervision of the Slovak news media became the responsibility of the Slovak Office of Press and Information, subsumed in 1980 under the Federal Office of Press and Information (FÚTI). Journalists were provided with guidelines about when and how to write about chapters of Slovak history, usually on the occasion of anniversaries. The original distortions of the history of the Slovak National Uprising and the purges were eliminated to some degree.

The revolt of the journalists and the challenge it provided to contemporary history deserves special attention because it shows not only how a historical event or historical period became important in politics, but also how the reexamination of that period changed its original meaning. Marína Zavacká is right to remind us that the "bourgeois nationalists" celebrated by the journalists were nonetheless communists.[10] But in the process the "bourgeois nationalists" became a national symbol, and the treatment of what happened to them could be used as a justification to raise other historical questions.

The fall of communist rule in Czechoslovakia in 1989 opened the door to a less-politicized study of history, but politicized history did not disappear. In fact, it inserted itself vigorously into the public square where professional historians tread carefully.

The study of the history of the World War II Slovak State, established at the behest of Nazi Germany, provides ample opportunity to examine how post-communist Slovakia, or at least its historians and journalists, are reexamining the past. Thomas E. Fischer has argued that coming to terms with what happened in the Slovak State is crucial for the development of a democratic society.[11]

The face of Slovak journalism is quite different today than it was before Communism fell, perhaps more so than anywhere else in the former communist bloc. Almost the entire enterprise is staffed by people who came of age after the Velvet Revolution. Several years ago, one researcher commented that it used to be that anyone who had been in journalism less than five years was considered a beginner, whereas today anyone with five years of experience is considered a veteran. Political influence in the press has dropped dramatically since the fall of Vladimír Mečiar from power in 1998. In 2005, the organization Reporters sans frontières listed Slovakia as having the eighth freest journalism in the world, just behind a seven-way tie for first. That ranking would have improved even further a short time later, when the politician Pavol Rusko lost control of the Markíza television channel, which for the previous decade had been the most-watched channel in the country and in whose news reports Rusko was known to have intervened. It might be argued, however, that the freedom that is generally evident in the Slovak news media today reflects a certain neutering of the role of the press. In recent years the Slovak news media have primarily reflected the public debate, rather than being involved in it in their own right. (Many American journalists would argue that that is the proper role of the news media, although that clashes with the commitment to "watchdogism" by modern American journalism.)

Stan Kirschbaum points out that "in post-1989 Slovak politics, the Slovak State was the object of vigorous public discussion, quite polemical at times...."[12] During most of the communist period, the Slovak State had, in contrast, been off limits, sometimes practically a *terra incognita*.[13] This immediate post-communist debate often took place in the press, but it was generated by politicians and publicist historians, not by journalists, who usually only reported on it. Historians who supported the nationalist Prime Minister Vladimír Mečiar saw themselves as "guardians of collective memory and identity," not as people whose professional values are above the nation.[14] What emerged first was not a careful historical, sociological, or ethnological study, but prosecutorial charges and counter-charges, a not surprising development when it is remembered that people who had experienced these life-and-death matters were being allowed for the first time in 40 years to discuss them.[15] Supporters and defenders of the Slovak State, including several people who had played leading roles in that state, as well as amateur historians, were able for the first time to present their arguments to the Slovak public. They blamed individuals for the "mistakes" that were made, and said that the system of the time itself should not be criticized. The deportation of Jews was blamed on Prime Minister Vojtech Tuka, or other radicals.[16] The arguments combined a latent anti-Semitism with a strong nationalist accent and a commitment to a Roman Catholic Slovakia.

Defenders of the Slovak State's treatment of the Jews tried to strengthen their arguments by demeaning the qualifications of professional historians who had exercised their craft during the communist period. The Slovak State's apologists rarely addressed the specific questions raised by such historians, arguing instead that the latter had written history during communist rule and were thus tainted. In reality, some of Slovakia's best communist-era historians had operated in a gray zone, on some occasions writing ideological material on the orders of party authorities while on other occasions trying to stretch the boundaries of what was permitted.[17] Under the Mečiar regime the primacy of the publicist historian drained away some of the resources from professional historians.[18]

The debate seems to have changed few minds because it was, in essence, a political debate, not a historical one. A poll by Zora Bútorová in 1993 included several questions about the wartime Slovak State. One of them asked whether the new post-communist Slovakia should consider itself a successor of the Slovak State. Just over 20 percent said "yes" or "more yes than no," while 58 percent said "no" or "more no than yes." The evaluation of Jozef Tiso was more complicated. In it 25 percent said that he should be viewed positively or more positively than negatively, while 42.5 percent said he should be viewed negatively or more negatively than positively, and 18 percent said both.[19] The more moderate view of Tiso probably reflects two things: first, that he was a Roman Catholic priest; and second, that he was executed in 1947, which some people believe was the result of Czech pressure.

The populist and nationalist historians achieved their greatest success with the publication, with the assistance of the European Union PHARE fund, of 80,000 copies of *Dejiny Slovenska a Slovákov* in 1996, designated for use as a history handbook in Slovak schools, part of the triumph of nationalist populism.[20] Professional Slovak historians issued a stronglyworded protest.[21] After an international uproar, the then prime minister Vladimír Mečiar acknowledged that "some parts of the book are inadequate or historically incorrect," and promised to remove it from schools, although he left copies in teachers' libraries.[22] After Mečiar's defeat a year later, the divisions among historians narrowed.[23]

In contrast, attitudes to the Slovak National Uprising were much more positive, despite the vigorous efforts of émigré historians.[24] More than 80 percent agreed with the statement that the Uprising "was an expression of resistance of the Slovaks to Fascism and we should therefore be proud of it," 11.4 percent disagreed.[25]

In spring 2004, Slovak Television, after a delay by its director, showed a moving documentary, "Love Your Neighbor," (Miluj blížneho svojho), about a pogrom, on 24 September 1945, against Jews in Topol'čany.[26] The program traced the history of Slovak–Jewish relations in the spa town and reviewed the extensive wartime deportations, then focused on the pogrom itself. The producers found some locals who still speak chillingly against Jews, even when there are no longer any in the town. Following the program, eight intellectuals, including historian Ivan Kamenec, discussed it. Only Ján Čarnogurský took issue with the program, saying that it unfairly blamed the Roman Catholic Church. In spite of the efforts of partisans of the Slovak State to blame individuals or Nazis for the deportation and murder of Slovak Jews during World War II, it is clear that this pogrom was carried out by Slovaks. In effect, it challenged the Slovak State's defenders. In the fall of 2005, nearly a year and a half after the program was aired, the Mayor of Topoľčany, on behalf of the city council, apologized for the pogrom.

The documentary, by its nature a form of journalism that takes a position, cast the Holocaust in Slovakia in black-and-white terms, and got past some careful media presentations that tried to contextualize the Slovak State and its leaders.[27] In April 2005, a one-man play about Tiso opened in Bratislava, based mostly on Tiso's writings and speeches, in one of which Tiso remarks that he will not allow Slovaks to die to save the Jews. Press coverage was modest because Actor Marian Labuda refused to give interviews. Neo-fascists threatened to blow up the theatre.[28]

Public debate on pre-communist Slovak history continues in intellectual publications.[29] The evidence about the Holocaust, however, has become undeniable in public life, as evidenced when President Ivan Gašparovič apologized in 2006 to Israel: "I come from a country that did not avoid the brown plague—as we call Fascism—and, unfortunately, did not avoid deportations of Jews either ... The Holocaust is the darkest stain in human history."[30]

In the modern world, the relationship of mass media, especially journalism, to nation is complex. Some scholars argue that nationalism in the press can help provide a defense against globalization.[31] In the Slovak case, one could argue that a national agenda had moved to the fore after 1968, strengthened in 1989, and moved to a position of crucial importance in 1992 because of the uncertainties related to the division of Czechoslovakia and the loss of its state identity, as well as the disappearance of the required socialist identity of communist days.[32] Thus initially, journalism provided a sympathetic ear to a nationalist agenda, represented especially by the efforts of nationalist politicians to praise the wartime Slovak State. As the future of the new Slovak Republic seemed more assured, however, journalists became less sympathetic, especially when professional historians aggressively presented a more nuanced view of the Slovak State.[33]

Coming to terms with the communist experience has been more difficult. The re-runs of the communist-era spy-thriller "Major Zeman" that began on Czech television a couple of years ago received international attention.[34] Critics wondered how programs that glorify the communist system could be shown again. It reflected nostalgia for the popular culture of late Communism, which had been nearly empty of ideology.[35] Public television in Slovakia showed its own communist-era series, a historical portrayal of the Slovak National Uprising of 1944. The series is based on the writings of Viliam Plevza, an adviser to the late communist leader Gustáv Husák, and reflects Husak's view of the Uprising.[36] It is no different than a US film that glorifies the pre-Civil War South, but when public understanding of the past in Slovakia is distorted, it only confuses the issue, particularly when entertainment programs are watched by more people than are news broadcasts, and most importantly, when television generally carries more impact than any other medium.

Much remains to be learned about the communist period. This is much more characteristic of Slovakia than the Czech Republic because the post-1968 regime had greater legitimacy in Slovakia than in the Czech Republic, ironically in part because of the success of the journalists' protests discussed above.[37] The republics' differing views on the legitimacy of the post-1968 regime also reflects the fact that many Czechs who had initially supported the communist regime after 1948, felt especially betrayed by the Soviet invasion.[38]

Even historians who toiled in the fields of Clio during the communist era are difficult to characterize. While a few collaborated closely with the regime, others quietly published important work in out-of-the-way journals, while some—mostly in the Czech Lands—engaged in dissident history.[39] Like other people in Czechoslovakia, they were "tangibly influenced by fear in their activities and achievements."[40] After 1989 some historians acknowledged their complicity, but rarely studied it.[41]

What has not been examined so much is the daily life of compromise and avoidance. This determined forgetting has remained the dominant public stance on the history of the communist period. It is hard enough to write about ordinary lives, particularly when confronted with the knowledge of how people dealt with fear and ambition or the desire to make the best of the situation in which they found themselves. Such topics are not suitable material for journalistic treatment.

Historians in Slovakia writing about the communist period not only first have to gather factual information, but they are also faced with the challenge of learning new historical approaches developed in the profession abroad, and they must also engage in some comparative history.[42]

Most Slovak historiography about the communist period has focused on the periods of crisis or dramatic change, where it is easier to ascribe guilt and innocence to individuals. The crackdown on various institutions, particularly the church, following the commencement of communist rule, is a gripping story.[43] Most of its perpetrators have either died, or had already retired to private life in the 1950s, and in some respects have been forgotten. The people most responsible for cooperation with the Soviet masters following the invasion of Czechoslovakia in 1968 are few in number, and also often advanced in years. The heroes of the reforms of the 1960s received their appreciations very soon after 1989, although their association with communist rule complicated judgments about their merits. Some of them became dissidents out of necessity, so they were not strictly speaking anti-communist heroes. The public wanted to distance itself from its own involvement with Communism.

A wedge pushing journalists and the public into coming to terms with behavior during the communist period is the Institute for the Memory of the Nation, established in 2003. On its website are records both of the World War II Center of State Security, and of the secret police of the communist period.[44] Its journal, the quarterly *Pamät národa*, provides a venue for historians who wish to delve into the topic of individual collaboration with the Nazi and communist regimes. The institute provides journalists with a legitimate public institution that can discuss issues of the communist period, thus overcoming the problems caused by the reluctance of public figures to introduce these topics.

In early 2005, Ján Langoš, then the institute's head, reported that Archbishop Ján Sokol, vice-chair of the Conference of Slovak Bishops, had been registered in secret police records as an agent.[45] By July, the newspaper *Sme* reported that more than a quarter of the deans in Sokol's archdiocese had also been agents.[46] After a few church denials, the issue disappeared from view until an interview aired on 27 December 2006 by the all-news channel TA3, in which Sokol praised the wartime Slovak State and its president, Jozef Tiso. This statement, combined with the earlier reports of Sokol's cooperation with the secret police, again brought to the forefront the issue of individual behavior during the communist period. Journalists contrasted statements by Sokol and other church officials with comments by historians and politicians of differing outlooks. Daniel C. Hallin has argued persuasively that that the media in the United States did not persuade the people of the US to turn against the Vietnam War.[47] The emergence of alternative official points of view in Slovakia is providing journalists there with the opportunity to begin to report the complicated history of the communist period.

In spring 2004, I was a guest speaker in a journalism history class at Comenius University. The discussion moved beyond history to politics and the place of media coverage of politics. The students had learned the theoretical lesson that the press should not be in bed with politicians, but should play the watchdog role. These students have no memory of living under Communism; they were four years old at the time of the Velvet Revolution. I asked them whether they would have been party members or dissidents if they had been living in those days. Dissidents, they all answered. Children often don't know what went on in their parents' lives before they were born or for the early years of their lives.[48] But these Slovak parents, having been complicit in the communist system, are not likely to talk about those days either. If parents aren't interested, and the children aren't interested, the news media will not pursue these topics. Coming to terms with the past will happen only when people outside the media raise the issues in such a way that the media are compelled to address them. This occurred with the occasional publication of the names of secret agents.

How Slovaks think about history and the past, and the meaning and use that it has for them, derives largely from the mediated versions of history disseminated through the media. Generally, analyses and discussions of complex, controversial and difficult issues do not lend themselves to media treatment. The clear connection of the historical evaluation of the Slovak State with contemporary politics finally helped journalism and journalists to address historical issues of complicity. Few professional historians joined the defenders of the Slovak State.

Much of the period of communist rule in Slovakia, however, remains an enigma. Today's historians grew up in that period. So did the majority of adult Slovaks. They have different memories and believe different truths. Most of Slovakia's journalists are young enough to not have adult memories of the communist period. On their own they are unlikely to follow up stories about that period. But the gradual democratization of Slovakia is leading to the development of a variety of official institutions and political outlooks, laying the groundwork for a debate about the past, a debate that will reach much further through society in Slovakia because the news media will be able to report alternative and conflicting viewpoints.

NOTES

1 Beata Balogova, "History Marches On at SNP Ceremonies—How Will Officials Respond to Neo-Nazi tendencies?" *Slovak Spectator*, (11 September 2005). In a not fully successful effort to present a similar demonstration the following year, 150 police officers and security officials were sent to protect 800 participants. Daniel Vražda, "Fašisti provokovali na oslavách." *Sme*, (30 August 2006).

2 Elena Mannová, ed., *A Concise History of Slovakia* (Bratislava: Historický ústav, 2000): 7.

3 Yen Le, "The 'We-Win-Even-When-We-Lose' Syndrome: U.S. Press Coverage of the Twenty-Fifth Anniversary of the 'Fall of Saigon,'" *American Quarterly* 58, No. 2 (June 2006): 329–52.

4 E.g., John E Haynes, "The Cold War Debate Continues: A Traditionalist View of Historical Writing on Domestic Communism & Anti-Communism," *Journal of Cold War Studies* 2, No. 1 (Winter 2000): 76–115.

5 Stanislav J. Kirschbaum, "Slovakia: Whose History, What History?" *Canadian Slavonic Papers* 45, Nos. 3–4 (September–December 2003): 459–67.

6 Costica Bradatan, "A Time of Crisis—A Crisis of (the Sense of) Time: The Political Production of Time in Communism & Its Relevance for the Postcommunist Debates," *East European Politics & Societies* 19, No. 2 (Spring 2005): 260.

7 Ibid.

8 It is now possible to examine the communist-era background of the current Slovak elite through the website Leaders.sk. See "Baring the Slovak Elite & Its 'Fascinating Past.'" *Slovak Spectator*, (17 October 2005).

9 Letter from "Akčný vybor pri Sväzu slovenských novinárov" [Action Committee of the Union of Slovak Journalists] 164/48 of 12 April 1948, 150 BV 52, *Archív literatúry a umení*, Slovenská národná knižnica, Martin. Elsewhere in Hušek's papers (150 BX 25) is the draft of a letter of March 2 from Hušek to Hysko. Ironically, Hysko himself would be ousted from the Union following the 1968 Soviet invasion.

10 Marína Zavacká, "Buržoázní nacionalisti? Slovenskí komunisti." [Bourgeois Nationalists? Slovak Communists] *Česko-Slovenská historická ročenka* (1998): 75–78.

11 Thomas E. Fischer, "Der slowakische Sonderweg: Zur Geschichtskultur in einer Transformationsgesellschaft." [The Slovak Way: On Historical Culture in a Transforming Society] *Ethnos—Nation* 6 (1998): 145–57.

12 Kirschbaum, "Slovakia: Whose History…," p. 464. Also see Stan Kirschbaum, "The First Slovak Republic (1939–1945): Some Thoughts on Its Meaning in Slovak History." *Österreichische Osthefte* 41, Nos. 3–4 (1999): 405–25.

13 In contrast, East Germany, another country under communist rule, could not avoid the Holocaust since the topic was discussed in West Germany. For an interesting take on the role of media in this process, see René Wolf, "'Mass Deception without Deceivers'? The Holocaust on East & West German Radio in the 1960s." *Journal of Contemporary History* 41, No. 4 (October 2006): 741–55.

14 Gil Eyal, "Identity & Trauma." *History & Memory* 16, No. 1 (Spring/Summer 2004): 5–36.

15 Ivan Kamenec, "Sedemdesiattisíc Židov: Holokaust na Slovensku, jeho reflexie v literatúre a spoločnosti." [Seventy Thousand Jews: The Holocaust in Slovakia (and) its Reflection in Literature & Society] *OS: Forum občianskej spoločnosti* 9, Nos. 1–2 (2005): 14–22.

16 Michael Shafir, "Deflective Negationism of the Holocaust in Postcommunist East-Central Europe (Part 3): "Deflections to 'The Fringe,'" *RFE/RL East European Perspectives* 4, No. 20 (2 October 2002); Gabriel Hoffmann, *Zamlčaná pravdu o Slovensku* [Silenced Truths About Slovakia] (Partizánske: Garmond, 1996).

17 Chad Bryant, "Whose Nation? Czech Dissidents & History Writing from a Post-1989 Perspective," *History & Memory* 12, No. 1 (Spring/Summer 2000): 39–40, describes Czech historians who worked in the gray zone.

18 Ivan Kamenec, "Niekoľko poznámok k vývoju slovenskej historiografie po roku 1989, alebo o peripetiách jednej novej tradície," [Some Notes on the Development of Slovak Historiography After 1989, Or About the Peripatetic of a New Tradition] *Česko-Slovenská historická ročenka 1998*, p. 225.

19 Zora Bútorová et al., *Current Problems of Slovakia After the Split of the CSFR—October 1993* (Bratislava: Focus, 1993).

20 Michael Carpenter discusses the nationalist populism that by 1997 was backed by ultranationalists in the Slovak National Party, populists, and former communists, in "Slovakia & the Triumph of Nationalist Populism," *Communist & Post-Communist Studies* 30, No. 2 (June 1997): 205–20. Kevin Deegan-Krause argues convincingly that this nationalism was not a Slovak characteristic, but rather a characteristic of the particular coalition. See his *Elected Affinities: Democracy & Party Competition in Slovakia & the Czech Republic* (Stanford, CA.: Stanford University Press, 2006).

21 *Práca*, (19 April 1997).

22 "Slovak Premier Raps Book Denying Hounding of Jews," (Reuters, 27 June 1997, 11:07 a.m. EDT). A detailed English-language website followed the developments regarding this book: www.angelfire.com/hi/xcampaign/engversion.html.

23 Elena Mannová, "Clio na slovenský spôsob: Problémy a nové prístupy historiografie na Slovensku po roku 1989," [Clio Slovak Style: Problems and New Approaches of Historiography in Slovakia After 1989] *Historický časopis* 52, No. 2 (2004): 245.

24 For one of the more interesting debates with representatives from several sides, see M. Janek and M. Straka, eds., "Aké si bolo, povstanie?" [What Was It Like, the Uprising] *Slovensko* 17, No. 4 (July–August 1994): 6–10, 26–27. For a more critical discussion of the use and misuse of the Uprising, see Martina Krénová and Michal Ač, eds., "Zneužité dejiny." *Kultúrny život* 24, No. 20 (30 August 1990): 6–8.

25 Zora Bútorová et al., *Current Problems of Slovakia After the Split of the CSFR—October 1993* (Bratislava: Focus, 1993), Supplement, 33–36.

26 A newsweekly referred to it as "The Film That Shook Slovakia." Andrej Bán, "Film, ktorý zatriasol Slovenskom," *Format* 3, No. 22 (31 May 2004): 51.

27 See the special section, "Ľudácky režim." [People's Party Regime] *Format* 3, No. 10 (8 March 2004): 48–55.

28 Milada Čechová, "V hlavnej úlohe Jozef Tiso." [Jozef Tiso in the Leading Role] *Sme*, (11 April 2005).

29 For example, see Rudolf Chmel, "Aj v tej Černovej strieľali Slováci." [Even in Černova, the Slovaks Did the Shooting] *Sme*, (3 September 2005).

30 Quoted in Beata Balogová, "Let's End the Silence About the Wartime Slovak State." *Slovak Spectator*, (6 March 2006).

31 Silvio Waisbord, "Media & the Reinvention of the Nation," in *The SAGE Handbook of Media Studies*, John D.H. Downing, ed., (Thousand Oaks, CA: Sage, 2004), pp. 375–92.

32 Owen V. Johnson, "Failing Democracy: Journalists, the Mass Media, and the Dissolution of Czechoslovakia," in *Irreconcilable Differences?: Explaining Czechoslovakia's Dissolution*, Michael Kraus and Allison K. Stanger, eds., (Lanham, Maryland: Rowman and Littlefield, 2000), pp. 163–82; Eric M. Eisenberg, "Building a Mystery: Toward a New Theory of Communication & Identity." *Journal of Communication* 51, No. 3 (September 2001): 534–52.

33 Ivan Kamenec, *Hľadanie a blúdenie v dejinách* [Seeking and Groping in History] (Bratislava: Kalligram, 2000), pp. 227–29.

34 Matt Reynolds, "The Spy Who Came in From the Cold." *New York Times*, (24 October 2005): 1; Charles W. Holmes, "Reruns of Communist-era Show Inflame Czechs: On the Anniversary of the 'Velvet Revolution,' a Dissident-busting '70s TV Cop Has Viewers Tuning In and On a Tirade." *Atlanta Journal and Constitution*, (17 November 1999); Peter Finn, "Prague's Mannix for the Masses: 'Major Zeman,' Rehabilitated?" *Washington Post*, (30 November 1998): C1.

35 Andrew Roberts, "The Politics & Anti-Politics of Nostalgia," *East European Politics and Societies* 16, No. 3 (Fall 2002): 764–809; Mirka Kernová, "Socialistický nerealizmus: Prečo ľudia pozerajú normalizačné seriály," [Seeking and Groping in History] *Sme*, (11 August 2005); Victor Gomez, "Nostalgia for the Communist Past," *Transitions Online*, (17 November 2004).

36 "Major Zeman po Povstaleckej histórii nepríde," [Major Zeman Doesn't Come After the Uprising History] *Sme*, (20 July 2005).

37 Nadya Nedelsky, "Divergent Responses to a Common Past: Transitional Justice in the Czech Republic & Slovakia." *Theory & Society* 33, No. 1 (February 2004): 65–115.

38 Muriel Blave, *Une destalinisation manqué: Tchécoslovaquie 1956* [A Missing Destalinization: Czechoslovakia 1956] (Paris: Editions Complexe, 2005).

39 Pavel Seifter and František Svátek. "L'historiographie et le pouvoir: l'exemple tchècoslovaque (1969–1990)," [Historiography and Power: The Czechoslovak Example (1969–1990)] *Relations internationals* 67 (Autumn 1997): 273–94; and Stanley B. Winters, "Science & Politics: The Rise & Fall of the Czechoslovak Academy of Sciences." *Bohemia* 35, No. 2 (1994): 268–99.

40 Ivan Kamenec, "Phenomenon of Fear in Modern Slovak History?" *Studia historica Slovaca* 19 (1995): 128.

41 Dušan Kováč, "Zamyslenie sa nad Slovenskou historiografiou deväťdesiatych rokov." [Thoughts on Slovak Historiography of the 1990s] *Česko-Slovenská historická ročenka* (2003): 225–31.

42 A useful commentary is Peter Haslinger, "Národné alebo nadnárodné dejiny? Historiografie o Slovenska v evropskom kontexte," *Historický časopis* 52, No. 2 (2004): 269–80.

43 Jan Pešek is the most prominent contemporary historian in this area.

44 www.upn.gov.sk

45 "Arcibiskup Sokol bol asi agent." *Sme*, (10 February 2005).

46 Monika Žemlová, "V Bratislave sú kňazí agenti stále vysoko," *Sme*, (7 July 2005).

47 Daniel C. Hallin, "The Media, the War in Vietnam, & Political Support: A Critique of the Thesis of an Oppositional Media," *Journal of Politics* 46, No. 1 (February 1984): 2–24.

48 Nicholas Wood, "Young Bulgarians Know Their Nation's History, Sort Of," *New York Times*, (15 November 2004): A4.

The Many Moralists and the Few Communists

Approaching Morality and Politics in Post-Communist Hungary

FERENC LACZÓ

INTRODUCTION

This piece is intended as a contribution to the classic debate over the relationship between morality and politics. On a general level, it deals with the intriguing way in which this relationship has evolved in the contemporary era especially since 1989 in former communist countries, and with the profound manner in which this evolving relationship is bound up with the perception of the recent, communist past. In my opinion, simultaneous reflection on morality and politics should be seen as central to the understanding of post-communist revisionism, since moralistic as well as moralizing discourses have greatly increased their force and are enormously widespread in the political lives of countries which once belonged to the Soviet bloc. Moral credibility is conceived as a crucial form of capital, and moral blackmail often proves a most effective tool in the hands of those aiming to discredit others.

More specifically, I shall explore the continuities and discontinuities in the ways the two realms are connected in Hungary, and how this is interrelated with current Hungarian historical culture, which is also highly relevant politically.[1] In doing this, I will point both to the announced "revision of ourselves" and the attempted revision of morals, consensually supported and, what is more, established as one of the central promises of the change of regime, *and* to the striking continuities. These can sometimes appear in novel forms which, however, barely hide the essential similarities of content. I shall use the complex and telling case of perceptions of the political and moral role that János Kádár played in Hungarian history, to illustrate a number of my more abstract points and to make some further ones. At the end of my paper, I shall make a number of recommendations.

Let me first clarify my stance on the issue of moralizing politics and the understanding of the recent past, which I conceive of as simultaneous and interrelated processes in post-communist countries. The overall impression one gets is that even though manifold revisions were thought necessary in the transition/transformation period, with moral revisionism in particular declared as the normative preference, and thus continuities have been ritually condemned when they have been addressed, various sides have tended to accuse other sides of exhibiting continuity. Self-examination has remained the exception rather than the rule, and therefore I would argue that self-righteousness still prevails almost unchallenged, while the superficial and seemingly enormous changes hide deeper continuities. The major trend in post-communist Hungary is to externalize blame and find others guilty, without groups and individuals openly questioning themselves or examining their own involvement. This type of thinking was described by Péter Nádas, among others, as the logic of dictatorships, which function precisely because they can often enough make people look for problems not in themselves but in their (human) environment.[2] Moreover, they are able to deflect criticism from systematic problems and the mechanisms that perpetuate the dictatorship to individual sinners. This anthropomorphic conception of problems as human shortcomings makes people express dissatisfaction with their rulers in a way that sees their replacement as individuals the most they can hope for. In other words, attention is shifted to secondary issues.[3] Moreover, the constant complaints uttered in the absence of the person who is held responsible, or even accused, are basic to such political cultures that are interrelated with the broader "cultures of complaint" so characteristic of Eastern Europe. Instead of creating forums to help solve problems, people often stick to forums which they know are not suited to such purposes. It is ironic that a habit which was one of the defense mechanisms under the former dictatorship (namely blaming) that could often be justified in that political environment (after all, it often represented the search for the responsibility of those who were unaccountable, and was thus, even if politically insufficient, certainly not unnecessary), survived the fall of the dictatorship to assume a more questionable role. Adam Michnik, among others, reflected on several occasions on the different status of the attempts to moralize (about) Communism and politics prior to and after 1989, claiming that many arguments that under the dictatorship could qualify as moralistic, afterwards would be no more than moralizing, even if they were used by the same people—which has by no means always been the case.[4]

MORALITY AND POLITICS: MAJOR TRENDS

In this section I shall reflect on the major transformation in the way moral questions began to be related to politics. This had already started in the later decades of the communist regimes, when it was done most significantly by people who belonged to the opposition. The collapse of Communism and the way it has been understood in the mainstream, crucially including Communism's moral delegitimization, enormously strengthened the novel way of relating the two fields, and moralized politics, at least on the surface.

In mainstream Western political theory a certain difference between the spheres of morality and politics tends to be accepted. Since Machiavelli, as the history of political theory is conventionally narrated, the basic canon has been that what is politically good is not necessarily morally righteous, and vice versa. Politics is about the common good and power, and political acts should be measured by the utilitarian criteria of their usefulness in the first place—the end to a certain extent justifying the means. Thus, when we analyze these two spheres and their relationship, we ought to remember that politics is about good and bad, while morality is about good and evil. Common sense tells us that though the two standards cannot be completely separated, neither moral, nor political criteria can be strictly applied to judge the "other sphere." Only a pure idealist would conflate these two types of criteria, and only a complete cynic would deny their interrelation.

Starting with the war crimes trials that followed the Allied victory in the Second World War and the acceptance of the Universal Declaration of Human Rights, and more forcefully in the 1970s with the signing of the Helsinki accords, Carter's increased (presidential) stress on human rights issues and the emergence of democratic oppositions in East Central Europe, the idea of keeping morality and politics apart came under attack. How to reconnect them properly, how to promote a new, moral kind of politics, was high on the agenda of many individuals and groups in opposition already prior to 1989. Questions of dignity (which can and ought to be maintained in the face of political defeat), and the vision of history in which moral righteousness also has (at least some) political validity, were crucial to the self-understanding of the marginalized though often extraordinary intellectuals who comprised the democratic opposition in Hungary, a national case in some ways similar to those of Czechoslovakia and Poland. This revision of the relationship between politics and morality under Communism was clearly polemical in intent.

While in power, communist rulers legitimized themselves in grandiose historical fashion, claiming that all history inevitably led up to their attainment of power. They claimed to think of human history as working according to knowable mechanisms towards progress and the ultimate attainment of an ideal society, and, in line with this, considered history to be an amoral court of judgment, distinguishing essentially only between progressives and reactionaries. In this epic struggle everything and anything was permitted on the part of the historically righteous, while their opponents were classified as enemies of human liberation. The supposition of their evil nature could then occasionally be scaled down to regarding them as people who had been misled into supporting the wrong side, who deviated from the right line and the good political nature of the "communist political animal." Sometimes subjective supporters were uncovered as objective enemies (the "self-purification of the communists" was initiated), at other times subjective enemies were judged to have no objectively harmful impact (the "delay of complete purification" was allowed).

In short, the communist project was a fundamentally moral one, but communists accepted a version of history that was meaningfully designed but fundamentally amoral in its unfolding. Hence, in the self-presentation of these regimes, communist crimes were without moral significance and deeds were to be judged only according to the utilitarian criterion of whether they had helped the greater cause (of progress and the ultimate attainment of an ideal society). The bet for or against Communism was more than somewhat Pascalian.

Living under communist regimes and in such a(n) (a)moral environment, members of the democratic opposition proposed a revolution of morals and human dignity. Dissidents in various countries of the Soviet bloc wanted to attain the recognition of communist crimes as crimes. This struggle for recognition was among their top priorities. Their consistently applied moral standard implied that the distinction between crimes and "progressive crimes" ought to be discarded, and that there should be no more political abuse of morals. A firm moralistic discourse ought to replace the communist type of moralizing, evidently based on double standards, on politically charged, only seemingly moral, judgments. With the (re-)introduction of a pure moral standard, they aimed at moral improvements, and at a widespread "revision of ourselves." This moralistic wish for recognition was the strongest means of oppressed (and otherwise politically disarmed) minorities courageous enough to oppose the dictatorship which made claims on their lives. These people aimed at a non-violent confrontation with the Soviet Behemoth, and ultimately at a moral delegitimization of the Soviet-type regimes, which would in turn trigger political changes.

What the major intellectual trend critical of the regime used to do was to measure the regime's realities against its own professed ideals, and to point to shortcomings. Though this type of socialist dissidence could at times be extremely powerful, it can still be regarded as internal criticism, since it shared the ideals of the regime it criticized. It was revisionist in intent. With the fading of reformist hopes, which suffered a severe blow with the suppression of the Prague Spring, this was gradually replaced by an external type of criticism, aiming to hold the regime responsible for upholding standards it did not declare as its own. This novel opposition strategy was first designed by Polish dissidents in the mid-1970s, whose ideas and practices clearly influenced Czechoslovak and Hungarian dissidents. Its most famous formulation can be found in Adam Michnik's seminal essay "A New Evolutionism." To use metaphors taken from the sports world, the most respected dissidents first tried to defeat communist regimes in what was a home game to such regimes, before they brought them to play an away game. In Hungary this trend could be observed with particular clarity, since several of the most important members of the liberally-oriented Democratic Opposition were previously disciples of Lukács, and wrote significant Marxist revisionist tracts. In Hungary, the turning point came around 1977. The volume *Marx a negyedik évtizedben* revealed that many former "revisionists" had reached the limits of Marxist criticism, and accepted its limited usefulness in understanding the world.

Parallel to the emergence of democratic oppositions proposing and propagating a revolution of morals, which in some cases can be seen as replacing their former belief in the communist utopia, in recent decades, and not only in formerly communist countries, there has been much focus on oppression, crimes, suffering and immorality. This has led to the emergence of an historical-cultural environment abundant with demands for the recognition of crimes, usually the ones committed against one's own group, however defined. Frequently, this has also led to severe competitions over which crime to recognize, on what level (with questions such as "genocide or not" high on the agenda), and in what way (providing restitution or not, to whom, in what measure or form, etc.). Though mutual recognition of oppression, humiliation, suffering, and dignity would be ideal, the current environment can be better understood analytically by using the approach and methods of *comparative martyrology*, as various (organized) groups are fighting for the recognition of their claim to martyrdom, while not being eager to recognize other groups' claims, even if of similar nature. This is why much of this practice can be called moralizing; many lack the willingness to apply one single standard, and wish to further political aims with their morally charged arguments. Given the narcissistic nature of memory, which makes us remember the pain inflicted on us more strongly than pain which we inflict on others, some of this is understandable. I have to add though that agents aiming to establish what should be the relevant, remembered crimes are frequently not from among those who have personal memories of their cause. In sum, and generally speaking, the current environment is characterized by an unfortunate lack of interest and respect for others' suffering (that would be similar to what is demanded of others), and only relatively few cases of conscious and honest self-positioning, in spite of the abundance of moral claims. It is an environment in which battles over memory and victimhood assume central legitimating importance. Therefore, both cultural *and* political stakes are simply too high for this practice not to turn almost completely into a competition over power.

However we may assess such developments, they clearly imply that the question of evil is moving ever closer to the center of the stage, as the main political and historical problem of our age. Evil is now something we have to understand, condemn, and fight. Once again it seems to have become an unavoidable political problem, no longer a mere moral criterion. For Leibniz, the question might have been how to explain the (seeming) existence of evil in a world that is fundamentally good. For us, with the experience of the 20th century behind us, the problem is likely to take a different form: how can we recognize and try to understand evil without accepting it, and how can we best defend ourselves against its real presence?

The recognition of the presence of evil—this fundamental moral (as well as ontological) issue—seems to have played a significant role in the collapse of communist regimes, or at least it certainly influences the ways this process, culminating in the *annus mirabilis* of 1989, tends to be narrated in much of mainstream scholarship. Besides the story of economic irrationality, insufficiency, and bankruptcy, the focus is on crimes and what is presented as a moralistic (and post factum) opposition to the communist dictatorship, which can be called "human self-defense against evil." This has a counterpart in the idea of resistance through culture, used by some prestigious intellectuals, notably in Romania, such as Patapievici.[5]

In the case of Hungary, the significant presence of this moralistic discourse is understandable in a certain sense, as it provides the only way to narrate how people from within and outside (divided over their judgments of the role of those working within the system and the merits of that system as well) could come to an agreement in 1989. Denying that what happened constituted an unprincipled, pragmatic agreement of elite groups, this agreement *had to happen* through a moral improvement in terms of the sides relating to each other while this improvement also *had* to take place on the communist side itself. The communist's authority was rather weak, and insufficient without the addition of a source of justification in the form of a promise, a promise to improve. One might say that 1989 constituted a crucial chapter in their lengthy *Bildungsroman*. From a moral point of view, based on ideas of repentance and forgiveness, and an investment of hope in an increasing role for moral conscience, one can hardly deny them the right to attempt this. Curiously, with this shared acceptance of the need for moral improvement, the moral illegitimacy of Communism was accepted even by the (successors of the) communists. There was a curious moral self-delegitimization in 1989 in order to make a claim to starting anew, which from a critical perspective could appear like a general assigning of blame to one's own side in order to pre-empt what would then be judged as mere "scapegoating."

Though its essential function is understandable, on the other hand, this discourse of the moral delegitimization of Communism does not make much analytical sense if one looks at the historical record. Skeptically, one might ask how it can be that certain crimes committed in the 1930s or 1950s did not delegitimize the communist establishment in the 1960s and 1970s, while they did so in the late 1980s? The intense moral questioning was preceded by the recognition of the system's failure, and this bankruptcy made the immorality obvious, as the communist project with fundamentally moral aims and immoral means turned out to have achieved none of its aims—while unquestionably relying on immoral means. The events of major importance in 1956, starting with Khruschev's secret speech, initiated an ambiguous admission of moral bankruptcy from the top, but in the absence of powerful enough reasons in other realms it failed to lead to a moral (and political) discrediting of the system. In 1989, the crucial difference was *not* the novel recognition of moral insufficiency, but the admission of political and economic failure, which was then automatically understood as a moral failure too. In sum, the centrality of moral discourse made sense politically, and its use was politically motivated. At the same time, being primarily politically motivated, it does not make so much sense analytically.

It is of special significance that the morally dubious character of the communist era as such, its unacceptable immorality and unbearable moral record, have emerged as major discursive ways to address the period. One might go as far as to claim that while in power, the communist authorities took responsibility for everything (not necessarily in detail, but in general), so now that their project has proven a failure they have to take the blame for all the imperfections. Some claim that this is only logical; there is a certain logic in assigning blame and responsibility to them, taking their promises as the basis of judgment. However, this might lead to absurd conclusions, such as the not only false, but also (within core Western countries) anachronistic idealization of some other path of development, notably the essentialized "Western" one.

BASIC POLITICAL AND SOCIAL TRANSFORMATIONS, AND THE ROLE OF HISTORIANS

To approach the new role of moral arguments in politics and the question of how this phenomenon is interrelated with our understanding of Communism in a more comprehensive manner, a brief presentation of the basics of societal transformation in the period under question focusing on public opinion is needed, together with some thoughts on the changes in the role of the historian. Let us now turn to these issues.

The period since 1989 is often presented as constituting a major transformation, and even as an unprecedented wave of simultaneous major political and economic reorganization. On the other hand it can also be pictured as the time of the "great miracle of the small transformation," since it has offered few opportunities for upward social mobility (though many might have converted various forms of capital into other kinds—primarily political into economic) and cultural change (as usual) has taken place at a much slower pace than political and economic change, and often in "unpredictable" (unforeseen, perhaps even unforeseeable) directions.[6] Since the acceptance of capitalism and of growing inequality among citizens has certainly remained a minority position, the (by no means overwhelming, to say the least) support for the post-1989 transformation was to a significant extent based on optimistic predictions about the future. The failure of the new epoch to fulfill many of these expectations led to growing skepticism and disappointment within a few years after 1989.[7] According to opinion polls, in the case of Hungary by 1992–1993, negative sentiments concerning the changes were much more common than positive ones. Since then, this generally negative evaluation has become less widespread, but the initial trend (higher numbers of disappointed than of contented people) has never been reversed. In Hungary, the transition failed people exactly in the areas where they had strongest hopes: for example, that living standards would increase and life would become easier. Only a tiny minority feel such changes have actually occurred. Linked to this is the fact that favorable assessments (typically and somewhat enigmatically assumed to be based on nostalgia) of the previous regime and era (strangely enough, these two terms are often used interchangeably in Hungarian) remain strong, especially among the older and less educated parts of the population. Etatist and anti-capitalist opinions are shared by majorities on both sides of the major political divide, commonly referred to as the left and the right, while the number of people with liberal convictions has barely increased over the almost two decades that have now passed since 1989.

What divides the two sides in Hungary most strongly is their relationship with the past, especially Communism and symbolic matters above all national ones. Since cultural issues have been moving to the center of contemporary political and academic discourse, as can be seen both in the unexpected revival of religious conceptions of differences and in the forcefulness of ethnicist biases surrounding the novel ways of dealing with "ethnic others" (emerging for instance in the enormous attention devoted to migrants and their specificities), it is little wonder that the issue of Communism polarizes people in post-communist times, especially if we also consider that meaningful options and alternative action plans are largely absent. Considerable political and cultural capital has been invested in order to create and strengthen this divide, and sometimes consciously, sometimes not, since it serves as one of the surest ways to strengthen allegiances, and to mobilize people in case of perceived need. In Hungary, the right-wing tends to maintain that its "righteous supporters" are still unfairly suffering from oppression inflicted under Communism and by the continuing dominance of people who profit from the legacy of those times, while the left can be held together by the fear of anti-communist, right-wing radicalism, aroused by regularly pointing to threats which can seem quite real in the light of the shaking of the previous (communist) anti-fascist consensus. The defense of the anti-fascist consensus, which has actually undergone multiple revisions since an openended discussion of the relationship between Communism and Fascism began immediately after freedom was won, is a major political demand in post-communist times. Given that right-wing conservatism and radicalism are related in ways that are rare in more solidly established Western democracies, where the level of knowledge concerning what is democratic and acceptable is higher, this threat is partly real. However, it is also frequently exaggerated for political purposes by the left.

In such an environment of high hopes and constant promises coupled with the (on the surface almost universally agreed upon) agenda of moral renewal and political and cultural investment in divisions over matters of the past, it is easy to understand that moral questioning becomes all the more severe. Disappointed people who feel cheated and see much hypocrisy more easily become morally outraged when morally charged arguments are so widespread. Politicians employ such arguments frequently, and thereby try to control them, but they are often turned against them whenever they are not judged credible. It is a paradoxical though widespread phenomenon that people do not trust politicians but apply idealistic standards when assessing their performances.

The growing gap between moral discourses and social practices is confirmed by the *growing* strength of anti-Communism in Hungary, including its radical variety The idea of holding people responsible for communist crimes specifically, or for Communism in general, has become more popular over time, though how one judges such questions depends largely on ideological and party preferences—so the change might be at least partly due to the growing political polarization in Hungary. Around 80 percent of right-wing voters favor the idea of some form of punishment being meted out. Around two-thirds of them would also support the exclusion of communists (though attempts to define this concept could lead to endless debate) from public life.[8] Note that this would mean a huge change in the system, causing massive disruption to the other side while (if applied consistently) harming many in their own ranks too. It is difficult to write of a stable, established democracy when a substantial majority on one side questions the fundamental legitimacy of a large number of crucial current actors, and when both sides display great readiness to "uncover" the "criminal historical background" of the other side as well as the anti-democratic implications of having such a background.

Having addressed the question of the role of Communism in the public and political life of post-communist Hungary, let me now turn to the case of professional historians. They have traditionally claimed to enjoy a calm isolation which allows them to research and write on more remote topics, and in earlier times many of them would not have felt comfortable having to offer politically relevant assessments. The role of the historian was traditionally understood as providing objective observations, balanced presentations and assessments. This detached scholarly practice crucially entailed the generally known and widely accepted norm of refraining from passing judgments, including moral judgments. To use Weber's coinage, history was meant to be a value-free scientific pursuit as well. This ideal of the historian/scholar prescribes a high level of consensus, as it is understood that if two people were to be similarly objective they could hardly fail to come to similar conclusions and assessments, once they addressed their disagreements earnestly. This self-image and self-presentation as objective observer and presenter is based on a self-assured (and often unreflected) epistemological stance. It leads to the understanding of history as a set of answers and not as a relevant and intriguing set of questions addressed by an interpretative historical scientific engagement.

1989 also challenged the established, officially sanctioned (and therefore previously basically unquestionable) role of the historian, as self-declared, detached scholarly pursuits began to be uncovered, and the "hermeneutics of suspicion" attracted many in the humanities, especially among the younger cohorts. What the "hermeneutics of less naïvety" already reveals to us is that value choices and judgments, moral positions and agency are intricately bound up with the historian's work, even if this has often been denied in the name of a "higher scientific rationality."

On top of this change in the climate of opinion, the study of the recent past provides historians with additional challenges to their traditional professional identity: How can they seem detached and objective when the political connotations of their opinions can be identified rapidly and with little difficulty? What is the "special access" that a historian has to the recent past, which is not granted the "ordinary concerned citizen"? Is the historian an expert of superior value on matters of the recent past or is he only one among many with different and equally relevant perspectives? These are all fundamental questions worth reflecting on.

It is striking how closely one's own (usually hidden, effaced) position as a historian tends to correlate strongly with one's (explicitly formulated) general assessments, especially in highly contested political environments and where interpretations of the recent past can assume decisive force. History might be regarded as not much more than past politics, but then what if the politics of the present are so crucially connected with those of the past? This is characteristic of post-communist political environments, in most of which no political side possesses legitimacy that would not be profoundly questioned and ultimately denied by some, and attempts to obtain historical (or, more broadly, symbolic) legitimization often assume far greater importance than is customary in more firmly established liberal democracies.

Both of these are the case in contemporary Hungary, making the ideal of an apolitical historian of the recent past almost unattainable in practice, even if it was theoretically possible. Still, even though the possibility of apolitical positions is difficult to defend even in theory, and few have recently tried to argue for it, convictions at the heart of the discipline warn us against moralizing in our argumentation. Through the language of their texts historians still aim at impartiality, as they did in the period when the traditional ideals were much more widely shared and were still considered attainable. This creates a paradoxical environment in which political stances and motivations are constantly exposed, although attempts are still made to hide them, as the ideal is to deny them as much as possible instead of spelling them out explicitly.

THE TWO KINDS OF MORAL REVISIONISM IN HUNGARY

Having discussed the current, novel interrelation between the realms of morality and politics and briefly contextualized this problem area in post-Communism (through reflecting on the perceptions of the legitimacy and credibility of the new regime, as well as of the historian of the recent past), let me turn to more specific Hungarian developments, the issues of greatest relevance in terms of morality and politics in this historical-political culture. As mentioned earlier, 1989 presented Hungarian society with the agenda of revising our ways (and ultimately ourselves), which featured a crucial moral component as well. 1989 and its symbolic apogee in Hungary, the reburial of Imre Nagy and his fellow sufferers, meant that though rules were broken at some point, they remained rules and were enforceable, even if only with significant delay. 1989 offered the comforting thought that although temporarily injustice might reign and immoral politicians might seem successful, ultimately the force of justice would prove stronger as immorality was, unavoidably, uncovered. This revision reached in 1989 was meant to express on the moral level that the original sin of Kádárism was without doubt a mortal sin, and the chance to recognize this was provided by *history* and by *people's untainted moral sense*. In other words, the morally comforting thought was that historical justice existed, and to many this also implied that "history has proved *us* right."[9]

As dealt with in several previous in-depth studies, 1956 provided a crucial reference point in 1989. In my assessment, it served as *the symbol of "no moral compromise" while a political compromise* was struck. Contrary to its simplistic interpretation, 1989 was not a reenactment of 1956 which finally achieved its goals, although this is one of the claims most frequently made in political speeches delivered on commemorative occasions such as anniversaries. As has been pointed out by János Rainer, 1956 served as a warning and a threat in 1989, and recalling it pointed to the need to compromise.[10] Strangely, already under Kádár the memory of 1956 (significantly suppressed and subject to many imposed taboos even when it was mentioned) served a similar function. It was meant to illustrate the superiority of *Realpolitik* over the irresponsible making of demands, to show that there were "walls," to use the metaphor made popular by the movie by András Kovács from 1968—and it helped to show roughly where these walls stood.

This real political lesson is also the great lesson of Polish history in the eyes of many. Heroism might be counter-productive even when coupled with righteousness, so goes the tragic conclusion that was drawn under Communism and that in many ways influences our present sense of realism. This is *the realism of the resigned*, which one ought to possess and bear with dignity, and which is often directly credited for the achievements of 1989. At the same time, I find it worth remembering István Bibó's claim, which can be used to counter this attitude of resigned realism. Bibó points out that it can also be politically severely limiting to accept too much as inevitable, to rate one's chances too lowly. In other words, one should not overestimate one's possibilities (against which there are constant warnings), but neither should one underestimate them. In Romania, for instance, the constant references to terror under Communism, which are typical of the country's post-communist anti-Communism (currently, in late 2006, receiving official sanction), and the accompanying perception of the "rationality of fearing the regime" back then, might be seen as the reproduction of what perhaps prevented the development of a political opposition—people did not believe that it could be done. Obviously, whether they could have (and therefore should have) had more faith, we shall never know. I only mean to point to one of the greatest analytical problems of the totalitarian model, namely its inability to incorporate anti-systemic realities and the emergence of oppositions and how it in some ways justifies the latter's absence. In no sense do I wish to have the final word on this dilemma of what constituted over- and underestimation. I only wish to point out that what we need to ponder more is which of the two might have proved more damaging in Eastern European history under Communism, and which is the source of greater danger to democratic developments today.

To return to Hungarian historical culture, as mentioned earlier, the Kádárist memory of 1956 was limiting, similar to its role in 1989. But in 1989 *the element of "no moral compromise" was added to it*, while the political compromises of the round-table negotiations were made. This can be judged as a moral pretense, a fictitious moral high ground, especially when the question arises: What was the legitimacy of the side representing the authorities? Who or what authorized these discredited and self-discrediting authorities? This is where the moral improvement argument plays such an important role. The authorities could be there because of their intentions—their declaration that they would seriously improve and change the ways of their discredited past.

On the other hand, if we question this moral pretense, which undeniably played a role in the achievement of the agreement of 1989 and was required for the framing of the political compromise, the political compromise itself automatically becomes suspect as well. Those who question it also champion themselves as representing the "true (moral) spirit of 1989" (typically phrased as the "spirit of the changing of systems"). They are referring only to the "no moral compromise" part of the larger story, which also includes the curious (in theory unseemly though in practice possible) combination of "no moral compromise" and political compromise.

1989 presented Hungarian society with an agenda of revising our ways that featured a crucial moral component as well. There was agreement on this much, but how this revision ought to be carried out divided people and political forces from the start. This division (perhaps counterintuitively) grew even stronger over time. The nature of the polarization could be described as follows. One side argues that one could no longer (nor should one) believe in amoral politics. One should condemn those who did so and practiced it, and that *justice* needs to be served through our *purification from Communism*. The other side argues against what they perceive as a continuing political abuse of morals (in other words, others' moralizing), and for the acceptance of "unavoidable continuities." This is the program of the constitutional revolution, with *lawfulness* as its key term, which would also mean *purification from the spirit of Communism*, and its politically charged moralizing. This side, with "constitutional consciousness" on its banner, has maintained its dominance though it feels its values are under serious attack and not only because of actions taken by political forces, but also since they see too few people ready to defend them more than passively.

The one side recurrently uses the rhetoric of furthering the revolution, which in its permanent form is in all likelihood the logic of civil war as well. Its picture of the recent historical world is painted mostly in black and white. It conceives of Communism as a megalomaniac attempt, an irrational and evil temptation caused by human hubris that meant the "rape of society" by a determined, fanatical minority. It prefers to focus on the symbolic parts over the real ones. The other picture we are offered is overwhelmingly gray. It prefers to look at the pettiness of the way the communist regime functioned, the abundant "compromises with reality," the endemic corruption and widespread adaptations, and the multiple strategies of involvement. One might say the former upholds the image of Stalinism as representing Communism (Stalinism as the "ideal type"), and the latter that of post-Stalinism, which in Hungary's case can be characterized more by pragmatism than dogmatism, and by power considerations based on the status quo rather than on the ideological commitment to transform and remodel.

The one side judges before making sufficient efforts to assess, the other aims to assess in order not to judge. It aims to provide explanations in order not to enter the terrain of justifications (and no excuses). The one side is primarily moralist, connecting the two standards (that of good and bad, and good and evil), the other primarily realist, aiming to show their difference. In their extreme manifestations, moralizing can lead to wholesale condemnation (implying that one "cannot look for the sources of legitimacy and valuable achievements of an evil system")—the realistic approach to essential acquittal (it may have been evil, but more importantly it was good, not bad).[11] Even in their more moderate versions they barely touch, as their fundamental principles are not the same.

These two perspectives are connected to and, what is more, sometimes based on, the self-understanding (potentially invented) of the past behavior of the two sides. One side accepts no claim (i.e., accusation) about their involvement. Instead, they maintain that they represented the other (anti- or at least non-communist, and by implication better and more authentic) Hungary then, and still do so now. The other side sees its history as largely unproblematic too, as it is narrated as a story of continuous improvements, or reforms, which is not surprisingly the Hungarian left's favorite word. They rely on a revised edition of the convergence thesis popular in the 1960s, which presupposed the conciliability of reform Communism and Social Democracy. The Hungarian left claims that this tendency of reform communists to become social democrats was the major engine of change in Hungary, stating both that it is beneficial to the country and that they can take credit for having done it. Though Hungarian communists have some evidence to support their claim to having possessed the strongest reformist tradition (the only really serious contestant before Gorbachev's rise to power was Czechoslovakia in the 1960s), it would be false to believe that their reformism was aimed at the collapse of the system and the establishment of the present regime. Their failure (to reform the system) should not be accepted as their success (in overcoming it).

It is striking how much of what one observes is shadowboxing related to Communism and communists. How many times are *they* condemned and accused without the label also being used as self-identification by others to whom this purportedly refers? This is a problem of great relevance, since it also points to the fact that the terms *Communism* and *communist* underwent so much reinterpretation that enormous confusion about them developed in the minds of many, and there is no consensus in sight about their basic meaning. Can *communists* refer to self-sacrificing idealists, opportunistic careerists, and immoral murderers and thieves at the same time?

In my assessment, many people's repositioning towards communists "out there" and the communist "within" has ended up being both confused (inconsistent) and opportunistic. Opportunistic in the sense that many perceive a need to falsify their pasts to some extent, to make it appear in a more favorable light and adapt it to the new situation and its requirements. At the same time, as they wish to defend themselves, they also feel the need to justify at least part of their past behavior and beliefs. This dual need (to defend and to give up) creates an exceptionally suitable environment for confusion when people are thinking of themselves, which in the Hungarian case is furthered by politically motivated accusations and denials of any guilt that would have to be associated with involvement. An apologetically disposed discourse claims that moral awakening has already taken place and there is now no need for moral questioning, while an accusatory discourse condemns this view of 1989 as moral pretense. It propagates the need for total moral questioning, which usually includes almost everyone, except the propagators of such questioning themselves—who instead of *having* a moral conscience aim to *become* the moral conscience, as Odo Marquard so aptly put it.[12] This polarized public space makes people relate simultaneously to the apologetic discourse and the criminalizing one. Except for a minority of the convinced (communists and anti-communists) who are consistent, people tend to employ elements of both understandings, which are in theory mutually exclusive.

Thus, the question many individuals began to face in the post-1989 climate of opinion can be posed in the following way: How much to adapt and/or falsify and how much to defend and try to justify? They were not really helped by public discussions which might have set clear standards for them, since only few sustained dialogues emerged on patterns and strategies of involvement, collaboration and resistance, on how and why one was or was not implicated. These dialogical engagements tended to be restricted to smaller circles, to organs of small outreach, even though these are the relevant questions for the majority. They did not experience the extreme practices of communist regimes on the basis of which one can condemn them unequivocally and *as regimes*. To express this on a different level, ritual condemnations relate only vaguely to the lived experiences of "ordinary majorities." Their focus (and basis) in the case of Hungary is primarily the 1950s, and since then a sufficient amount of time has passed so that it is no longer the actual memory of the majority.

While the historical amnesia imposed by the Kádár regime (which desperately needed to forget, especially the dictator's own past) is a source of common concern, the historical amnesia related to the Kádár regime itself is much less frequently a target of attack in this new morally charged environment.[13] Polemically, one might claim that the early post-communist years meant more of an attempt to erase the past, to move beyond by forgetting or unlearning it, than through a sustained engagement with it—overcoming through painful though needed remembrance. Michnik would often refer back to his belief in "amnesty, not amnesia," perhaps exactly because what was much more widespread was the opposite—amnesia without the certainty of amnesty. At the same time, this habit of "pretending to be Western, denying 'Easternhood'" has begun to change in the past few years, as promises of quick Westernization have not materialized, while the communist period is increasingly integrated into attempts at writing coherent national histories. This admittance also leads to growing skepticism towards the chances of full Westernization, and the realization that the Eastern (and also the specifically communist) features (such as the built environment much of which has been effaced from sight for a while, but some of which is now being rediscovered) are "here to stay."

THE CASE OF THE PERCEPTIONS OF JÁNOS KÁDÁR

Let me relate what I have so far described in rather general and abstract terms to the concrete case of the understandings as well as the historical and moral evaluation of the role of János Kádár. On the one hand, Kádár has been judged as a mass murderer and as a traitor to his country. Both of these are accurate statements. The latter accusation has clearly been overused in various explanations of Eastern European history, which far too often aim to assign blame for not making it great and successful ("Western") by pointing to the workings of the "enemies of greatness and success." Let me remark that the popularity of the traitor theses is related to the interesting paradox at the heart of much of Eastern European history writing: the double agenda to show "our" history's basic Westernness while at the same time to continuously point out (and lament on) what we, as Easterners, lack to fully qualify as Western. There is a permanent oscillation between claims to Westernness and Easternness, typically hoping Westerners would regard us uncritically as their equals while being more critical among ourselves as Easterners (the Turkish variant of which is nicely exposed by Orhan Pamuk in his *Istanbul: Memories of a City*). In the case of Kádár the accusation holds; he undoubtedly proved to be a traitor, though in a moment in Hungarian history when a traitor *had* to come to power. In Kádár's case the gravity of this fundamentally flawed moral behavior is even greater, since he initially supported the revolution. As Péter György remarked, he had to walk the thinnest of lines to arrive at his decisive judgment of 1956, an infamous counter-revolution. However, from a moral point of view, his case is indefensible.

At the same time, he has also been praised not only for his rare political talent, but also for his "achievements in fostering Hungarian development" and "inclination to reform the socialist system." The evidence we have also shows that his popularity was at times quite exceptional. Many in contemporary Hungary would like to forget about the masses that showed up for the May Day parade in 1957 and also those who paid their respects to him in the summer of 1989 after he passed away at the time of the collapse of the regime and a severe crisis in the economy. Kádár is no doubt a somewhat uncomfortable figure for the forces with democratic convictions in post-communist Hungary, since he possessed something peculiar, which could best be labeled "relative legitimacy." Like his strange predecessors in Hungarian history, Francis Joseph and Miklós Horthy, Kádár consolidated power through executions, to become relatively widely accepted afterwards as the "comparably preferable option." In other words, he might have been evil rather than good, but good rather than bad according to common perception. From a democratic point of view, it would be more comfortable to focus on the immoral beginnings of his rule and its final collapse (leaving out the May Day parade of 1957, the masses paying tribute in 1989, and the years in between), though this focus would exclude far too much of Hungarian history, and would aim to eliminate complexities that are disturbing precisely because they are so real.

The two perspectives (mass murderer and traitor versus great politician with relative legitimacy, and the most successful agenda that was conceivable, and could be implemented under the given circumstances) illustrate the unlikely coexistence of contemporary perspectives on Communism in Hungary, which oscillate between charged forms of moralizing and relativizing, and in which the moral and the political judgments are still largely separate, in spite of the reintegration of the two discourses that I described earlier. Kádár proved not only that he possessed no moral scruples whatsoever (though, perhaps surprisingly, a sense of guilt was not alien to him, as 1989 was to reveal, and was later to become the theme of Mihály Kornis' famous play *A Kádár-beszéd*), but also as the political winner, for a very long time—nearly all his life.[14] The moral discourse aims to overwhelm, to teach a lesson about morality (and immorality), but unfortunately the Kádár story is not the most suitable example with which to educate citizens. This moral discourse apparently shows that Hungarian history has a certain logic which we need to overcome (the logic of Francis Joseph, Horthy and Kádár). It teaches us not *from* the "pages of history," but *against* what we can find there on our record. Ultimately, it teaches us to either blame history, or simply escape from it. Neither of these options offers us the chance for the needed confrontation with the past—a more substantial way of dealing with it.

Though 1989 reversed the roles assigned to Imre Nagy and János Kádár in mainstream discourse, turning Kádár into the traitor, the clear opposition between the two of them, in terms of how their moral choices are judged, remained. Prior to 1989, immorality was politically irrelevant since communist politics replaced morality (Kádár had to be a moral agent in history since he was the communist political winner), now it is supposed to be politically decisive. In turn, the aim in 1989 was to make morality a substitute for politics, but since it did not really succeed (nor could it, since morality cannot replace politics), attempts are still made to achieve it. The parallel story of these two exceptional (and exceptionally important, and not only symbolically) figures in Hungarian history, whose fate was so intricately interwoven, remains to be conceived and written. When the painters of the historical picture of Communism start to use colors other than black, white or gray, a depiction of this intricate story that is not based on the opposition of the two of them (and the identification of one with evil politics and the other with high morality) is likely to emerge as one of their primary tasks. Then, the current belief in the possibility of effortlessly arriving at historically accurate and politically helpful moral lessons will finally be exposed and discredited.

To gain a sense of 1956 as a valuable lesson, it somehow needs to be framed as a success, not a defeat, as many evidently understood it previously. Success is perhaps too strong a word, and I would prefer to use the word achievement, or contribution. A tendency towards this understanding is evident in the internationalization of 1956, a central feature of the 50th anniversary commemorations of the revolution which are taking place at the time of writing. The Hungarian Revolution of 1956 is being turned into Hungary's current claim to have contributed to global historical development, and to have helped to achieve positive changes by its people's heroism and political righteousness. Unfortunately, this story of achievement and contribution is based on a naïve moral reading of the past, which the American-dominated, post-Cold War master-narrative strongly supports, but which is largely external to the Hungarian story—the story of those who lived through it. Their strongest memories and focus are often on the painful period starting on 4 November 1956, not on the sadly short weeks of the revolution.

As is currently becoming evident to many, 1956 is an unhappy moral foundation for post-communist Hungary. Though its moralistic message ought to be remembered, the immorality of the story overshadows the (often exceptional) morality of some of the heroes of 1956, and crucially, the connections between politics and morality are not what one would wish. After all, the morally righteous and the politically successful diverged drastically, and 1989 could achieve no more than a symbolic reinterpretation of the realities of previous Hungarian history. 1956 might have been an exceptional, "blessed" moment of moral awakening, but then again it was followed by a process of much humiliation and widespread moral degradation. This survival of the sense of humiliation alongside the awareness of the symbolic reinterpretation allows much space to claim victimhood, and to justify a political agenda with historical and moral claims. Therefore, efforts are still constantly made to moralize politics in post-Communism, and (usually self-serving) moral and political claims are regularly made which pretend to serve historical justice "against Communism and communists." This is what I regard as the central dynamics in the evolving relationship between morality and politics in post-communist Hungary as it relates to the communist past of the country. The full consequences of this tendency are yet to emerge.

I would conclude with two proposals concerning the way I imagine the music of the future. One is that we should refrain from ultimate judgments, that we should replace the logic of the courtroom with attempts to understand the logic of various processes. It is not so interesting (if it is even possible) to attempt to classify someone as a good or evil person. It is much more fruitful to reflect on moral changes under Communism. This would mean that we finally ask questions in the following vein: How did someone who was originally entirely unwilling to collaborate end up as a diligent and "useful" informant? How did someone supportive of the communist revolution, a justifier of Stalinist practices, end up morally and firmly revolting against Communism (as the case of Miklós Gimes, among many other intellectuals involved in the preparation of the 1956 Hungarian revolution and in the revolution itself, attest)?[15]

In other words, my recommendation is that establishing what constitutes a crime ought not to be regarded first of all as an issue of legal or institutional application, and thereby automatically as a question of power, which has been the standard line of public inquiry. This predominant line may be captured in the question: Who has a legitimate claim to power and thus the right to implement decisions about the (possible) criminality of Communism? Instead, I propose a public discussion of what was ethically and morally unacceptable and what was innocent, and morally pardonable, since in spite of the superficial reintegration of the moral and political discourses in post-communist societies, sustained public debate of people's moral performance under Communism has been lacking. This lack is actually *all the more* unfortunate because of the superficial reintegration of the two realms.

My second recommendation is related to the first. It is a call to incorporate the two moral standards, the normative and the contextualist, simultaneously. One is an external standard to the communist era, conceived with absolutist aims. The other relates to what was perceived and accepted as normal at the time, and how moral norms were internalized and moral practices performed by contemporaries of the period. These two standards drastically diverge, and thereby offer the chance for recurrent condemnations and measuring of the real against the ideal. I believe it would be more appropriate, firstly, to argue on multiple and delineated levels, and secondly, possibly to relate these two standards more, in order not to judge people acting in constrained moral environments by unfairly high standards. We cannot do without moral standards, nor can we be moral without aiming to understand other people's situations from the inside.

NOTES

1 Some illuminating pieces on the connections between power and morality, especially the way morality was assumed to have a political role in the eyes of various significant authors of the Hungarian political traditions of previous centuries, particularly the 19th, can be found in the collection of Péter Dávidházi: *Per passivam resistentiam: Változatok hatalom és írás témájára* [Per passiva resistentiam: Variation on the theme of power and the pen] (Budapest: Argumentum, 1998). The pieces are more or less unified by their treatment of the relationship between power and writing, but morality is hardly ever excluded from consideration. Recently, a book-length discussion of this major theme was published by the leading moral philosopher (and as some would claim, moral authority) of Hungary, János Kis, as *A politika mint erkölcsi probléma* [Politics as a moral problem] (Budapest: Irodalom Kft., 2004).

2 For more detailed description of this, see Péter Nádas's *Esszék* (Pécs: Jelenkor, 1995), and his *Kritikák* [Critiques] (Pécs: Jelenkor, 1999).

3 Miklós Szabó elaborated this theory, claiming that when systemic questions cannot be addressed, such as "how society should be ruled," as in a dictatorship, then secondary questions, such as "who should rule," become central. He uses his theory to (partly) account for anti-Semitism, for instance. It can be found in several of his works, see for instance, Miklós Szabó's *Múmiák öröksége* [The heritage of mummies] (Budapest: Új Mandátum, 1995).

4 With the recent release of selected Michnik pieces from the past decade, there are now two collections in Hungarian, which between them cover most of his important writings. Adam Michnik, *Gondban a bohóc* (Bratislava: Kalligram, 1996), and *Harag és szégyen, büszkeség és szomorúság* [Anger and shame, pride and sadness] (Bratislava: Kalligram, 2006).

5 The work is one of the few important Romanian documents on the period, now available in English translation. See Patapievici, Horia-Roman. *Flying against the Arrow: An Intellectual in Ceausescu's Romania* (Budapest: CEU Press, 2003).

6 The different pace of change in post-Communism was introduced by Ralf Dahrendorf in his famous open letter: *Reflections on the Revolution in Europe: In a Letter intended to have been sent to a Gentleman in Warsaw, 1990* (London: Chatto and Windus, 1990).

7 This could be reflected in scholarship by more attention to the basic failures to Westernize, such as absences, like the near absence of gender role changes (with some notable exceptions, though with restricted scope) or the weakness of environmentalism in the post-communist part of the world. However, it is rarely reflected, as the main focus is still on places where achievements in terms of Westernization could be noted.

8 Mária Vásárhelyi, *Csalódások Kora: Rendszerváltás alulnézetben* [The era of disappointment: The change of regimes as seen from down under] (Budapest: MTA Társadalomtud. Közp., 2005), pp. 59–61.

9 Péter Balassa substantially criticized this distorted though unfortunately common relationship with oneself based on the unwillingness to face one's mistakes and admit one's weaknesses to others. He claims that it is typically a sign of strength to admit and show weakness and should be perceived as that by others as well, which is usually not done. Since people are afraid of appearing weak and do not hope for understanding, this crucial point often remains unrecognized. Such an exposition can be found in his publication that was contemporaneous with the major events: *Hiába: valóság* [In vain: reality]

(Pécs: Jelenkor, 1989), but recurs also in several places of his posthumously released volume of collected interviews. Péter Balassa, *Végtelen beszélgetés* [Endless conversation] (Budapest: Palatinus: 2004).

10 The point is made in János M. Rainer's *Ötvenhat után* [After fifty-six] (Budapest: 1956-os Intézet, 2003).

11 In terms of historical scholarship, social historical writings are rather typical in this vein, tracking modernization under Communism in a "neutral sense," but usually (and paradoxically) at the same time attaching positive value to more modernization than less.

12 The Hungarian collection of some of his best texts is: Odo Marquard, *Az egyetemes történelem és más mesék* [Universal history and other tall tales] (Budapest: Atlantisz, 2001). In the pages of this volume, Marquard proves himself a sharp and witty critic of leftist moralizing, often at levels of quality that have been reached by few (notably by Leszek Kołakowski, for instance in his justly famous reply to E.P. Thompson).

13 The theme of historical amnesia was made more widely known and discussed in Hungary (where historical awareness and consciousness are rather highly valued, at least in recurrent declarations) by the controversial book of Péter György, *Néma hagyomány: kollektív felejtés és kései múltértelmezés. 1956 1989-ben* [Mute tradition: Collective forgetting and belated interpretations of history] (Budapest: Magvető, 2000). He deals with the historical amnesia of the Kádár era, which he sees as one of the crucial compromises between rulers and ruled, a consensual "deafening silence" from which seemingly both sides benefited while much was lost.

14 This justly famous play can be found in Kornis' collected plays. See Mihály Kornis, *Drámák* [Dramas] (Budapest: Magvető, 1999).

15 The complex and shattering story of Gimes, the Stalinist journalist who converted into a supporter of pluralist democracy (to be executed after the Imre Nagy trial) was written by Sándor Révész. See Sándor Révész, *Egyetlen élet: Gimes Miklós története* [One life only: the story of Miklós Gimes] (Budapest: 1956-os Intézet/Sík Kiadó, 1999).

The Revisions of the 1956 Hungarian Revolution

ANDRÁS MINK

INTRODUCTION

The tradition of the 1956 Hungarian revolution played a major role in undermining the legitimacy of the one-party state in 1988–89. However, the post-mortem victory of Imre Nagy over János Kádár, the glorious revival of the tradition of the revolution, coincided with the dissolution of the very same tradition. Recently, as the 50th anniversary of the revolution approached, the memory and celebration of 1956 became the most controversial historical and ideological issue in the Hungarian public domain. Interestingly enough, the official "counter-revolutionary" narrative of the Kádár era greatly influenced the post-transitional memory of 1956, in various perverted ways.

On the 50th anniversary of the revolution, foreign and domestic observers witnessed an attempt to recreate the historical events of 50 years before. On this noble occasion the whole gamut of the cultural and ideological flora and fauna of the interwar far-right mythology was displayed in front of the Hungarian Parliament, on Kossuth Square in Budapest. The demonstrators not only intended to replace the government and its head, but demanded the revision of the constitutional system and the reestablishment of the Hungarian political community on the basis of the Holy Crown. In this paper I will not discuss either the political developments that led to the public protests, or the tactical considerations that might have led the opposition parties to consider these protests useful. My interest is more limited: What made it possible for the memory of the 1956 Hungarian revolution to be linked to the traditional symbols of the extreme right-wing movements and ideologies of the prewar period? In order to understand this grotesque and peculiar phenomenon, we must cast a glance over the early "counter-revolutionary" period of 1956–1957, and its lengthy aftermath. In the first part of this chapter I will briefly describe the main elements of the "counter-revolutionary" narrative and its democratic counterpart during the communist dictatorship. In the eyes of the police-historians of the Kádár regime, 1956 in its character belonged to the past, to the prewar political regime and its campaign against progressive forces: first and foremost the communists. In the dissident tradition of the Kádár era, 1956, with its strong leftist (democratic-socialist) inclination, was the prelude to a desired post-communist democratic development.

The second part of this chapter will analyze one aspect of the question of how and why the democratic tradition of the 1956 revolution fell apart. This did not happen only because the inherent tradition of the revolution was very hard to identify and proved to be discontinuous with post-transitional social and political developments. Other factors also made the tradition controversial. It seems that the contrasting interpretations of the revolution are closely linked to the various and irreconcilable images not only of the communist regime itself, but of the prewar political system and its tradition. The main question has become again whether 1956 was a return to the natural—meaning anti-communist and nationalistic—stream of Hungarian history, or whether it belongs to post-1945 historical development.

THE KÁDÁRIST COUNTER-REVOLUTION AND ITS DEMOCRATIC COUNTERPART

Kádárist propaganda regarded and depicted 1956 as a revolt organized and directed off-scene by Hungarian reactionaries (former landowners, the clergy, former members of the pro-Nazi Arrow Cross movement, and Horthy's followers), whose aim was the restoration of the previous, part-feudal and part-capitalist order and/or the Arrow Cross regime.[1] Their false allegations about an ongoing organized underground conspiracy after the war, and their emphasis on the continuity of 1919, 1944, and 1956, the three successive but eventually unsuccessful blows against Communism, served to promote this conception. In their interpretation Fascism was identical with anti-Communism, consequently the revolt against the socialist state could not be anything but a fascist one. Many of the repressive post-1956 trials had the sole function of demonstrating this continuity. The trials of former gendarmerie and police officers for crimes they committed or allegedly committed before 1945, and the trial and execution of Mihaly Francia Kiss, the mass killer of the 1920 "white terror" massacres, 37 years later in 1957, are obvious examples.[2]

The scale of the repression, the number of arrests and executions had the function not only of terrorizing the population but also of proving that the counter-revolution was a strong and dangerous one. The people's courts were not only judging individual perpetrators but also delivering a verdict on the criminal nature of the prewar period. According to this, the counter-revolution started with the repression of the first Hungarian communist state in 1919, with the emergence of the white terror, and it continued with the Horthy regime, which inevitably culminated in the Holocaust and a fascist Arrow Cross coup d'etat and dictatorship in 1944. The final stage was 1956, with its christian-national, anti-communist ideology and revisionist chauvinism. Indeed, Francia and those others who were convicted and executed for prewar misdeeds, were presented as the forerunners of German Nazism.

That image of the "counter-revolution" served not only to justify the Soviet intervention and the restoration of the dictatorial regime, but also to distance people from what happened. It was both a threat and redeeming offer. Those who accepted the Kádár government were saved from being associated with the fascists of 1944, even if they had "naïvely" supported the Nagy government. They maintained the fiction that the forces behind the counter-revolution were not the same as the forces the people believed in and saw in action during the 1956 revolution. Nothing was really what it seemed to be.

The police-historians of the Kádár era wrote:

The composition of the armed groups in these days changed in the following way: Those forces that were loyal to the cause of socialism and were indeed motivated by the wish to correct mistakes, and believed that they could influence the armed groups in a beneficial way, quit the groups. Young students also left the insurgents en masse … At the same time newly released ordinary and political criminals, the lumpen and the servants of the old regime drifted into the armed groups … The lead was taken everywhere by extreme right-wingers, and in many cases, by officers of the former Horthy regime.[3]

Similarly, the Workers' Councils could not represent the working class. Another official historian put it as follows:

The leadership of the newly reorganised workers' councils fell into the hands of openly counter-revolutionary elements, cashiered military officers, judges, gendarmes, priests, or in the best cases, confused laborers who had fallen under the spell of counter-revolutionary and revisionist ideas … The lumpen elements could not for long resist the attraction of pretending to be freedom-fighters and national guards. They became comfortable with themselves only after they returned to their own methods, which, from a political point of view meant arrest, murder, lynching and brutality.[4]

Behind the curtain, the story went, a fundamental evil was emerging, about which the Hungarian people did not know: the restoration of the pre-war political and social order. The Nagy government was an agent of the counter-revolution that treacherously helped to cover the real nature of events. The reestablished non-communist parties—their announced political programs envisioning national independence, the restoration of private property on a (very) limited scale, and the restoration of a multi-party system (bourgeois democracy) were only the initial steps on a path back to the dark past. These politicians either cautiously hid their real intentions behind the veil of these popular demands, or they themselves were the veil.

It was on these issues that Hungarian dissident authors both at home or in exile and Western observers unanimously repudiated the allegations of the Kádár regime, pointing out that the spontaneous popular uprising of 1956 had been sparked off by the deceit and brutality of Mátyás Rákosi's Stalinist regime. The insurgents fought against dictatorship and for national independence, and not for any restoration of the old social order. The uprising was spontaneous and had an essentially democratic character; atrocities were marginal accompaniments. Most of the observers belonging to the democratic side stressed and tried to prove that the mainstream of the revolutionary movement: including the Imre Nagy circle; the reform communist intellectuals; the Writer's Association, which included authors who had previously been enthusiastic supporters of communist ideas; the students; the worker's and revolutionary councils; and even the re-established non-communist parties, remained within the vaguely defined but still clearly recognizable political and ideological framework of a kind of democratic socialism.

Indeed, the demands of these groups that were made public in those hectic days tended in that direction. This certainly does not mean that the historian can retrospectively limit the potential outcomes of a consolidated and victorious regime change to this framework, supposing that the revolution had succeeded. But we have strong evidence, most importantly the sociological interviews conducted with Hungarian refugees in Western Europe and in the United States in 1957 and 1958,[5] that even the average Hungarian held this sort of egalitarian vision of the future of Hungary. However, the political content of 1956 is not the topic of this paper. It seems sufficient to conclude here that in 1956 and afterwards, those who tried to keep alive the democratic memory of 1956 at home and abroad would certainly not have wished to be compromised by charges of alleged leanings towards liberal democracy and free market capitalism, or even worse, towards the prewar Hungarian autocratic regime or Fascism (This conclusion, by the way, disappointed some of the American analysts of the refugee interviews). I think it is more important to stress that for those who aimed to defend the dignity of 1956 against the accusations of Kádárist propaganda up to 1989, the democratic socialist image, apart from their personal political sympathies, seemed to offer a better way of exposing the hypocritical nature of Soviet-style dictatorship. The Soviet regime and its Hungarian puppets crushed and liquidated exactly those individuals who took the idea of a democratic, egalitarian society seriously. The democratic nature of the revolution could be demonstrated most efficiently by strictly separating it from the reminiscences of old-fashioned anti-communist narratives that were characteristic of prewar times. Let me note here that Kádárist propaganda was also aware of this and targeted the Western democratic public from exactly the opposite direction; it was David Irving who enjoyed the support of the Hungarian authorities in writing an evil book which depicted the revolution as a pogrom against communists of Jewish origin in Hungary.[6]

However, one of the consequences of this was that the 1956 revolution took on a certain democratic socialist profile which had become not only outdated in political terms by the time the communist regime collapsed, but also a little suspicious in the eyes of many Hungarians. Moreover, mainstream anti-Kádárist narratives of 1956 before 1989 tended to focus on Imre Nagy and his fellow martyrs, the *anti-Stalinist* and *reform-communist* resistance within the party prior to the outbreak of the uprising, i.e., the *grand process* of the disillusionment of former communist intellectuals. The so called "Pest lads," the then young and enthusiastic freedom fighters who had nothing to do with "Communism" before the revolution and who were hit hardest by the post-revolutionary terror, felt that they were ignored. This was made even worse by the attempts of the successor party to adjust itself to the new situation and hide its own responsibility for the previous crimes.

1956 AFTER 1989

"The problem of 1956 should be—and could be—solved immediately, in brackets, if we accepted György Lukács' formula … in accordance with which Hungary's 1956 should be called neither a counter-revolution nor a revolution, but an uprising … this formula would be equally acceptable to those who witnessed the counter-revolutionary aspect of the uprising and those who experienced its revolutionary aspect," said Ferenc Tőkei, philosopher and sinologist and a member of the Central Committee of the Hungarian Socialist Workers Party at the 12–13 February 1989 session, which set itself the task of debating Imre Pozsgay's public statement of January 18, when he defined 1956 as an uprising.[7] Tőkei and the more clear-sighted members of the Central Committee were interested in finding a way to incorporate 1956 (crushed by the HSWP) into the HSWP heritage and to make Imre Nagy (hanged by the HSWP in 1958), into a founder of the same party in 1989 (*de facto* he was among the founders). The Central Committee's statement on Imre Nagy's reburial on 16 June 1989 contained the following passage:

> Nowadays, when representatives of certain parties and movements speak in public and in the media, they make an attempt to appropriate Imre Nagy's heritage without mentioning his communist commitment … The HSWP's Central Committee finds it important to point out that the reform policies of 1953–54, including Imre Nagy's activities, form the historical origins of the HSWP's political course.[8]

In July, 1989 the Central Committee discussed the idea of declaring October 23 a day of national reconciliation, in order to forestall greater complications. The draft statement by the Central Committee went as follows:

> The renewing HSWP regards 23 October 1956 as the symbol of the movement aimed at democratic socialism, national independence and sweeping and radical reforms. We cherish the political heritage of those who participated in the fateful events of those days under the banner of these ideals. We wish to bring justice to those who fought, and laid down their lives, to humanize and democratize social relations and to defend our national interests. We also wish to pay homage to the memory of those who, guided by good intentions and personal beliefs, fell victim to the shootings and the atrocities while fighting on the other side of the barricade.

László Kovács, later Minister of Foreign Affairs, and recently appointed Hungarian representative in the European Commission, who was also a member of the CC, added a short comment to this passage in the debate: "This statement only makes sense if we were on both sides of the barricade."[9]

With these declarations the HWSP was making a clear attempt to embrace and even expropriate the democratic socialist interpretation of 1956. They did it in a moment when one-party rule had not yet been formally shaken and the Party itself was not completely prepared to accept liberal constitutionalism and the free market economy. The decisive sessions of the round table negotiations that eventually led to the regime change started only after the reburial of Imre Nagy, and the successor Hungarian Socialist Party was founded only in October, 1989. The attempt to expropriate the democratic tradition of 1956 took place at a moment when it apparently served the survival of the former elite and the avoidance of fundamental political changes. This move not only cast a shadow on the democratic image of 1956 but also added fuel to the radical anti-communist narratives of the revolution. The former defenders of the memory of 1956 found themselves once more in a defensive position *vis-à-vis* the new radicals. A new political struggle for the heritage of 1956 began.

REVISIONS ON THE RIGHT

It is not easy to decide when the right-wing revision of 1956 actually started. Most probably, the traditional, nationalist-ethnicist, extreme right-wing form of anti-Communism had never completely disappeared from the post-war Eastern European and Hungarian scene and certainly gave some signs of its existence during the revolution as well. The proper identification of these attitudes is problematic for at least two reasons: first, the communist narrative regarded and depicted the non-commmunist political domain as a continuation of Fascism. Second, we know much better now than we did some decades ago that the communist interpretation of Fascism was surely mistaken in another respect as well, prewar extreme right-wing movements and ideas were much more revolutionary, and had much stronger anti-capitalist (i.e., anti-parliamentarian, anti-liberal) tendencies than was recognised earlier. In Hungary the Hungarist and Arrow Cross movements were strongest within the trade union of miners and iron workers, and among the poorer peasantry. A large number of disaffected intellectuals crossed over from the extreme left to the extreme right and back again repeatedly throughout the 1930s with amazing nonchalance. One may add that this kind of vague uncertainty would be even more characteristic in 1956 when anti-capitalism and anti-Communism could easily be combined in a sort of anti-elitism. As we read the testimonies of Hungarian refugees it is salient that while they expressed a surprising consensus of sympathy towards egalitarian, socialistic ideas, they regarded the Hungarian communists not as people with political convictions but rather as a gang of mafiosi, conspiring to preserve their own privileges and material welfare. In his memoirs, published in the US in the early 1980, Gergely Pongrátz, legendary commander of the Corvin köz rebel group in Budapest, clearly stated that they were fighting for democratic socialism, a kind of fair and free society. It is quite revealing that Pongrátz, who became the cult figure of right-wing anti-communist resistance after 1989, carefully ommitted this paragraph from post-1989 editions of his book.[10]

Radical anti-Communism received a new impetus after the fall of the communist regimes throughout the post-Soviet bloc. There were attempts everywhere to rehabilitate former fascist, extreme-right leaders, war-criminals, military commanders, anti-Semitic publicists, etc., as heroes of the struggle against the threat of "Red Bolshevism." It is easy to see that in part it was the former communist narrative that made this possible. Those who wanted to see justice for the "martyrs" of communist repression, had to do nothing else than take the communist arguments seriously: the martyrs were not fascists: this was only an allegation made by the communist courts in order to discredit their heroic struggle against the communist threat.[11] In these narratives Fascism as an independent phenomenon suddenly disappeared. What perhaps makes the Hungarian case unique in this respect is that Hungary, unlike Poland or Czechoslovakia, did not belong to the anti-fascist camp prior to the Soviet occupation and the anti-fascist tradition was imported into Hungary by the Red Army and the Hungarian communists. In Hungary, instead of commemorating the end of World War II every year, we have a recurring ideological debate about the meaning and relevance of 1945. The front lines of this debate are the same as the front lines in the debates on 1956.

The reevaluation of 1956 by the right obviously started with the reinterpretation of the Hungarian role in World War II ("Hungary took part in the great struggle against Bolshevism"), the denial of the responsibility of the prewar political elite and the Hungarian state in the Hungarian Holocaust, and of course the reassessment of the prewar Horthy regime. From the perspective of this new anti-communist revisionism, after the regime change in 1989 Hungary should have turned back to its genuine historical roots and to the national character of the pre-1945 period. The revision is a justifiable reversal of the distortions and the false charges about the past inspired by communist ideology. Consequently, the heroes of 1956 were not the disappointed reform-communist intellectuals but the young freedom fighters, and the revolution was an attempt to return to Hungary's pre-1945 roots.[12] This is precisely the view of the "real character" of 1956 that communist propaganda was trying to impose throughout the Kádár era. As I indicated above, the question has once again come to this: Was 1956 a return to prewar times, or a prelude to the democratic dénouement of post-communist Hungary?

NOTES

1 "Resolution of the Provisional Central Committee of the Hungarian Socialist Workers' Party, December 5, 1956," in Csaba Békés, Byrne Malcolm and János M. Rainer, eds., *The 1956 Hungarian Revolution: A History in Documents. A National Security Archive Cold War Reader* (Budapest: Central European University Press, 2002), pp. 460–463.

2 Mihály Francia Kiss was a member of the white terror death brigades after the crushing of the Hungarian Soviet Republic in 1919–1920. He and his cronies committed brutal murders against alleged "Bolsheviks." In 1923, he was tried and sentenced but soon released. He was tried again *in absentia* in 1947 and sentenced to capital punishment by the People's Tribunal that was established after World War II for prosecuting war criminals. In March 1957, he was arrested and sentenced to death again. He was hanged in 1957. On his case see: István Rév, "A Rule of Law," in Rév, *Retroactive Justice*, (Stanford, CA: Stanford University Press, 2005), pp. 202–239.

3 Sándor Geréb, and Pál Hajdú, *Az ellenforradalom utóvédharca* [The rear-guard action of the counterrevolution] (Budapest: Kossuth Kiadó, 1986), p. 13.

4 János Molnár, "Fegyveres ellenforradalmi csoportok" (Armed counter-revolutionary groups) *Századunk* (1966): 1151.

5 See the interviews of the Columbia Research Project Hungary (CURPH) at the Archives of the Columbia University, New York. A copy of the interviews and their background materials was recently made public by OSA Archives, Budapest: www.osa.ceu.hu, or www.archivum.ws.

6 David Irving, *Uprising!* (London: Hodder and Stoughton, 1981); and András Mink, "David Irving and the 1956 Revolution," *New Hungarian Quarterly*, (Fall 2000).

7 László Soós, ed., *A Magyar Szocialista Munkáspárt Központi Bizottságának 1989. évi jegyzőkönyvei, I–II.* [The minutes of the central committee of the Hungarian Socialist Workers' Party, 1989. Vol. 1–2.] (Budapest: Hungarian National Archive, 1993), Vol. 1, 1079–1080.

8 "Javaslat a Központi Bizottságnak a Nagy Imre temetésével kapcsolatos KB-közleményre" [Proposal on the Central Committee's statement regarding Imre Nagy's reburial], in *The Minutes...*, Vol. 1, pp. 1079–1080.

9 "Javaslat az MSZMP Központi Bizottságának állásfoglalására a nemzeti megbékélés napjáról" [Proposal to the MSZMP's central committee on the declaration of the day of national reconciliation], in *A Magyar Szocialista...,* Vol. 2, p. 1359. At that time the conditions of the later, "all-embracing" solution, i.e. the proclamation of the Republic on 23 October, were still not available since the round-table negotiations between the Party and the opposition on the constitutional changes had not been concluded yet.

10 Gergely Pongrátz, *Corvin köz —1956* [Corvin alley—1956]. (Chicago: G. Pongrátz, 1982), p. 13. Pongrátz was the commander of the largest insurgent group in Budapest, with its headquarters at Corvin köz, in the 9th district. After the Soviet intervention on 4 November he fled to the US, and returned to Hungary in 1991.

11 István Rév, "Ellenforradalom" ["Counterrevolution"], *Beszélő* 3 (November 1999) pp. 47–59.

12 For the most eloquent summary of this revised 1956 see: Róbert Szalay, *A forradalom igaz története* [The real story of the revolution] (Budapest: 56-os Magyarok Világtanácsa, 1999). Szalay stated that 1956 continued the "anti-Bolshevik fight" started by Ferenc Szálasi and the Arrow-Cross movement in October 1944, and that the representatives of the Nagy government in 1956—in particular Pál Maléter, Minister of Defense, who was later hanged after a show trial together with Imre Nagy in 1958—were in reality traitors of the 1956 revolution who tried to help the Russian invasion. Szalay's book was promoted in the semi-official political daily (*Új Magyarország*) of the right-wing conservative Orbán government in 1999 as a proposed textbook for secondary schools.

Historians Facing Politics of History

The Case of Poland

RAFAŁ STOBIECKI

I.

From a certain point of view one may risk the thesis that the current discussion regarding historical policy is the third great debate among historians since Poland regained independence at the turn of the 1980s and the 1990s. The first debate is usually called "the discussion about the Polish People's Republic (PRL)." It started when the communist system collapsed and continues more or less intensely today.[1] It was and still is a mixture of cognitive, ideological, and ethical themes. From the historiographical point of view the most important questions were those regarding the status of the Polish state after 1945—its regime, relations between the authorities and society, and finally the balance of the development of civilization during the PRL. The second dispute is the debate on the subject of Jedwabne initiated by Jan Tomasz Gross's book *Sąsiedzi. Historia zagłady pewnego miasteczka.* (Neighbors. The story of the annihilation of a small Jewish town). The book deals with the extermination of Jews in July 1941 at the hands of "ordinary Poles" inspired by the Nazi occupying forces. Its significance lies mostly in the fact that, by questioning the image of Polish people as solely the victims of World War II, it raises the issue of Polish participation in the Holocaust and initiates a very serious discussion about Polish–Jewish relations throughout the 20th century.[2] In a broader context both these debates and the one presented below are part of the discussion which started at the beginning of the 1990s in Europe regarding the role of history in public life, the significance of ideology in historical discourse and finally the relationship between historiography and individual as well as collective memory.

II.

I would like to present a more detailed description of the field of my considerations. If we agree that politics of history in its broadest sense is a synonym for conscious and purposeful activity by the authorities, conducted in order to preserve a certain image of the past in society, then with some simplification we may mention two traditional ways of understanding this category. The first is commonly associated with the totalitarian state, where the authorities use mass propaganda and various forms of repression and pressure to try to impose their own version of history on society, with the aim of eliminating any competitive discourse about the past. In such circumstances the "totalitarianization" of history or historiography becomes part of the disempowerment of the whole society. From this point of view history is deprived of its multi-dimensional aspect and becomes one of the most important ideological instruments of totalitarianism, serving to legitimize the current sociopolitical regime. The second tradition relates to the democratic state. In this case, as Michel Foucault puts it, "History is the discourse of authority," but in a different sense. The relationship between authority and knowledge becomes a particular game, played on the field of culture, and both concepts are interlinked. In this tradition any social group may become the victim of certain value systems which obscure their position. Besides, different discourses about the past compete and conflict with each other. To sum up, in the first case historical policy becomes a unilateral and often primitive form of propaganda based on the state monopoly of information, while in the second it becomes an uninterrupted dispute between various interest groups, each trying to promote its own vision of the past or "impose" it on society. From the present perspective it seems obvious that the politics of history of the PRL belonged unequivocally to the first tradition, while the current debate about the role of the state in creating one vision of the past or another, belongs to the second. This should be clearly emphasized because among the critics of historical policy, including students of the past, the objection is sometimes raised that the present way of treating this issue (i.e., historical policy) more or less resembles the practices of the PRL.

III.

In this debate about historical policy, which has gone on for years and is now particularly fervent, an increasingly active part is being taken by those who are naturally closely involved in the issue: the historians themselves. In sociopolitical magazines of different shades the most prominent researchers publish their articles, while editorial committees organize debates about political history in which its opponents and supporters expound their conflicting views.[3] The aims of the present chapter are: first, to present the main issues under debate; second, to reconstruct the most important arguments in the discussion; and third, to answer the question of what this debate is saying about us, historians, participating in it.

In the current discussion the three main disputable issues, to simplify slightly, are: the actual term "historical policy," its merits, and the function it should perform. The very use of the term "historical policy" or "politics of history" is open to debate as such. According to its supporters, it is rather neutral category, which appeared in Polish public discourse via Germany (from the German *Geschichtspolitik*), referring to a particular intentional attitude towards the past among some sections of the Polish intellectual elite. Marek Cichocki, commonly regarded not only as the inventor of the term historical policy but also as its main supporter, says in an interview:

> I can hardly be considered either the author of the term or the initiator of the discussion. I might, however, attempt to offer my own definition. Historical policy functions in various countries in many different ways. In Poland it seems to lie in the search of a term capable of capturing a certain phenomena that can be observed both in our country and abroad. The phenomenon is more important than the term. But if I were to offer a definition ... I would say that it consisted in reinvigorating public discourse about the past by means of different forms of institutionalizing it. The institutionalization occurs on the level of both state as well as local, that is, regional and self-governmental, institutions.[4]

According to the supporters of the term, historical policy is not only an obligation of the state and its government, but results from a natural state of affairs. They think that it is impossible to separate collective memory from politics because it provides a strong basis for any community, whether institutional or national. From this perspective historical policy is a set of activities similar to those involved in social and economic policy.[5] It is needed to enable society to identify more strongly with the state and its structures and for the Polish people to integrate with the great motherland in an ideological sense as well as to strengthen their bonds with small local motherlands. Besides this, historical policy is treated as a challenge, which "Poland needs to face if it does not want to become in United Europe a mere consumer of the benefits that result from the support of its partners, but an active participant in creating a common European identity."[6]

This notion of historical policy is based on a certain analysis, whether explicitly articulated or not, of the nature of the systemic transformation which took place at the turn of the 1980s and the 1990s and the following years. According to its supporters, who are to be found mainly among historians of ideas, the Third Republic of Poland as a state placed little trust in issues of collective memory and identity and consequently such issues were regarded as a threat to democracy and liberal projects for Polish state modernization. The characteristic feature of this period was "collective amnesia" about the past, especially the recent past, which was sacrificed on the altar of the future (cf., the famous election slogan of Aleksander Kwaśniewski, "let's choose the future") and relegated to the margins of public debate.[7] In the framework of this notion of sociopolitical reality, historical policy becomes a national issue, a symbol of the hope for a moral change in society and the chance to build a new and better historical identity for the Polish people. So it is not surprising that supporters of this project are somewhat wary of historians. Marek Cichocki states this very clearly: "there are important reasons why we cannot leave history to the historians, and memory must remain a living substance of every policy."[8]

But how do the opponents of historical policy see the issue? First of all they reject the neutral character of the term. In public debate it is often emphasized that "historical policy" has naturally become a slogan of the program of that part of the intellectual elite that is associated with the *Prawo i Sprawiedliwość* (Law and Justice) party, and has therefore gained currency in the political and ideological context. Marcin Kula gave three reasons why he is skeptical about this. Firstly, the very term seems unfortunate, because it associates politics and history on a semantic level. This not only implies a close relationship between historiography and politics, but also positively evaluates this phenomenon. Secondly, Kula notes that in numerous statements by supporters of historical policy "the one and only right image of history which would be introduced into life, memory and social identity"[9] is always implicitly or explicitly present. Thirdly, according to the Warsaw researcher, the very term presumes an instrumental attitude towards history; arises out of a desire "to concentrate on what belongs to us and disguise national complexes."[10] Similar ideas have appeared in other contributions to the debate.[11] In general, the objections of the opponents of historical policy could be summarized as follows: according to them, it embodies a positive approach to the national past, which excludes any form of criticism, may lead to the manipulation of history by rejecting its autonomous status, and moreover, safeguards the party's interests. This point of view implies the fear that the term will or at least may become one more aspect of the political exploitation of different spheres of life such as the media or culture. The opponents of historical policy run the whole gamut of opinions, ranging from concerns, expressed more or less clearly, about the extent to which the state may want to interfere in historical research to strong objections raised against any form of political initiatives undertaken with a view to supporting a given interpretation of the past. One significant problem which arises here is how to determine the limits of historical policy in such a way as to preserve state responsibility for the shape of historical knowledge and at the same time to prevent history from being nationalized altogether.

The critics of historical policy also oppose the opinion that the Third Republic of Poland "rejected history" and did not perform a symbolic "de-communization" in the field of collective memory. According to Paweł Machcewicz, the very dawn of independence witnessed a series of activities which constituted historical policy *avant la lettre*. The researcher mentioned the changing of the national anthem and the national coat of arms, the liquidation of the old celebration commemorating the foundation of the PRL on 22 July and its replacement by celebrations on 3 May and 11 November, and fundamental changes in the symbolic sphere (renaming streets and squares, demolishing old statues and erecting new ones).[12]

So, there is an apparent clash between the two camps engaged in a dispute over the notion of historical policy, with each of them rarely willing to go beyond the trench lines determining the legitimacy of their own definitions characterizing the object of contention. It seems clear that these lines of division are strengthened by generational differences, political preferences and finally by the image of the historian and his social role imprinted in his milieu. Why is this happening? Why is it that the discussions of the usefulness of the term lack intellectual sophistication and offer little insight into the problem, resembling slanging matches rather than a serious debate? It seems that Anna Wolff-Powęska rightly pointed out two reasons for this state of affairs. In an essay with the title "The state must leave history" she says that "historical policy lies in the field of permanent tension between science and politics."[13] These categories are not only linked to each other but are also related to other spheres of action and behavior. We may add that while politics are dominated by short periods of time, sometimes from one election to another, history or the culture of history, according to Wolff-Powęska, is a field of slow changes resulting from long-lasting mental processes. Moreover, in the researcher's opinion:

> the slogan of historical policy, which became a frequent guest in Polish parlors, is used in different contexts; often as a media slogan, the topic of numerous conferences or as a way to describe historical science under dictatorship … it still lacks cognitive values because as a subject of research it is in very preliminary phase.[14]

Literary historian Andrzej Mencwel presents one of the few attempts to conceptualize the category "political history" in a series of articles.[15] The researcher mentions three meanings or spheres of political history. In the first, narrow sphere, it relates to the authorities and to administrative activities; this is the most common meaning presented in the media. It is reflected, for example, in decisions to reward some people and lustrate others. In the second, medium sphere, according to Mencwel, politics of history becomes the domain of activities "in the field of values and symbols, the construction and choice of tradition, the creation or recreation of collective identity including national identity." In this sense, the changes in the names of streets and squares can serve as a good example. Finally the researcher mentions the third "great" sphere of historical policy, to which no conscious citizen can remain indifferent. It means a thorough vision of the past, which suggests a new interpretation, from the perspective of permanent historical changes; the sense of national history.[16] Obviously according to Mencwel this last meaning of historical policy should become the focus of public debate. It is "the supreme arena in which the shape of national identity can be decided, it is the foundation of a new scheme of memory and tradition or a means of deconstructing the old one." The author is also specific about a social mechanism which, in his opinion, is responsible for creating historical policy. According to him any deliberate attempt to constitute such a "coherent narration about our whole history" would fail. It is created through a natural process of trial and error "in individual work and social activities, in local initiatives and regional associations, in religious feasts and national rituals because we all feel that we are becoming different in a new Poland and a new Europe, never seen before."[17]

Now I will turn to the next item of the discussion—to that concerned with a contention over the specific issues dealt with in the conduct of historical policy. It seems that the debate is focused on the question of the shape of Polish patriotism at the beginning of the 21st century. On the symbolic level the subject of the dispute is well illustrated by the titles of two articles published in *Rzeczpospolita* during the discussion about Jan T. Gross's book *Sąsiedzi* (The Neighbors). Andrzej Nowak published an article entitled "Westerplatte or Jedwabne?", which provoked a response from Paweł Machcewicz's "Westerplatte and Jedwabne."[18] A good example of the discussion about content is a polemic started by D. Gawin and D. Karłowicz against Jan Józef Lipski's famous essay "Dwie ojczyzny. Dwa patriotyzmy / uwagi o megalomanii narodowej i ksenofobii Polaków" (Two motherlands. Two patriotisms. Remarks on the national megalomania and xenophobia of Polish people), published in 1981. Gavin claimed that the model of critical patriotism proposed by Lipski combined hostility and suspicion towards all forms of megalomania or xenophobia with the evangelical imperative of love and forgiveness. Consequently it eliminated from the discourse any possibility of using the category of collective interest because the latter is by its nature marked with egoism. In Gawin's opinion "Historical policy from this perspective is totally dominated by ethics, it becomes the field in which not only is collective identity being created but where through a painful process of auto-psychomachy one rejects the possibility of sin which belongs inherently to the community and the political sphere."[19]

D. Karłowicz used different arguments. In his opinion Lipski's proposal, like the rest of his ideas about Polish patriotisms, is aimed against what the author calls "axiological memory." "It is the record of a value system embedded in the collective memory that constitutes a spiritual dimension of a community."[20] From this point of view immoderate criticism of the national past rejects the axiological sphere and therefore destroys the basis of the community, leading to the tribalization of collective memory.

The idea of reinterpreting the category of patriotism proposed by these two historians of ideas did not win much favor. In most cases the proponents of stronger state activity in the field of historical memory do not relate to the above-mentioned source of inspiration but to the 19th-century vision of patriotism, which is based on the following beliefs. Firstly, the uniqueness of Polish historical experience against the European background. It is no accident that the brochure popularizing the idea of opening a Museum of Polish History says:

In the Museum's activities the emphasis should lie on what was unique, specific and fascinating in Polish history. Poland is a country with one of the longest republican and parliamentary traditions in Europe, the country of citizens' freedom, which reached a unique level of religious tolerance in modern history, the country of a unique culture and customs.[21]

Secondly, by emphasizing the relationship between modern patriotism, Christianity and the Catholic Church. One of the researchers from the Krakow magazine "Arcana" notes:

It is high time to realize the point we have reached. It is time to reconsider our past. That is the necessity we are facing today. In this respect, we cannot count on any support from the West. They seem even less capable of recognizing the real problems of our times and lag behind us in returning to normality and right principles. We need to reject and deny the whole left-wing tradition – starting with Jacobinism. Because this tradition and this mentality contradict the foundations of our identity: Catholic, Christian, Polish, national but also Latin, Western. It is an urgent and inexorable imperative … We cannot free ourselves intellectually, morally and therefore politically unless we realize what is enslaving us. It is only by exploring the ideological debris of today that we will be able to find our way to the future.[22]

And thirdly, the concept of patriotism popularized by political history supporters in most cases relates to nationalism in its narrow sense, based on the simple dichotomy "us—them" in its most extreme form, or patronizing "the others" in its gentler form. Generally the aim of the supporters of historical memory is to restore pride in the national past, and—what is equally important and necessary for them—to reinterpret chosen subjects from the history of Poland, both ancient and recent. They see an urgent need to reject that kind of historical consciousness which one of the authors named "the PRL version of a conservative or Jester school". It is necessary, they claim, to break with a negative perception of the old Polish-Lithuanian Commonwealth symbolized by Bobrzyński`s synthesis and to show "the real heroes who remained for the last 70 years in the garbage of history, where they were kept over the last 15 years.[23]

Critics of this notion of "tomorrow's patriotism" point out its numerous weaknesses and limitations. Some historians try to contrast the vision of an affirmative concept of national history with critical patriotism, not antagonistic but respecting the subjectivity of others. This notion of patriotism relates to the nation as a kind of political and civic community, not an ethnic one. According to Robert Traba in a historical policy program there is no room for what he describes as "'not our'[24] national history" and further on he adds "If those who are involved in creating a historical policy fail to adopt a clear stance on the problem of regional patriotism and do not do justice to the multinational character and the heritage of the old Poland, their project will never be credible. It will remain a short-sighted political action of no consequences for historical debates in Poland." Andrzej Romanowski is even more radical in his attempt to sound the alarm and warn the public that the postulate of creating national pride is based on "a huge dose of hypocrisy and deceit." In his opinion it should be discredited for two reasons. First, it leads inevitably to the disguising of Polish national complexes. Secondly, it conflicts with the truth and naturally "has a touch of propaganda."[25] It is in this context that the idea of liberal nationalism, formed by Andrzej Walicki, appears.[26] With some simplification we may say that it is derived from the criticism of ethnic nationalism and proposes replacing it with a notion of national ideology in which "nation" means a pluralistic community. In this interpreted vision the natural state involves the presence of many memories complementing one another and creating a community based on plural identity. As Walicki says: "It is not a nation in the name of which one may request the unification of opinions and moreover institutionalize a catechism of common memory. In such a community it is impossible to impose identical memories or to use state institutions for this purpose."[27]

One of the few positive (though not uncritical) attempts to interpret the slogan "tomorrow's patriotism" and the essays of Cichocki, Gawin, and Karłowicz came in the series of articles by Mencwel that we have already mentioned. Accepting the social need for public debate on the postulated content of historical policy, the researcher linked it to Jerzy Giedroyc's well-known saying about the two coffins, in the shadow of which the debate about Polish tradition has been taking place for years. In his opinion the starting point of the debate on Polish identity and the vision of patriotism should be the final and critical evaluation of the thought of Józef Piłsudski and Roman Dmowski, not in their literal meaning but as "the concentration of meanings," which expresses two main models of nation: society and state.[28] I will not present Mencwel's argumentation in detail, but in his opinion the continuation and verification of Dmowski's model after 1945 was "the program of agreement with the communists proposed by "national Catholic" leader Bolesław Piasecki, and Piłsudki's model was creatively developed by the creator of Parisian "Culture," Jerzy Giedroyc. According to the above-mentioned historian the former transformation was "adaptational, totalitarian and satellite," while the latter was "creative, democratic and independent."[29] Obviously those two traditions imply exclusive visions of Poland and patriotism with their respective cultural systems, educational ideas and practices. Mencwel's conclusion is not very revealing, but undoubtedly unequivocal. In the debate on historical policy we are in a situation; *tertium non datur.*

Now let us turn to the politics of history. Based on the statements heard so far there are at least three, the first of which is the legitimizing or ideological function. From today's perspective it should support democratic order, the freedom of public discussion and the debate between different traditions. It is especially important at times of danger coming from the state, as can be illustrated by the French experience: both the petition published on 13 December 2005 about "Freedom for History," protesting against the so-called "Memory Acts" and the recent law condemning the Turkish massacre of Armenians in 1915.[30] Secondly, there is the integrative-activist function: in this case the intention underlying historical policy is to unite the Polish people around a commonly accepted vision of the past and to inspire its approval and support. Thirdly, we find the "uncovering" function, with the aim of showing strange, false contents and defining the enemy (enemies) both in internal and foreign affairs. In the debate that we are now analyzing only the first of these functions seems not to be controversial;[31] the other two divide historians. According to the supporters of memory policy its role is to oppose the false images of the national past that were formed under the PRL and to counter the sometimes aggressive decisions to ignore the Polish perspective on historical policy of our neighbors (especially Russia).[32] From this perspective, some of them do not hesitate to speak openly of "counterpropaganda" as an antidote to the nihilism of propaganda activities during the PRL and their continuation after 1989.[33] Critics of memory policy relate to the same clichés but evaluate them *a rebours.* For them the contemporary form of historical policy, both in its program and methods, means a return to communist times.[34] These historians also shun the idea of applying "direct" historical policy in diplomatic activity. They emphasize the inefficiency of actions based on reinforcing mutual conflicts, the need for empathy, and rejection of the temptation to treat Poland as the core of all things. Walicki's statement on Polish–Russian relations is a good example of this context:

> Both nations, Polish and Russians, have suffered and are extremely sensitive in questions of historical memory. Our mutual relations are often marked by hysterical reactions. The Russians too present similar behavior. If we reopen our own wounds, it is not so big a problem. The real problems crop up when the Poles set about reopening Russian wounds and Russians begin to reopen the Polish ones. A war over historical memory will do the Poles no good. That is why I think it is better advised to abstain from making it the object of great politics.[35]

There is another interesting question about historical policy: What does it say about us historians? I have already mentioned the two images of historians derived from the 19th century which still predominate in research circles.[36] The first one is related to the figure of the "neutral observer," "the impartial searcher for truth" who is guided only by cognitive pursuits. The second identifies the historian as the "spiritual guide and the educator of the nation," who would like to transform history into a treasury of useful knowledge and an important part of common opinion.

We may get the impression that in the debate on historical policy both images are somehow being up-dated and gaining new justification. Obviously the supporters of historical policy most often identify themselves with the latter image. The key issue in this context remains the relationship between historiography and social life, especially politics. As usual, the starting point is the diagnosis of everything that happened in Poland after 1989. According to one side of the debate the characteristic feature of this period was that historians believed that the role of the researcher could replace that of the judge and citizen, and politicians occupied themselves with historical policy, choosing a future without any reference to the past.[37] In the opinion of supporters of memory policy the division between the scientific and the public spheres is inherently false and artificial, and cannot be sustained. One characteristic statement of this point of view goes:

> I cannot completely understand how a historian can declare that in reality he does not belong to the political sphere. It is not only the question of the contrast between the historian and the politician, who comes from outside and is demanding or suggesting something, or wants to use his knowledge instrumentally. Politics in its broad sense is present in the historian's very activity, in such elementary issues as choosing a subject for research and presentation. I think that politics does not exist "somewhere else"; it is an inherent part of all human activity, and therefore of the activities of the historian. His decisions are political *par excellence* and should be treated as such.[38]

From this perspective one may add that the results of historical research are not used only for scientific purposes, but should also contain some educational aspect. Supporters of historical policy want to legitimize two types of historical discourse in regard to their social role: the academic and the popular-scientific. According to them historical research is a mission that is clearly described by one researcher as follows: "History implies some obligation (...) We cannot revive the imagination of young generations only with souvenirs. We must show them certain tasks through history, if they want to feel the value of being Polish."[39]

Opposing this, we find the voices of those representatives of historical circles who favor the first of the above-mentioned images of the historian. They are afraid of involving the historian in current politics, for presenting his political views and ideas clearly contradicts the idea of independent historiography. Here is one example: "The sphere of the past (...) should remain the autonomous domain of researchers and should not be given away to the prosecutors who rule memory according to the interests of the state or *raison d'etre*."[40] Other discussants note that there are two ways of dealing with history: gratuitous and mercenary. In the former case "even the worst truth is better than a lie"; in the latter the researcher favors the selective and instrumental aspect of science.[41] There are some radical opinions among the opponents of historical policy. The description "political historian" sometimes becomes the personification of someone who "knows what he knows and does not bother to prove it, and moreover insults others"; it is an image which contradicts the ideal of the historian's work, the pursuit of truth, and disregards the common rules of historical methodology.[42]

The moderate voices of those seeking a compromise between the world of politics and the historical community are in a minority. P. Machcewicz voiced such an idea: in his opinion both sides should be "longsighted and deliberate":

> politicians must appreciate the significance of history, support scientific research and educational activities relating to the past, but avoid an instrumental approach. But historians should recognize their civic obligations and the fact that the results of their work are important not only for them but for the whole community. At the same time they should guard their independence as they would protect their own eyes, avoid the temptations of "court historiography" and be able to say "no" to the politicians in certain situations ... I believe that such a model of co-operation is achievable, however difficult.[43]

It would simplify the picture if one thought that this layer of the discussion about historical policy revealed only a fundamental conflict between two images of the historian: "the independent scientist" and "the historian concerned about the spirit of the community." It is also an issue of the place of knowledge about the past in public debate and questions about the historian's responsibility. Consequently the following questions become significant: first, should the researcher remain indifferent towards different modern ways of using the past? Second, is it possible to limit the above-mentioned problem of responsibility only remaining faithful to truth in the most reasonable meaning of this word and historical methodology? Or should it reach beyond the purely scientific sphere and emphasize the historian's obligations towards the community: state, national or local?

IV.

The voices of historians presented above, emphasising differences rather than similarities with regard to the debate on historical policy, allow us to come to what are obviously provisional conclusions.

Firstly, there is no doubt that the debate, which has gone on for several years, has not only brought new life into academic circles but has also helped us to realize that the past exercises extraordinary power and constitutes an intrinsic component of our present culture. The atmosphere of the debate and its sometimes extremely emotional tone clearly show that the assumptions that were characteristic of the nineties, of a flexible future and a past which hardly imposes any limits, have disappeared. For some time it seemed that in the latter sphere there were no major issues to be debated. Today a significantly different opinion prevails. The discussions summarized above show spectacularly that arguments about the past have grown in importance and that this is no temporary trend. At the beginning of the 21st century the recent history of Poland has become the arena of major debates, which divide different generations of Polish people.

Secondly, the debate on historical policy has revealed, although only hazily so far, the controversy regarding the relationship between historiography and collective memory. The reason for this situation is an almost simultaneous change in the circumstances under which professional historians operate. As Wojciech Wrzosek observed in a slightly different context: "historians 'breathe in' the stereotypes of their profession and recognize the fact of breathing only when the circumstances in which they breathe change."[44] What was the sense of this change? French historian Pierre Nora describes the new situation as follows:

> The whole of history ... now transformed into a field with scientific ambitions, was built on the basis of memory, but memory was not perceived as individual, psychological and unreliable; it was useful only as a proof. History was the domain of the community, a memory of privacy. There was one history and *ex definitione* many kinds of memory, because memory is by nature individual. The idea of collective memory liberating and being praised means the exact opposite situation. Individuals had memory, communities had history. The idea that communities have memory implies a significant change in the place of individuals in community and their mutual relationships ...[45]

The identification of history with memory has two consequences. One is the rapid intensification of the use of the past in politics, tourism, and the economy, the other is the fact that the historian has lost his traditional monopoly over the interpretation of the past. Today the historian is not the only producer of the past. He shares this role with judges, witnesses, the media and legislators.[46] The boundary between common and scientific discourse naturally becomes blurred. Both contain the same categories, however differently understood. We are observing their fusion and mutual replacement. The very term "historical policy" is a significant example. From this perspective the debate on historical policy shows the tensions and conflicts between those who treat it as a way of manipulating collective memory and those who want it revived as a fundamental part of the Polish historical experience. The former case clearly shows the opposition between collective memory and historiography; the latter emphasizes their complementary relationship.[47]

Thirdly, the debate presented above has raised the question of which model of historical policy Poland should adopt, especially in relation to our neighbors. Undoubtedly every historical policy relates to a certain system of values. Therefore, it is worth wondering whether it should be a civic paradigm, based on notions of human rights, democracy and pluralism, or a national paradigm emphasizing the following issues: sovereignty; the interests of the nation; and the national state.[48] There are two reasons why it is hard to answer this question. On the one hand, Poland is in a difficult geopolitical position. Even if we assume that it would be easier to achieve a compromise with the Germans using the civic or multinational code, we still have to deal with the challenge of Russian historical policy; the celebrations of the 60th anniversary of the end of the Second World War two years ago show that we are facing a revival of national and imperialist rhetoric. On the other hand we must face the dilemma: on which axiology should we base a program of historical policy? Are we mentally prepared to use two systems of values simultaneously? Is it possible at all? Its consequences would involve compromises between the contradictory axiologies, priorities and methods used in different cases.

The debate about historical policy has already raised many such questions. Only by answering them can we move beyond well-known, comfortable ways of thinking and indirectly add a civic aspect to history, thus protecting Polish people from the always dangerous act of usurping it.

NOTES

1 For further reading see e.g., M. Pawłowski, ed., *Spór o PRL*, (The Debate about the Polish People's Republic) (Cracow: Wyd. Znak, 1996); S. Ciesielski, and W. Wrzesiński, *Uwagi o stanie badań nad dziejami powojennej Polski, "Polska 1944/1945–1989. Studia i materiały,"* [Remarks on the state of research on postwar Poland, "Poland 1944/1945/1989. Studies and Materials"] (Warsaw: 1995), pp. 217–240; A. Friszke, "Spór o PRL w III Rzeczypospolitej (1989–2001)" [The Debate on the PRL in the Third Republic of Poland (1989–2001)], *Pamięć i Sprawiedliwość* [Memory and Justice] 2002, No. 1, pp. 9–28; Ibid., "Polish Communism in Contemporary Debates," in *Stalinism in Poland. Selected Papers from the Fifth World Congress of Central and East European Studies, Warsaw 1995,* A. Kemp-Welch, ed. and trans. (London: Basingstoke, Macmillan, 1999), pp. 144–157; P. Machcewicz, "Spory o PRL w polskiej historiografii i publicystyce po 1989 r." [The Debates about the PRL in Polish Historiography and Writing after 1989], in *Historycy polscy i ukraińscy wobec problemów XX wieku* [Polish and Ukrainian historians facing 20th-century problems], in P. Kosiewski and G. Motyka, eds. (Crakow: Wyd. Universitas, 2000), pp. 68–81; R. Stobiecki, *Spór o interpretacje PRL w publicystyce i historiografii polskiej po 1989.* [The Debate on the interpretation of the PRL in Polish historiography and historical publicism after 1989], in *Historia, poznanie i przekaz.* B. Jakubowska, ed., (Rzeszów: Wyd. WSP, 2000), pp. 169–182.

2 The work summing up the debates and research related to the crimes in Jedwabne is *Wokół Jedwabnego* [Around Jedwabne], P. Machcewicz and K. Persak, eds., Vols. 1–2, (Warsaw: Wydawnictwo Instytutu Pamięci Narodowej, 2002). See also: *Jedwabne: Spór historyków wokół książki Jana T. Grossa "Sąsiedzi"* [Jedwabne. The Historians' Debate around Jan T. Gross' book "Neighbors"] (Warsaw: Wyd. Fronda, 2002); *"Thou Shalt not Kill": Poles on Jedwabne* (Warsaw: Wyd. Więź, 2001); B. Törnquist-Plewa, "The Jedwabne Killings—a challenge for Polish collective memory. The Polish Debate on Neighbours," in *Echoes of the Holocaust. Historical Cultures in Contemporary Europe,* K. G. Karlsson and U. Zander, eds., (Lund: Nordic Academic Press, 2003), pp. 141–176.

3 For examples of such debates see discussions published in *Mówią Wieki* No. 8 (2006), *Biuletyn IPN* No. 5 (2006), or *Gazeta Wyborcza"* Nos. 1–2 (October 2005).

4 Statement in the discussion "Historical policy—for and against," *Mówią Wieki* No. 8 (2006), See also, *Polityka pamięci* [The Memory Policy], *Rzeczpospolita* Nos. 10–11 (June 2006).

5 D. Gawin and P. Kowal, "Polska polityka historyczna" [Polish Historical policy], in *Polityka historyczna. Historycy—politycy—prasa*, (Warsaw: Muzeum Powstania Warszawskiego, 2005), p. 13. (Materials from the conference relating to this theme organized on 15 December 2004.)

6 Ibid.

7 M. Cichocki, "Czas silnych tożsamości" [The time of strong identities], in *Polityka historyczna...* [Historical policy...], p. 17. See also R. Kostro and K. M. Ujazdowski, "Odzyskać pamięć" [Regaining Memory], in *Pamięć i odpowiedzialność* [Memory and responsibility], R. Kostro and T. Merta, eds., (Cracow–Wrocław: OMP-Centrum Konserwatywne, 2005), p. 45.

8 M. Cichocki, "Czas silnych tożsamości", p. 15. Politicians express similar ideas. There is a characteristic statement by Jan Maria Rokita: "Historical memory is not only the property of the professors of history and academics, historical memory is a collective memory, not private Klio property," ibid., "Głos w dyskusi" [The voice in the discussion], in *Pamięć i polityka zagraniczna* [Memory and foreign affairs], P. Kosiewski, ed., (Warsaw: Fundacja im. Stefana Batorego, 2006), p. 135.

9 M. Kula, "Wypowiedź w dyskusji..." [Voice in Discussion...], p. 1.

10 M. Kula, "Wypowiedź w dyskusji," p. 2.

11 See "Głosy w dyskusji A. Juzwenki i D. Nałęcz" [Voices in discussion of A. Juzwenko and D. Nałęcz], in *Polityka historyczna...* [Historical policy...], pp. 45–46, 52–53; "Kicz patriotyczny. Wywiad J. Kurskiego z R. Trabą" [Patriotic kitsch. The interview of J. Kurski with R. Traba] *Gazeta Wyborcza* 7–8 (January 2006), R. Traba, "Walka o kulturę. Przestrzeń dialogu w najnowszej debacie o polskiej historii i pamięci" [The Battle on Culture. The Space for dialogue in recent debate about Polish history and memory], *Przegląd Polityczny* No. 75 (2006): pp. 45–53. After the publication of this text the whole collection of R. Traba studies appeared as *Historia—przestrzeń dialogu* [History—The Space for Dialogue], (Warsaw: Wyd. Instytutu Studiów Politycznych PAN, 2006); A. Romanowski, "Historia, kłamstwo i banał", *Gazeta Wyborcza* (15–16 July 2006); "Polityka kłamstw historycznych" [The Policy of Historical Lies], *Gazeta Wyborcza* (7–8 October 2006) (Trancript of UMSC in Lublin debate with the participation of K. Pomian, A. Michnik and J. Życiński).

12 P. Machcewicz, "Polityka historyczna to nic nowego" [Historical policy is nothing new], *Gazeta Wyborcza* (20 April 2006).

13 A. Wolff-Powęska, "Państwo precz od historii" [The state must leave history], *Gazeta Wyborcza* (3–4 May 2006).

14 Ibid.

15 I mean the three-part essay published in *Rzeczypospolita:* "Tradycja do remontu" [Tradition for Renovation], (16–17 September 2006), "Jak stwarza się naród" [How to Create a Nation], (23–24 September 2006), "Dwie trumny wiecznie żywe" [Two Coffins always alive], (30 September–1 October 2006).

16 A. Mencwel, "Tradycja do remontu" [Tradition for Renovation], *Rzeczpospolita* (16–17 September 2006).

17 Ibid.

18 The significance of this dilemma was pointed out by A. Dudek in his speech published in *Polityka historyczna...* [Historical Policy...], p. 104.

19 D. Gawin, *O pożytkach i szkodliwości historycznego rewizjonizmu* [On the advantages and disadvantages of Historical Revisionism] in: *Pamięć i odpowiedzialność...* [Memory and Responsibility], p. 20. It is worth mentioning that Gawin's criticism is not aimed directly at J.J. Lipski but rather at the social consequences of his ideas. "The attitude of Jan Józef Lipski may become a symbol of patriotism and civil obedience for the next generation of Polish people. He preferred not to mention his own patriotism, which could be a reason for pride... It was a noble and ethically radical position. At first not threatening anyone with consequences, but with time it has brought more and more significant results, because it contained some risk. The attitude of heroic ethically radical criticism was the basis of the bringing whole masses of intellectuals to use involuntary automatic criticism. Radical criticism becomes intellectual addiction, a mental disposition overcoming any thought." Ibid. p. 28.

20 D. Karłowicz, "Pamięć aksjologiczna a historia" [Axiological memory and history], in *Pamięć i odpowiedzialność...* [Memory and Responsibility], p. 35.

21 *Odkryć historię—zrozumieć wolność. Muzeum Historii Polski* [Discovering history— understanding freedom. The museum of Polish history] (Warsaw: Muzeum Historii Polski, 2006), p. 16.

22 T. Wituch, "Narodowy bilans XX wieku" [National Balance of the 20th Century], *Arcana* No. 2 (1999): 25. See also the opinions of T. Wituch and Marek K. Kamiński published in *Arcana* as the answer for their survey regarding historical patterns in contemporary Poland, *Arcana* No. 1 (1988): 20–25, 31–32 and the contributions of J. Żaryn, A. Nowak and Marek Jurek in the discussion "Polska polityka historyczna" [Polish Historical Policy] published in *Biuletyn IPN* No. 5 (2006): 2–3, 7–8, 11.

23 The first quotation is a statement by J. Choińska-Mika published in *Polityka historyczna...* [Historical Policy...], pp. 79–80, the second is part of A. Nowak's contribution to the discussion "Polska polityka historyczna" [Polish Historical Policy], *Biuletyn IPN* No. 5 (2006): 28.

24 *Kicz patriotyczny...* [Patriotic kitsch...] See also R. Traba, *Walka o kulturę* [The battle on culture], pp. 45–53.

25 A. Romanowski, "Historia, kłamstwo" [History, lie].

26 A. Walicki, "Czy możliwy jest nacjonalizm liberalny?" [Is Liberal Nationalism Possible?] *"Znak"* 1997, No. 3.

27 "O liberalizmie wspólnocie i historii." [Liberalism, community and history] Rozmowa "Łukasza Gałeckiego z Andrzejem Walickim," [Interview of Lukasz Galecki with Andrzej Walicki] *"Przegląd Polityczny"* No. 75/26 (2006).

28 A. Mencwel, "Dwie trumny wiecznie żywe..." [Two coffins always alive...].

29 Ibid.

30 The chapter, according to which negating Turkish genocide of Armenians is a crime, was voted on and accepted by the French parliament on 17 October 2006. For further reading see. E. Bieńkowska, "Demokracja—historia—cenzura" [Democracy— history—censorship], *Europa. Tygodnik Idei* 19 July 2006; L. Sonik, "Wojna o historię" [The war on history], *Rzeczpospolita* (11–12 March 2006); T. G. Ash, "Nie potrzebujemy nowych tabu" [We do not need new taboo topics], *Gazeta Wyborcza* 21–22.10. 2006.

31 See. D. Gawin, "Polityka historyczna i demokratyczne państwo" [Historical policy and democratic state], in *Polityka historyczna...* [Historical Policy...], pp. 22–27.

32 See. "Polityka zagraniczna—polityka zagraniczna?" [Foreign policy—foreign policy?], in *Polityka historyczna...* [Historical Policy], pp. 121–151, especially A. Nowak's statement regarding Polish–Russian relations, ibid., pp. 125–128. See also *Pamięć i polityka zagraniczna...* [Memory and Historical Policy].

33 A. Nowak, statement in the discussion "Polska polityka historyczna..." [Polish Historical Policy...], p. 33.

34 See A. Romanowski, "Historia, kłamstwo..." [History, Lie]; "Polityka kłamstw historycznych..." [The Policy of Historical Lies].

35 "O liberalizmie, wspólnocie i historii..." [Liberalism, community and history], p. 30. There are similar statements by other debaters. See B. Geremek, "Pamięć indywidualna a pamięć zbiorowa" [Individual and collective memory], in *Pamięć i polityka zagraniczna...* [Memory and historical policy], p. 125.

36 R. Stobiecki, "Historyk i jego rola we współczesnym świecie" [The historian and his role in the contemporary world], in *Gra i konieczność. Zbiór rozpraw z historii historiografii i filozofii histori* [The game and necessity. The compilation of writing on the history of historiography and history of philosophy], G. A. Dominiak, J. Ostoja-Zagórski, W. Wrzosek, eds., (Bydgoszcz: 2005), pp. 49–60.

37 Z. Krasnodębski, the statement in the discussion on "Historical Policy, the Role of Historians," in *Polityka historyczna*, p. 90.

38 T. Merta, the statement in the discussion on "Historical Policy, the Role of Historians," ibid., p. 98.

39 A. Nowak, statement in the discussion on "Polska polityka historyczna" [Polish historical policy], *Biuletyn IPN,* p. 8.

40 B. Geremek, "Pamięć…," p. 125.

41 D. Grinberg, contribution to the discussion "Could the State Rule over History?" *Gazeta Wyborcza* (17–18 June 2006). This is a shortened transcript of the discussion on "The Jewish Subject and Polish Historical Policy", which took place on 24 May 2006 during the IXth Days of the Jewish Book organized by the *Midrasz* association.

42 Romanowski, *Historia, kłamstwo…*

43 P. Machcewicz, statement made during the discussion on "Historical Policy, the Role of Historians," pp. 95–96.

44 W. Wrzosek, "Historiograficzny status historii narodowej" [The historiographical status of national history], in *Wielokulturowe środowisko historyczne Lwowa w XIX i XX w.* [The Multicultural Circle of Historians in Lvov 19th and 20th centuries] (Lvov—Rzeszów: Wydawnictwo Universytetu Rzeszowskiego, 2006), p.14.

45 P. Nora, *Czas pamięci* [The time of memory], *Res Publica Nowa* No. 7 (2001), p. 41.

46 Ibid., p. 43.

47 An example of a totally different opinion from Pierre Nore's is presented in the latest book by K. Pomian, *Historia. Nauka wobec pamięci* (History. The science towards memory) (Lublin: Wyd. UMCS, 2006), especially pp. 181–187.

48 Cf. K. Bachman's, *Długi cień Trzeciej Rzeszy. Jak Niemcy zmieniali swój charakter narodowy* [The Long shadow of the Third Reich. How the Germans changed their national character] (Wrocław: Wyd. Atut, 2005) and my review of this work was published in *Dzieje Najnowsze* No 2 (2006): 199–204.

Revisiting the Great Famine of 1932–1933

Politics of Memory and Public Consciousness (Ukraine after 1991)

GEORGIY KASIANOV

Rethinking the Soviet period has become one of the central problems involved in constructing a new model of collective memory in Ukraine within the framework of nationalized history. In contrast to more remote historical periods, the rethinking and rewriting of the Soviet past has had and continues to have special meaning in present-day historical mythology. First, the social and political meaning of that "past" has been actualized in the present; it has been used quite straightforwardly in political infighting. Second, the methods involved in the recollection of that past have gone considerably beyond the professional standards to which historians were accustomed at the time of the disintegration of the USSR. Third, for the authorities, as well as for most professional historians and a large part of the Ukrainian population, the Soviet "past" constitutes present reality in two senses. On the one hand, individual memory remains vital, reflecting the collective experience of the last ten to thirty years of Soviet rule (for many, memory goes back even further). On the other hand, the civic culture,[1] ideological power structures, and state institutional hierarchies, having undergone certain formal transformations, remain essentially unchanged, so that the "past" is still physically embodied in the "present" and naturally, influences the nature of change in historical memory. And even the "gains of Independence Square" proclaimed by the current authorities do not change this situation.

In evaluating the role of Soviet-era social institutions inherited by post-independence Ukrainian society, and the individuals who represent and embody those institutions when it comes to the formation of historical memory, some scholars advance explanations in the spirit of instrumentalism, along with a drop of conspiracy theory. Thus Professor George Grabowicz of Harvard University asserts:

... today the Ukrainian establishment is making strenuous efforts to carry out what I would call an amnesia project—a more or less conscious but consistently and success-fully realized program of actions and measures intended to obliterate the recent Soviet past forever and to ensure that it is not researched or reviewed. This is being done for perfectly obvious reasons: since the former Soviet *nomenklatura* continues to retain the leading positions in every single sector of social, institutional and, most particu-larly, political life, these people will hardly agree to support any program of remem-bering, rethinking and reevaluating the legacy of the past, with which they are associ-ated in the closest possible way.[2]

The political writer and essayist Mykola Riabchuk comments on the problem in a similar key. Analyzing the role of the authorities in com-memorating key dates of Soviet Ukrainian history (Volodymyr Shcherbyt-sky's 85th birth anniversary, the anniversary of the famine of 1932–33, or the "jubilee" of the Young Communist League of Ukraine, which is most often mentioned contextually), Riabchuk indicates that in one way or an-other their behavior is part of a "certain discursive strategy." If the anni-versaries of communist symbols are worked into a general linear scheme of "Ukrainian statehood," and thus directly legitimize the current admini-stration which still bears the hallmarks of the Soviet order, that admini-stration also makes use of key dates associated with anti-Communism (such as the famine of 1932–33) in order "to lend a certain respectability to the post-communist regime, which supposedly represents the interests of the whole nation and supposedly distances itself from the dubious prac-tices of its predecessors."[3]

The historian Stanislav Kulchytsky notes the "muffled disregard of the famine on the part of our bureaucratic elite"[4] and explains it by means of a psychological factor—incapacity to absorb the whole stream of negative information and a corresponding unwillingness to recall the "black pages" of the past.

These fairly similar approaches offer a generally sound explanation of the post-communist authorities' attitude to "the past in the present," citing their natural desire to legalize the new regime with the aid of historical arguments (or the conscious or unconscious desire to ignore those portions of the historical map that are considered undesirable, or perceived as such). Still, this treatment is clearly prone to exaggerate the element of planning in the authorities' actions, which in my view are fairly spontane-ous, situational and reflexive—hardly the results of a well-considered strategy. The thesis of conscious and deliberate "forgetting" (or amnesia) is at variance with the authorities' obvious desire to take part in "remem-brance" from time to time and, even more, to have an active influence on the nature of that remembrance (although here, too, the orientation and character of "remembrance" are determined situationally and expressed in utterly standard forms).

Moreover, the commentators cited above obviously exaggerate the degree to which the current authorities[5] realize and admit their direct link with the communist past and their fear, supposedly associated with this, of losing social legitimacy. Enough time has already passed for images of the current authorities and their communist predecessors to separate and become dissociated. Over 15 years of independence, despite the parallel existence of Soviet and post-Soviet structures of power that mimic one another, society has had time to form new notions of them. A whole complex of new images and *idées fixes* has arisen—a kind of ideological buffer zone that has afforded the oligarchs secure protection against the "attacks" of those who demanded a "trial of Communism" or a "second Nuremberg," with the obvious political subtext of discrediting those who held power at the time.[6] This buffer zone is all the more secure because Ukraine, like most of the former Soviet republics (with the exception, perhaps, only of the Baltics and Armenia), did not experience what was known in postwar Germany as "de-Nazification" and in the post-communist lands of East Central Europe as "de-communization," "lustration,"[7] and the like. The Noah's ark of the authorities survived both the right-wing anti-communist escapades of the 1990s and the *ersatz* orange Flood of 2004.

To be sure, it should not be forgotten that this buffer zone was built in comradely fashion both by the former communist *nomenklatura* who managed to stay in power and by their opponents from the national-democratic camp, some of whom entered the power structures themselves. In the early 1990s these two forces reached a tacit compromise based on a formal community of interests—the building of Ukrainian statehood. The former communists turned into nationalists and, with no less zeal than their recent opponents, set about publicly condemning the "crimes of the totalitarian regime," thereby neutralizing possible accusations against themselves. (The bellwether figure par excellence is Leonid Kravchuk. From 1980 to 1988 he headed the Department of Agitation and Propaganda of the Central Committee of the Communist Party of Ukraine (CC CPU) and was necessarily involved in counter-propaganda measures pertaining to the 50th anniversary of the famine of 1932–33. In 1989 he became head of the Department of Ideology of the CC CPU and, until the change of course, took an active part in debates with the national democrats. In 1991, he became president of Ukraine, winning far more votes than his competitor from the national-democratic camp, Viacheslav Chornovil. In 1993, Mykola Plawiuk, president of the Ukrainian People's Republic (UNR) "in exile" and leader of the Organization of Ukrainian Nationalists (Melnyk faction), transferred the powers of the president of the UNR to Kravchuk. This manifested the symbolic link between the UNR authorities and those of present-day Ukraine, as well as the extreme pragmatism or *naïveté* (or cynicism?) of some diaspora political figures (the cynicism of the Ukrainian oligarchs of the period goes without saying; in their moral frame of reference, this was a perfectly normal transition). Most Ukrainian diaspora organizations supported this policy openly or indirectly, clearly compromising their basic principles for the sake of the idea of statebuilding. As a parliamentary deputy serving continuously since 1994, Kravchuk invariably held to the principle of joining factions that directly or indirectly supported those in power. In Leonid Kuchma's times he belonged to the "oligarchic" faction—the (United) Social-Democratic Party. Under Viktor Yushchenko, he became a tribune of the "opposition" at the very time when "opposition" status became perfectly safe, that is, it presented no danger to his private capital or to his personal liberty, as it would have done in Kuchma's day. In 1993, it was Kravchuk, then holding presidential office, who gave his official blessing to government measures associated with the 60th anniversary of the famine of 1932–33. Kravchuk was also among the initiators of one of the most odious commemorations of the last few years, the 85th anniversary of the birth of Volodymyr Shcherbytsky, first secretary of the CC CPU from 1972 to 1989, responsible for the cruel persecution of the Ukrainian dissident movement, large-scale Russification, and the cover-up of the Chornobyl nuclear disaster.

Those who revived the Communist Party of Ukraine in 1993 inherited its real and imaginary "sins" and thus created an additional buffer for the oligarchs in their own persons.

What was the role of the community of professional historians in these developments? On the one hand, their actions were determined by the ideological market (which demanded the nationalization of history). On the other, they themselves formulated those demands, creating a kind of research opportunity. If in the latter half of the 1980s historians carried out ideological orders directly, on the cusp of the 1990s they largely began to determine those requirements themselves and to influence the conjuncture of the ideological market in their own right. The merging of these two functions remains one of the most notable features of the current state of official Ukrainian historiography.

This in turn is reflected in the formation of the collective memory of the Soviet past. On the level of social thought and everyday consciousness, we see the dominance of notions representing an alloy of personal experience and propaganda issued by various political forces with fragmentary information about the past communicated through the media. Naturally, the schools, with their systematized standard courses in Ukrainian history, play a significant role. It is quite difficult to establish the course of change in mass consciousness without systematic research, but available information in the form of letters to the editor, television programs and shows dealing with problems of Ukrainian history and the like indicates that many new ideological elements associated with the reevaluation of the Soviet past have become fairly well established as fixed stereotypes.[8]

All this is clearly illustrated by the "inscription" of notions about the famine of 1932–33 in "national" historical memory.

The calm and "dispassionate" scholarly analysis of problems associated with the famine of 1932–33 in Ukraine itself is complicated by a whole series of sociocultural and political factors. First of all, such a huge trauma as the loss of several million people on one's own territory in peacetime, with biological, social and sociopsychological consequences that have not yet been fully apprehended, can hardly be a subject of purely academic discussion. Since the topic itself was forbidden for decades, the compensation mechanism for that taboo is fairly obvious. It should also be remembered that for some ethnic Ukrainians the famine of 1932–33 remains part of living memory. Many of those still alive, including some scholars, know of it not only from scholarly works, political writings or archival sources,[9] but also from stories told by relatives and acquaintances (there are also those who survived the famine in early childhood, although, understandably, the number of direct witnesses is now very small). And the very fact of the demise of millions of people who died a terrible martyr's death in their own homes in peacetime, having entered mass consciousness, is beginning to influence the judgment even of those professionals most inclined to unprejudiced evaluation. Professional historians are also subject to pressure from society at large (especially when public statements are called for) and from the declarations of various political forces. Popular publications, literary works, television programs and films about the events of 1932–33, as well as a whole variety of public events, create a certain cultural setting in which the professional historian, who means to render a purely scholarly judgment on a historical phenomenon, finds it rather difficult to remain within the confines of a balanced academic style. Periodically, the strong emotional charge of the problem even brings out a measure of social hysteria, and in that context scholarly appeals for a sober and rational examination of the question may be regarded (and often are regarded by a segment of the public) as a challenge to public opinion or as a show of disrespect for the memory of the victims.

The famine of 1932–33 is an integral element of domestic political discussion and even of foreign-policy initiatives. In some cases it has been used to discredit part of the current political elite, which was brought up by the regime that organized the famine (this also helps explain the authorities' fairly "reserved" attitude to the problem and accusations leveled against them because of that attitude). In other cases the subject of the famine calls forth emotional parallels with the current state of the Ukrainian nation, allegedly the result of suffering and losses in the years of totalitarianism. Third, today's left-wingers have openly been called heirs to the party responsible for the famine of 1932–33—an obvious attempt to discredit them in the struggle for power.

There is one more important circumstance that has a direct bearing on the nature and orientation of interpretations of the events of 1932–33. During the years of Soviet rule, inhabitants of the Ukrainian lands had to endure mass famine three times, in 1921–23, 1932–33 and 1947. But the greatest famine—that of 1932–33, which has come to be known as the *holodomor* (a term with no exact English equivalent, but meaning a manmade famine) according to a tradition inherited from the Ukrainian diaspora—has been transformed through the efforts of political writers, historians and public activists into one of the most imposing symbols of national historical memory. It finds multifarious instrumental application in a variety of spheres, ranging from politics and social initiatives to art. This may be explained by the fact that the famine of 1921–23 was not covered up even in Soviet historiography. It was explained by postwar devastation and natural causes, and the state organized assistance to those suffering from starvation, including aid from abroad. The famine of 1947 was also not ignored by the authorities, although Soviet-era historical works that actually mentioned it spoke only of "food-supply problems" associated with the selfsame postwar devastation and drought. The famine of 1932–33 was set apart by the very fact that a cover-up was attempted. The population, according to popular knowledge, was not only left to its own devices but also became the object of actions that scholars designate as "terror by famine," while the international resonance of the disaster was muffled by the efforts of Western politicians, journalists, and broad circles of pro-Soviet Western intellectuals favorably disposed to cooperation with the USSR. It was this famine that the authorities tried to wipe out of collective memory; the subject was rendered taboo.

Understandably, historians dealing with this set of problems find themselves constantly drifting between two related discourses: ideological and scholarly, with the former clearly prevailing over the latter. Naturally, after 1991 efforts have been made to link the famines of 1921–23, 1932–33 and 1947 into a chain of related events. For example, in an article by an author whose high academic reputation is not in doubt, the famine of 1921–23 is called (metaphorically, to be sure) "a dress rehearsal for 1933."[10] In an introduction to a publication with the eloquent title *Famines in Ukraine, 1921–23, 1932–33, 1946–47: A Crime against the Nation*[11] S. V. Kulchytsky writes of the "establishment of a planned command economy adequate to the totalitarian regime" as the general cause of all three famines. In their afterword, the authors of the book assert that 20th-century famines were the "consequence of the functioning of dictatorial totalitarian regimes. And this is an almost *undeniable rule*"[12] To be sure, the causes (grain requisitions, droughts, etc.) are spelled out on the level of factual exposition, but in the general context and in the texts themselves there are direct statements to the effect that, to a greater or lesser degree, all three episodes are manifestations of one strategic line associated in one way or another with the "subjugation of freedom-loving Ukrainian peasant farmers." The idea of linear continuity has attained institutional embodiment; the Association of Researchers of the Famine-Genocide of 1932–33, a public organization established in June 1992, was renamed the Association of Researchers of Famines in Ukraine in 1998.

In the Soviet Union the subject of the famine of 1932–33 was absent from intellectual space even in the first years of the "thaw" of the 1950s, although the number of direct witnesses to the catastrophe of 1932–33 was still sufficient for it to register at the very least as a phenomenon of collective memory. According to contemporary testimony, talk of this famine was undesirable even within the family circle, as children might inadvertently mention it in school, with negative consequences for adults. The only attempt to make a partial concession and admit the famine as a fact dates to the late 1960s. Writing about the famine was confined to *samvydav*[13] or to oblique references in works of Soviet counterpropaganda intended to refute the "fabrications of bourgeois falsifiers" (direct polemical engagements on this subject were not recommended).[14]

In the late 1980s, given the general wave of revisionism with regard to the Stalinist period of Soviet history, the famine became, for the first time, a subject of public discussion and research in Ukraine itself. The scenario of its "restoration" was standard. The initiative came from political writers, and ideological institutions had to react, making the subject relevant and visible, which led to its recognition.

A strong external stimulus to the official recognition of the famine of 1932–33 was the activity of the Ukrainian diaspora. As early as 1983, Ukrainians in the United States established an organization called Americans for Human Rights in Ukraine. Owing to its active participation and the assistance of Ukrainian research centers in Canada and the United States, the problem of the famine of 1932–33 came to public attention. The initiative arose following the study of documents about the Holocaust; the parallels were all too obvious. Generally speaking, in considering the role of the diaspora in internationalizing the problem of the famine of 1932–33, it is important to bear in mind that efforts to endow the famine with weight and significance in international public opinion copied the example of the joint project of the Jewish diaspora and Israel to internationalize knowledge of the Holocaust. At the same time, this borrowing took place against the background of conflict between the Ukrainian and Jewish diasporas over questions of Ukrainian participation in the killing of Jews during the Second World War. On the other hand, it is well known that attempts to compare structurally similar tragedies of other peoples with the Holocaust have often met with resistance on the part of some Jewish historians, as in the case of efforts to treat the genocide of Armenians during the First World War as an atrocity on the same level as the Holocaust. All this has had its effect both on the methods of representatives of the Ukrainian diaspora and on perceptions of their activity. In 1985, after considerable bureaucratic delays and intensive lobbying on the part of the Ukrainian diaspora, a Congressional committee was established to research the famine (the American historian James Mace,[15] who specialized in Ukraine of the 1920s and 1930s, was appointed its executive director). The first volume of the committee's report, based mainly on the oral testimony of émigré Ukrainian survivors of the famine, appeared in 1987.

In 1988, an international commission of jurists was formed on the initiative of one of the largest Ukrainian diaspora organizations, the World Congress of Free Ukrainians. It confirmed the fact of large-scale famine in Ukraine in 1932–33, giving the "excessive grain requisition of July 1932" as its immediate cause and identifying forced collectivization, de-'kulak'ization and the central government's desire to combat traditional Ukrainian nationalism as the preconditions.[16]

In 1987, the CC CPU established a special commission composed of scholars from the Institute of History of the Ukrainian SSR Academy of

Sciences and from the Institute of Party History of the CC CPU, which was given the task of refuting the conclusions of the American Congressional committee on the basis of archival sources. Yet it was the very materials of the Ukrainian commission that confirmed the fact of large-scale famine in 1932–33 and became one of the arguments for public recognition of that tragedy by the authorities. According to the reminiscences of participants, the documents that they received were a revelation to them, as archival materials on the subject had not been available even to the most "faithful" researchers. As a result, Volodymyr Shcherbytsky, who then headed the CPU, was obliged to admit the fact of the famine's occurrence in his speech on the 70th anniversary of the October Revolution (giving drought as the cause). Understandably, this became possible only because the general level of revision of Stalinism in the USSR had already gone beyond the criticism of "particular failings" and "errors."

Since the initial purpose of the committee, that of counterpropaganda, had become irrelevant, it ceased working "to order," but certain scholars belonging to it continued their archival research. Some of their work was published in the press and, significantly, in journals that functioned as official party organs (for example, in the CC CPU journal *Pid praporom leninizmu* [Under the Banner of Leninism]). A general statement of their conclusions took the form of a documentary collection, *The Famine of 1932–1933 in Ukraine: Through the Eyes of Historians, In the Language of Documents.*[17] The materials contained therein became the subject of special discussion at a session of the Politburo of the CC CPU in January 1990: according to eyewitnesses, the attitude of Volodymyr Ivashko, then first secretary of the CC CPU, was decisive in clearing the book for publication.[18] In February 1990 the CC CPU adopted a resolution "On the Famine of 1932–1933 in Ukraine and the Publication of Associated Archival Materials." The rhetoric of the resolution was a mixture of conclusions—fairly radical for the time—on the cause of the famine (carrying out the policy of grain requisitions "on a compulsory basis, with the extensive use of repressive measures") and ritual references to the violation of "Leninist principles of peasant cooperation."[19] Later, at the level of the Politburo of the CC CPU, a decision was made to include the subject of "Total Collectivization and Famine among the Rural Population in 1932–33" in the "Republican Program for the Development of Historical Research and Improvement of the Study and Propaganda of the History of the Ukrainian SSR."

It may be said with certainty that it was these decisions and the publication of the documentary collection that initiated open and thoroughgoing discussion of the problem of the famine of 1932–33. The prohibition was lifted officially at the highest level. Public organizations became involved. In particular, with the active support of the Memorial Society, a number of public conferences, including regional ones, were organized in the early 1990s to "revive the memory" of 1932–33. The subject produced its enthusiasts, the writers Volodymyr Maniak and Liudmyla Kovalenko-Maniak, who carried out an extensive project to collect oral and documentary evidence, thought to have been lost, about the famine of 1932–33. A book of testimonies, *33: Famine. A People's Memorial Volume*, appeared under their editorship in 1991.[20]

That book marked the first instance of turning to everyday national consciousness as an alternative to official history. The method of its compilation was quite simple: Stanislav Kulchytsky drafted a list of questions that appeared in *Sil's'ki visti* (Village News), one of the largest mass-circulation newspapers, in December 1988. Appealing to its readers, Kulchytsky indicated that historians possessed very few documents (and access to them was minimal indeed); hence the testimony of eyewitnesses was particularly important. Readers were asked to "recall" instances of resistance to the requisition of foodstuffs on the part of local party and government representatives; repressive measures against leading workers and collective farmers because of their grain-requisition arrears; forms of decentralized assistance to the starving (at the local level) on the part of the authorities; the fate of villages blacklisted for failing to meet grain-requisition quotas; the numbers of fellow villagers who died of starvation; assistance from the cities during the spring sowing campaign of 1933; and, quite simply, their own observations.[21] Close to 6,000 letters were received,[22] a 1,000 of which were published in the book.

The appeal to "witnesses" through the newspaper created a precedent for commemorative practice unique in Ukrainian experience. This was, in effect, a program of "remembrance" that not only influenced the direction and nature of the whole process but also largely determined the way in which the events of 1932–33 were subsequently imagined in mass consciousness—indeed, in the formation of collective historical memory. The efforts of local enthusiasts to revive the memory of the famine met with active support, both institutional and financial, from the Ukrainian diaspora.[23] Such public organizations as Rukh, Memorial, the All-Ukrainian Prosvita Society, the Writers' Union of Ukraine, and the Ukraine Society, as well as academic institutions and the press, became involved in the organization of public events dedicated to the famine of 1932–33. It became apparent that for decades hundreds and thousands of people had kept their own reminiscences or those of people close to them, neighbors and acquaintances, and only the strict taboo on the subject had rendered it "invisible." The collection of testimonies in the regions of Ukraine, organized as a true grassroots initiative, and numerous community events in villages and towns that had suffered from the famine (memorial services, processions with crosses, the erection of memorial tablets, monuments, crosses, grave mounds and the exhibition of documents)—all this evoked mass "remembrance" of the events of 1932–33. This revival of memory was already taking place in a new context and flowing directly into the Ukrainian national historical narrative, which was then taking shape. By the same token, the process of "remembrance" had already taken on its own logic and dynamics. The public revelation of testimonies and documents created a corresponding sociopsychological atmosphere in which new testimonies and references were already contributing to a certain scenario and being dramatized either consciously or subconsciously.

Since history was being put into active service in the late 1980s to legitimize Ukraine's claim to sovereignty, a subject of such colossal emotional and political potential could not remain on the sidelines of practical politics. On the cusp of the 1990s, references to the famine became an obligatory element of virtually all public appearances, oral or written, dedicated to criticizing the Soviet system. This applied particularly to the condemnation of "external influences" on Ukraine, first and foremost those of communist ideology and the communist rule that it sustained, which were presented as "fundamentally alien" to the Ukrainian tradition and mentality. In conjunction with this, as Mykola Riabchuk has noted, a rather characteristic change of terminology took place over time in the rhetoric of politicians representing the authorities. The terms "Stalin regime," "totalitarian regime," "totalitarian system," and the like were used in official documents, appeals and speeches, but the word *communist* was generally absent.[24] Riabchuk considers this part of the above-mentioned strategy, although one might imagine that those responsible for composing the texts of politicians' public appearances made use of scholarly and popular literature in which this particular terminology is dominant. Moreover, there are instances of senior government officials referring to the "communist regime" as the organizer of the famine of 1932–33,[25] so it may be assumed that these nuances did not have the same symbolic meaning for the leadership of that day as they have for Riabchuk and other intellectuals.

During the years of independence, a certain algorithm was worked out for public references to the famine. As a rule, interest peaked in anniversary years: 1993, 1998 and 2002–3. In every instance, the subject of the *holodomor* was exploited for political purposes by a variety of forces (it should be noted that in all instances the "bursts" of interest in the subject coincided chronologically with pre-electoral or electoral campaigns, whether parliamentary or presidential). Some of the national-democratic forces and the more radical right-wingers made use of the subject in their struggle against the left, which managed to keep a stable hold on the sympathies of a significant part of the population, especially in eastern and southern Ukraine, until 2002. The left-wingers, for their part, periodically exploited references to the famine in their propaganda directed against the ruling authorities.[26] The authorities themselves, referring to the subject in connection with anniversary dates, issued directives enumerating commemorative events and persons responsible for them but were fairly stingy when it came to financial support for those events. Depending on the regional balance of political forces, the local authorities carried out those directives or ignored them. Quite often the local authorities simply carried out the directive, the population was "informed," and *pro forma* measures were taken so that a report could be prepared. For instance, on 20 November 2003 the authorities in Kharkiv oblast held a "residents' information day." The report on it noted that "those taking part included deputy heads of the *oblast* state administration, heads and deputy heads of *rayon* state administrations and city executive committees, as well as heads of enterprises, institutions and organizations of the region.[27] Interestingly enough, this tedious bureaucratic style is quite an accurate reflection of the wholly perfunctory attitude generally adopted by local authorities in response to such initiatives from the center, which were no less perfunctory to begin with. In other instances, such directives from the central authorities were sabotaged outright (the motives can only be guessed at)—needless to say, with no consequences for those responsible.

The first president of Ukraine, Leonid Kravchuk, who had been fairly successful in exploiting the slogans of the national-democratic opposition (Rukh) during the *perestroika* period, assisted personally in the organization of activities commemorating the 60th anniversary of the famine of 1932–33. The cause also gained considerable support from activists of the national-democratic movement of the late 1980s who became high-ranking government officials,[28] and from the diaspora, which gained a voice and moral weight in Ukrainian domestic politics for a time.[29] In September 1993, Kravchuk took part in an international conference on "The Famine of 1932–33 in Ukraine: Causes and Consequences." The leader's presence at the conference was considered substantial proof of the authorities' interest in the "revival of historical truth," although it may be assumed that the approach of the 1994 elections was also an (unadvertised) motive.

Still, the feigned or genuine enthusiasm of the supreme authorities and the civic courage of initiators close to those authorities had their limits. In May 1993, the official program of activities proposed by the organizing committee included an item on the trial of those responsible for the famine before a People's Court (Tribunal),[30] and the Days of Sorrow and Remembrance of Victims of the Famine were planned as a large-scale stage spectacle (with the best directorial talents—Yurii Illienko, Mykola Mashchenko, and Leonid Osyka—summoned to put it on). In July of the same year both the idea of the tribunal and the stage-spectacle component vanished from the program.[31]

With Leonid Kuchma's accession to power, the ideological sphere became less significant in government policy. (It was during his administration that the post of vice-premier for humanitarian issues was marginalized and, unlike in the previous period, became more technical. In the corridors of power, the holder of that office came to be known as "folksy" [*sharovarnyi*]). Accordingly, key dates and events took on narrowly pragmatic significance. It was difficult to get along without them, but they were more an auxiliary factor strengthening the authorities' hand than a principal element in the formation of their image, as had been the case in previous years. Still, this pragmatism had important systemic consequences; it was in Kuchma's times that the famine of 1932–33 was legitimized as part of official commemorative practice. In October 1998 the government adopted a special resolution on the 65th anniversary of the famine of 1932–33, and in November of that year President Kuchma signed a special decree establishing a Day of Remembrance of Famine Victims. In 2003 the Ukrainian authorities undertook foreign-policy initiatives in order to gain recognition of the famine of 1932–33 by the international community.

The social situation itself impelled the authorities to change their attitude: as the domestic political struggle grew more intense, the president's milieu had to devote more attention to gaining ideological legitimacy by exploiting the ideological construct generally known as the "national idea."

By the early 2000s, the famine of 1932–33 had become an important element of that idea. In February 2002 (a year of parliamentary elections regarded as a test of strength prior to the presidential elections of 2004), Leonid Kuchma signed a decree "On Measures Related to the 70th Anni-

versary of the Famine in Ukraine." The document is extraordinarily interesting because, on the one hand, it reproduced in detail all the ritual commemorative practices introduced by popular initiative during previous
years and, on the other, it contained standard bureaucratic rhetoric[32] intended to "recode" the play of symbols and seize the initiative from the
opposition.[33] On 6 December 2002, Kuchma issued a directive to establish
a Memorial to the Victims of Famine and Political Repression in Kyiv.[34]
The execution of that directive turned into an endless dispute between
various Kyiv offices, compounded by bureaucratic obstruction, that continues to this day.

The coming to power of political forces defining themselves as an opposition to the "Kuchma regime" was supposed to signal a change in the
attitude of the supreme authorities to the problem of the Famine of 1932–
33, if only because of the general image of the "new" administration and
the sincere desire of the new head of state to promote the restoration of
genuine historical memory. Nevertheless, the first declarations and actions
of the new authorities intended to commemorate the famine of 1932–33
and to endow it with genuine social significance were strangely reminiscent of the practices of the previous administration. On 4 November 2005,
President Viktor Yushchenko signed a decree "On Honoring the Victims
and Casualties of Famines in Ukraine," a mirror image of the standard
rhetoric found in similar documents issued by the Kuchma government. A
whole series of initiatives proposed in the document amounts to the same
standard scheme intended to ensure the "restoration of historical justice"
and "citizens' profound awareness of the causes and consequences of the
genocide of the Ukrainian people."[35] In 2005–2007 the presidential office
has issued seven 'commemorative' decrees devoted to 1932–1933.

What was the attitude to the problem on the part of the legislative authorities? In June 1993 the Association of Researchers of the Famine-
Genocide of 1932–33 in Ukraine initiated a proposal to establish a temporary commission of the Verkhovna Rada (Supreme Council or parliament)
of Ukraine. On the basis of documents available to scholars, the commission would determine that the famine was a crime against the Ukrainian
people, an act of outright genocide that had undermined the gene pool and
the spiritual and cultural potential of the Ukrainian nation. The matter was
to be referred to the International Court of Justice at the Hague.[36] "By way
of carrying out the decree of the president of Ukraine," the Institute of
Ukrainian History of the National Academy of Sciences of Ukraine proposed that the Verkhovna Rada "consider the question of the famine of
1932–33 in Ukraine and render an evaluation of that action that would not

be at variance with the truth … a situation has arisen that necessitates an official evaluation of the famine as a deliberate action on the part of a totalitarian state."[37]

The authors of the proposal referred to the conclusions of the American Congressional commission and the international commission of jurists and scholars (1988), noting that the official evaluation contained in the CC CPU resolution of 26 January 1990 "is not fully in accord with the truth." In July 1993 the organizing committee in charge of commemorating the 60th anniversary of the famine of 1932–33 (headed by Vice-Premier Mykola Zhulynsky) proposed to the leadership of the Verkhovna Rada that the problem be discussed at one of its sessions. A formal reply was received with a request to prepare a historical background paper and a draft parliamentary resolution, as well as to suggest someone qualified to speak about the famine. Further consultations with key figures in the leadership of the Verkhovna Rada made it apparent that there was no prospect of discussing the famine of 1932–33 during the current session. The elections of 1994, both parliamentary and presidential, were drawing near, and the deputies were interested in entirely different questions. Moreover, the composition of parliament, formed during the Soviet period, did not favor political scenarios promoting the thoroughgoing condemnation of the crimes of the communist regime. In addition, Ukraine was undergoing a large-scale economic and social crisis,[38] and social morale was already quite low. Consequently, when certain activists and amateur famine researchers insisted on emphasizing facts that were difficult to accept, the public response was one of sociopsychological rejection and fatigue with a surfeit of negativism.

In 2003, the situation looked different. By that time, the subject of the famine had reached the peak of its political and ideological significance. As in the past, the executive authorities approached the anniversary with restraint, although they mined the subject quite extensively to show their "unity with the people." One of the additional reasons for such restraint may well have been a desire not to worsen relations with Russia, especially in 2003, which was declared the year of Russia in Ukraine. Ideological rhetoric of the day often repeated such constructions as "the famine organized by Moscow" and references to centuries-old imperial (meaning Muscovite and Russian) policy in Ukraine. Popular writings of the time included works by authors such as A. Kulish.[39] The explanatory texts accompanying the photo exhibition on the walls of St. Michael's Golden-Domed Monastery in Kyiv, located near the monument to famine victims, include direct reminders that villages devastated by the famine of

1932–33 were repopulated by settlers from Russia. A work of popular history prepared by scholars (with a press run of 3,000 copies) indicates (with no reference to generalizations based on factual data) that the proletarians "sent to Ukrainian villages to collect grain" consisted mainly of ethnic Russians and that "military units and other power structures composed mainly of ethnic Russians were used to carry out forced collectivization, dekulakization and the requisition of foodstuffs in Ukraine during the famine period."[40] At the same time, parliament became extraordinarily active. Paradoxically enough, the very issue of the famine of 1932–33 became a cause of dissension in the ranks of the many-colored opposition, which included left- and right-wing elements. The communist faction, which formally belonged to the opposition, became the most active opponent of any consideration of the famine in parliament. Our Ukraine, a coalition of center-right forces recently allied with the communists in the struggle against the "Kuchma regime," became the major promoter of special parliamentary hearings. It was supported by some of the pro-presidential factions (with the consent of Leonid Kuchma, to be sure), deepening ideological fissures within the opposition. They were joined by the socialists, who thus violated the "unity of the left." The speaker of parliament, Volodymyr Lytvyn, also showed considerable activity. Since he was a historian by education, the organization of such hearings was a marvelous opportunity for him to consolidate his image as a scholar-politician and a nationally aware intellectual capable of reliving the tragedies of the past together with his people.

In February 2003 special hearings on the famine of 1932–33 were held at the Verkhovna Rada of Ukraine. A special session of parliament took place on 14 May 2003. The keynote speech was given by Vice-Premier Dmytro Tabachnyk, also an historian by education. By official standards, his declarations on behalf of the executive authorities were extraordinarily radical: in particular, the famine of 1932–33 was termed a "Ukrainian Holocaust."[41] Parliament approved an "Appeal to the Ukrainian People" in which the famine was called an act of genocide against the Ukrainian people.[42]

Also in 2003, the joint efforts of the Ministry of Foreign Affairs of Ukraine and the Ukrainian diaspora resulted in a number of initiatives (pursuant to a presidential decree) intended to obtain international recognition of the famine of 1932–33 as an act of genocide against the Ukrainian people. In September 2003, speaking at the 58th session of the UN General Assembly, Leonid Kuchma called on the delegates to render due respect to the memory of the famine victims. The Ministry of Foreign

Affairs and the Ukrainian mission to the UN prepared a draft resolution for the 58th session condemning the famine and terming it an act of genocide, but the attempt to secure adoption of the special resolution proved unsuccessful. The Ukrainian authorities had to content themselves with a joint declaration of 36 states that did not contain the word "genocide." It is hard to say whether this was an achievement or a failure: in any case, the events of 1932–33 became an object of (not particularly acute) attention on the part of the international community, but the desired resonance was not achieved. It is safe to predict that future efforts to secure recognition of the famine of 1932–33 as an act of genocide, especially on the international level, will be no less intense. President Yushchenko's above-mentioned decree includes a point on promoting "additional" measures intended to obtain "recognition by the international community of the famine of 1932–33 in Ukraine as a genocide of the Ukrainian people and one of the greatest tragedies in human history."[43] In November 2006 the Ukrainian Parliament has adopted the Law On Mane-Made Famine of 1932–1933 in Ukraine. Article 1 of the Law stated that 'The Man-Made Famine of 1932–1933 in Ukraine is a genocide of the Ukrainian People.' According to the Article 2 of the Law public denial of the Man-Made Famine of 1932–1933 was proclaimed as a contamination of the memory of the millions of victims' and 'humiliation of the dignity of the Ukrainian people.' The *Holodomor* 'denial' was labeled as 'unlawful' act, however, no further clarifications or legal provisions were introduced.[44]

Having emerged in Ukrainian intellectual and ideological space in the mid-1980s as part of the general critique of the Soviet past, the subject of the famine of 1932–33 became an important functional element of political disputes and ideological differences. It solidly established itself among popular historical notions of the Ukrainian past and became part of "textbook" history. The speed with which it entered collective memory is to be explained above all by its utility both for the incumbent authorities and for many of those who aspired to the role of opposition. At the same time, the efforts of those who helped construct images of the famine of 1932–33 at the professional scholarly or political/ideological levels found an echo in the segment of the population for which the famine was still part of inherited "popular memory" and those who were direct witnesses to the famine of 1946–47. Thanks to this, the already constructed memory of 1932–33 became more organic and natural, shedding the formal characteristics of "invented tradition."

Naturally, such a large-scale project could not have been completed without scholars. Their contribution to the formal scholarly elaboration of the problem can be grasped by means of the following figure: by 2001, the bibliographic total of publications about the famine of 1932–33 amounted to more than 6,000 items.[45] The scholarly study of the subject and its presence in collective consciousness are gradually drawing apart: in the first instance, there is a growing dominance of elements of rational analysis, while the second is stuck fast at the level of "lacrimogenesis"[46] and remembrance of a great national tragedy. To be sure, for many Ukrainians, regardless of ethnic origin, interest in the subject is also a matter of profound moral and ethical significance based on the desire to render due respect to the memory of the victims of the terror-famine. That said, it should be noted that precisely on the level of everyday consciousness one does not encounter any explicit demands, even symbolic ones, to punish those responsible for organizing the famine.

On the level of practical politics, the subject of the famine remains a matter of political speculation and pragmatic exploitation; its moral significance becomes lost in political squabbles or is discredited by those attempting to exploit it. It is not identified in social consciousness with high moral and ethical standards. For politicians, references to "national traumas" generally serve to promote immediate political goals and mobilize the populace in the short term. Naturally, Ukrainian politicians are no exception to the norm.

Turning to long-term prospects, the evolution of collective national memory with regard to the "revived" subject of the famine of 1932–33, as analyzed in this article, attests to the complete absence of strategies both on the level of public organizations and on that of the state policy of remembrance. We are not speaking here of anything resembling the huge "Holocaust industry," for which Ukraine has neither the financial resources nor the requisite cultural tradition (unless the latter can be invented). One can hardly speak even of something on the scale of the Institute of National Memory created by Ukraine's closest neighbors, the Poles. Attempts to establish similar structures in Ukraine look like inept parodies. In May 2002 the people's deputy Lev Lukianenko presented Vice-Premier Volodymyr Semynozhenko with an official project for the establishment of a Research Institute on the Genocide of the Ukrainian People. He proposed an institute with a staff of 30 (20 of whom would be scholarly researchers and assistants) with an annual budget of approx. 500,000 hryvnias (close to US $90,000 at the time). It would concentrate on three areas of research: 1) *holodomory* ("man-made famines"), 2) large-scale repressions, and 3) deportations. The proposal was not approved, for, according to an official note from the Institute of History of the Academy of Sciences of Ukraine, "the problem of large-scale repressions and deportations is being studied as part of the program 'Rehabilitated by History,'" which already comprised "hundreds of research works and several defended candidate and doctoral dissertations. Dozens of books and many hundreds of articles have been published." The same document proposed the establishment of a Center for the Study of Famines as part of the Institute of Ukrainian History, with a staff of ten researchers.[47] As a result, the above-mentioned Center for the Study of Genocide in Ukraine, with a staff of three, was indeed established. It constitutes the most active and productive element of the Association of Researchers of Famines in Ukraine. The center, which functions as a subunit of the Institute of Ukrainian History, is currently occupied with the subject of "The Genocide of National, Ethnic and Religious Groups in Ukraine in the 20th Century: A Historical, Political and Legal Analysis."

On 11 July 2005 President Viktor Yushchenko signed a Decree on the Establishment of an Institute of National Memory, the realization of which turned into an extraordinarily unedifying spectacle involving politicians, businessmen and community activists. The clash of personal ambitions, material interests and political speculation with regard to the institute itself, its ideology, location, financing, and so on serves to discredit an idea of uncommon importance to society. By the end of 2006 the institute still exists in a form of two rooms in the Cabinet of Ministers premises with the staff comprised of the director and his two deputies.

The new Ukrainian political and intellectual elites are not prepared to mobilize public opinion by exercising their potential for symbolic politics (which have their subjective and objective limitations in Ukraine) in a well-considered and consistent manner. In some cases, the elites mistakenly consider symbolic politics to be of secondary importance; in others, their purely ethical or narrow ideological interests limit the social significance of particular symbols.

NOTES

1 In the present context, the term "culture" refers to certain standards of social behavior, communication, collective reactions, traditions and hierarchies of values.

2 H. Hrabovych, "Ukraïna: pidsumky stolittia,"[Ukraine: The Summary of the Century] *Krytyka*, No. 11 (1999): 7. Professor Grabowicz disagrees with my treatment of his comments quoted in this article, especially with the term "conspiracy theory." He explained in a private discussion (August 2005) that he was referring not so much to a deliberate rational strategy on the part of the authorities as to the general attitude of the current establishment. The establishment he had in mind was of course that of the Ku-

chma period, but it seems to my understanding that the post-Kuchma authorities are re-
acting in the same way. What psychologists call the "dynamic stereotype" remains unchanged. My comments in the present article refer only to Professor Grabowicz's text,
not to his subsequent remarks.

3 M. Riabchuk, "Pot'omkins'kyi iuvilei, abo shche raz pro amnistiiu, amneziiu ta 'spad-
koiemnist' postkomunistychnoï vlady v Ukraïni" [Potiomkin's Jubilee or Once Again
About Amnesty, Amnesia and 'Legacy' of Post-Communist Power In Ukraine] *Suchasnist'*, No. 3 (2004): 74.

4 S. Kul'chyts'kyi, "Demohrafichni naslidky holodu-henotsydu 1933 r. v Ukraïni,"
[Demographic Consequences of Famine-Genocide of 1933 in Ukraine] in: *Henotsyd
ukraïns'koho narodu: istorychna pam'iat' ta politychno-pravova otsinka. Mizhnarodna
naukovo-teoretychna konferentsiia. Materialy* (Kyiv, 25 November 2000) (Kyiv and
New York: Vydavnyctvo M.P. Kots, 2003), p. 5.

5 The basic text of this article was written in 2004, but the term "current authorities" still
applies to much of the present-day political milieu, especially those from the middle
ranks of the post-communist *nomenklatura*.

6 The "Nuremberg-2" Ukrainian National Committee to Organize an International Trial of
the CPSU was established in March 1996 at the initiative of the All-Ukrainian Society of
Political Prisoners and Victims of Repressions, the Association of Famine Researchers,
and the Vasyl Stus Memorial Society. The public tribunal was held in Lithuania in 2000
but had no serious resonance whatever in Ukraine, its time had passed.

7 The subject of lustrations emerged immediately after the events of the autumn and
winter of 2004, which came to be known as the Orange Revolution, but it was regarded
as an attempt to settle accounts with the old regime and came to nought, receiving neither broad popular support nor the blessing of the new oligarchs.

8 Quite interesting in this regard are the analytical studies of pupils' papers on Ukrainian
history written for a contest during the 1998–99 school year. Among the negative aspects of Ukrainian history, pupils clearly identified the "bloody specter of communism"
and the "totalitarian Bolshevik system" *(sic)*. See Fisher Claudia "Chy mozhna pysaty
pro istoriiu bez heroïchnoho pafosu?" [Is it possible to write about history without pa-
thos?] *Doba*, No. 2 (2002): 9.

9 The mere reading of certain archival documents about the famine of 1932–33 can suffice to bring about psychological trauma.

10 See O. Movchan, "Holod 1921–1923 rr.: 'heneral'na repetytsiia' 1933-ho," [Famine of
1922-1923: A Dress Rehearsal of 1933] in *Holod 1932–1933 rokiv v Ukraïni: prychyny
i naslidky* [Famine 1932-1933 in Ukraine. Reasons and results] (Kyiv: Naukova
Dumka, 2003): 220–245.

11 O.M. Veselova, V.I.Marochko, and O.M Movchan, eds., *Holodomory v Ukraïni 1921–
1923, 1932–1933, 1946–1947. Zlochyny proty narodu*, [Man-made Famines in Ukraine
1921-1923, 1932 – 1933, 1946-1947. [Crimes Against the People] (Kyiv and New
York: Vydavnyctvo M.P. Kots, 2002)

12 Ibid., p. 257 (emphasis added).

13 It is worth mentioning the book *Ethnocide of Ukrainians in the U.S.S.R. (The Ukrainian
Herald,* Nos. 7–8 (Baltimore, Md.: Smoloskyp Publishers, 1978), an English translation
of Ukrainian *samvydav* (self-published) materials probably written by Stepan Khmara.
The famine of 1932–33 receives particular attention in the chapter devoted to the
demographic losses of ethnic Ukrainians during the years of Soviet rule.

14 The Russian-language CC CPU document "On Propagandistic Measures to Counteract the Anti-Soviet Campaign Unleashed by Reactionary Centers of the Ukrainian Emigration in Connection with Food-Supply Difficulties in Ukraine in the Early 1930s" states openly that "it is inconvenient for us to enter into direct polemics with foreign nationalist scribblers on this question." Cited according to Dzh. Meis (James Mace), "Diial'nist' Komisiï Konhresu SShA z vyvchennia holodu v Ukraïni," [Work of the Commission of the USA Congress on Study of Famine in Ukraine] in *Holod 1932–1933*, p. 805.

15 James Mace settled in Ukraine in the 1990s. He died in Kyiv on 2 May 2004. His fairly explicit endorsement of the interpretation of the famine of 1932–33 as an act of genocide, which was based on personal conviction and clearly made no pretense of "objectivity," was exploited by politicians and political writers of the national-patriotic camp as an argument advanced by an "unbiased" professional historian and a foreigner to boot.

16 *Mezhdunarodnaia komissiia po rassledovaniiu goloda na Ukraine 1932–1933 godov. Itogovyi otchet 1990* [International Commission for Investigation of the Famine in Ukraine of 1932-1933. Final report 1990] (Kiev: 1992), p. 15.

17 *Holod 1932–1933 rokiv na Ukraïni: ochyma istorykiv, movoiu dokumentiv* [Famine of 1932-1933 in Ukraine. Through the eyes of historians, in the language of documents] (Kyiv: Politvydav Ukrainy, 1990).

18 S. Kul'chyts'kyi, "Demohrafichni naslidky holodu-henotsydu 1933 r. v Ukraïni," [Demographic Consequences of Famine-Genocide of 1933 in Ukraine] in *Henotsyd ukraïns'koho narodu: istorychna pam'iat' ta polityko-pravova otsinka (Mizhnarodna naukovo-teoretychna konferentsiia, Kyiv, 25 lystopada 2000 r.)* (Kyiv and New York: Vydavnyctvo M. Kots, 2003), p. 20.

19 "U TsK Kompartiï Ukraïny. Pravda pro narodnu trahediiu," [In the Central Committee of the Communist Party of Ukraine. The Truth About People's Tragedy] *Radians'ka Ukraïna*, 7 February 1990.

20 *33-i: Holod. Narodna knyha-memorial* [The Year 33: A Famine. A People's Book-Memorial] (Kyiv: Radians'kyj pys'mennyk, 1991).

21 S. V. Kul'chyts'kyi, "33-i: holod. Zaproshuiemo do stvorennia knyhy-memorialu," [The Year 3: A Famine. An Invitation to Take Part in the Book-Memorial] *Sil's'ki visti*, (9 December 1988).

22 Dzh. Meis "Henotsyd v Ukraïni—dovedeno!" [The genocide in Ukraine – Proven!] *Den'*, (22 November 2000).

23 Suffice it to note that ten publications on the famine were sponsored by Marian Kots, an American publisher of Ukrainian descent.

24 M. Riabchuk "Pot'omkins'kyi iuvilei, abo shche raz pro amnistiiu, amneziiu ta 'spad koiemnist' postkomunistychnoï vlady v Ukraïn." [Potiomkin's Jubilee or Once Again About Amnesty, Amnesia and 'Legacy' of Post-Communist Power In Ukraine] *Suchasnist'*, No. 3. (2004): 77.

25 For example, in President Leonid Kuchma's appeal to the Ukrainian people of 24 November 2003 in connection with the Day of Remembrance of Victims of Famine and Political Repression, we read: "The Famine and mass political repressions planned and carried out by the communist regime placed the very existence of the nation in question." See the official Internet site of President L. D. Kuchma of Ukraine, www.president.gov.ua/activity/zayavinterv/speakto/114407592.html.

26 The central organ of the Communist Party of Ukraine, the newspaper *Komunist*, periodically printed letters and appeals from pensioners, articles, and even humorous pieces (!) in which the famine of 1932–33 figured in the context of the current situation of most of the Ukrainian population, most notably pensioners. When the communists were preparing public actions in 2000, one of their slogans was "No to the sale of land and famine in 2000!" For a detailed discussion, see S. Kostyleva, "Novitnia kompartiina presa Ukraïny pro storinky radians'koho mynuloho," [The Contemporary Ukrainian Communist Media Speak About Soviet Past] in *Henotsyd ukraïns'koho narodu: istorychna pam'iat' ta polityko-pravova otsinka* [Genocide of Ukrainian people: Historical Memory and Political/Legal Assessment] (2003), pp. 573–82.

27 [Official Site of the President of Ukraine Accessed 23 June 2004] www.president.gov. ua/authofstate/prezidlist/localrada/diyalcommonely21/ 209325915.htm.

28 To name some of them: Mykola Zhulynsky, vice-premier of Ukraine in 1993; Ivan Dziuba, minister of culture; Dmytro Pavlychko, head of the Verkhovna Rada Commission on Foreign Affairs; Ivan Drach, head of the council of the Society for Relations with Ukrainians Abroad. See the Decree of the President of Ukraine "Pro zakhody u zv'iazku z 60-my rokovynamy holodomoru v Ukraïni," [On Measures in Connection with the 60th Anniversary of the Famine in Ukraine] *Holos Ukraïny,* (20 March 1993).

29 Given the composition of the organizing committee responsible for preparing and carrying out the program of activities in connection with the 60th anniversary of the famine in Ukraine, it is possible to identify the organizations whose ideas were voiced by representatives of the national-democratic forces: the Ukrainian Congress Committee of America, the Ukrainian National Aid Association (USA), the Ukrainian Canadian Congress, the Ukrainian World Congress (Canada), and the Australian Federation of Ukrainian Organizations.

30 The group organizing the tribunal included the selfsame representatives of the writers' "fronde" of the late 1980s who had enjoyed a fairly comfortable existence under the "macabre communist regime" and established themselves just as comfortably among the post-communist authorities: Ivan Drach, Pavlo Movchan and Volodymyr Yavorivsky. This very circumstance may be assumed to have deprived the idea of a public tribunal of the requisite moral weight.

31 "Protokol narady u vitse-prem'ier ministra Ukraïny, Holovy Orhkomitetu z pidhotovky ta provedennia zakhodiv u zv'iazku z 60-my rokovynamy holodomoru v Ukraïni 17 travnia 1993" [Minutes of the Meeting at the Deputy Prime-Minister's Office, the Head of the Organizational Committee for 60th Anniversary of Man-Made Famine in Ukraine, 17 May, 1993]; "Plan osnovnykh zakhodiv u zv'iazku z 60-my rokovynamy holodomoru v Ukraïni (2 chervnia 1993 roku)" (documents from the private archive of S. V. Kulchytsky).

32 "Pro zakhody u zv'iazku z 70-my rokovynamy holodomoru v Ukraïni," *Uriadovyi kur'ier* (29 March 2002).

33 The document includes detailed instructions on the organization of activities, down to such details as placing flowers before monuments, memorial tablets and places of burial of famine victims. Also noteworthy is the section of the decree proposing that local authorities "increase attention to the daily needs of citizens who survived the famine, improve medical and social services for them, help them tend their household gardens, and find ways of providing material assistance to such people." Those who drafted the decree were aware of the impossibility of carrying out this section of it (and many others).

34 There was even a contest of architectural and sculptural designs, which presented quite a sorry spectacle from the aesthetic viewpoint.

35 Ukaz Prezydenta Ukraïny "Pro vshanuvannia zhertv ta postrazhdalykh vid holodomoriv v Ukraïni." (Copy of original document from Author's archive).

36 "Propozytsiï shchodo vshanuvannia 60-kh rokovyn holodomoru v Ukraïni" (document from the private archive of S. V. Kulchytsky).

37 Document from the private archive of S. V. Kulchytsky.

38 This may be illustrated by the expense of the planned activities themselves: one international scholarly conference alone, scheduled for September 1993, was to cost 12 million *kupono-karbovantsi*, while the total budget for the Days of Sorrow was to be 288,580,000 *kupono-karbovantsi* (US \$2.9 million) (draft estimates from the private archive of S. V. Kulchytsky).

39 See A. Kulish, *Knyha pam'iati ukraïntsiv: Ukraïna 1932–1933 rr. Korotkyi perelik zlochyniv moskovs'koho imperializmu v Rusi-Ukraïni* [A Book of Ukrainian memory: Ukraine, 1932–33: A brief account of the crimes of muscovite imperialism in Rus'-Ukraine] (Kharkiv, 1996)

40 See P.P. Panchenko, et al., *Smertiu smert' podolaly: Holodomor v Ukraïni 1932–1933* [The Death Overcame the Death. Man-Made Famine in Ukraine in 1932–1933] (Kyiv: Ukraina, 2003), p. 48.

41 Tabachnyk began his career as a professional historian and wrote both his candidate and doctoral dissertations on the political repression of the 1920s and 1930s. The defense of his doctoral dissertation took place when he was already a senior government official and became one of the first instances of the attainment of an academic degree by a government official of the highest rank.

42 The communist faction boycotted the session. Characteristically, the pro-presidential parliamentary majority also ignored it. Two hundred twenty-six out of 450 deputies voted in favor of the appeal.

43 In March 2006 the upper house of the Polish Diet (Senate) approved a resolution recognizing the famine of 1932–33 as an act of genocide against the Ukrainian people (Ukrinform, 17 March 2006).

44 *Vidomosti Verkhovnoï Rady*, No. 50 (2006): 504.

45 L.M. Burjan and I.E. Rikun, eds., *Holodomor v Ukraïni. 1932–1933 rr.: Bibliohrafichnyi pokazhchyk* [Famine in Ukraine 1932-1933. A bibliography] (Odesa and Lviv: ODNB im. M. Gor'kogo, Instytut istorii Ukrainy NAN Ukrainy, Fundatsija ukrainoznavchykh studij Avstralii, 2001).

46 This term was used by the American historian Mark von Hagen to characterize a tendency in Ukrainian historiography of the 1990s associated with elements of incessant "mournful lamentation" over the losses and sufferings of Ukrainians since time immemorial. Let us note that this is not an invention or significant feature of Ukrainian historiography alone. The myth of the great suffering of this or that nation is common to almost all historiographies of the period of "national revival" not only in Europe but throughout the world (indeed, it is an indispensable component of the "national revival" scenario). It enjoys considerable popularity in post-Soviet space.

47 Inventory control card no. 4452/2, dated 12 July 2002; document from the private archive of S. V. Kulchytsky.

The Struggle for Official Recognition of 'Displaced' Group Memories in Post-Soviet Estonia

MEIKE WULF

"All history is the history of past politics"
F. R. Ankersmit

INTRODUCTORY COMMENTS

The revision of the events of the Second World War played a crucial role before and after the change of regime in post-socialist and post-Soviet societies. I argue that this is largely because the interpretation of certain historical events strongly affected the reconfiguration of collective identities in Central and Eastern Europe after 1989.[1] Daniel Levy points to this very connection, when he writes that "historical revisionism does not directly cause new identities, but it does generate public attention to identity deficits and suggest alternative frames of identification... It is in this capacity that historical revisionism has come to serve as a crucial link between collective memory and the nation, as the crisis of collective identities continues."[2]

Turning to the case study of Estonia, the overriding question, therefore, is how the transformed sociopolitical and spatial frameworks affect post-Soviet identities.[3] In this article I examine three separate landmarks of Estonia's contemporary "historical culture" that are all examples of the continuous reinterpretation of historical facts that has taken place since the society underwent political reframing;[4] namely: 1) the work of the Estonian Occupation Museum; 2) the "Estonian International Commission for the Investigation of Crimes against Humanity"; and 3) the conflict over memorial monuments to different veteran groups in Estonia. All these cases concern public ways of dealing with the enduring ambiguities of Estonia's recent past; particularly with the controversial issues of indigenous collaboration and complicity with the Soviet regime and the Nazi occupiers, as well as with traumatic memories of the war and postwar years. Within the realm of memory politics they represent attempts at agreeing on a codification of how to officially remember Estonia's past. In the background of my discussion stands the question of *what* makes them instances of "historical revisionism." To scrutinize this question, I consider historical revisionism in relation to five different "public uses" of history, namely the moral, ideological, political, existential and emblematic dimension of history.[5]

HISTORICAL REVISIONISM

I begin by proposing that revising conventional historical interpretations in the light of subsequent knowledge is an essential part of what Alexander von Humboldt termed "the historian's task"; that is, the (self-) reflexivity of a scholar and his or her discipline. In this the interpretation of historical facts is not simply corrected and erased; it is rather a case of adding layers to an existing body of knowledge. To put it differently, the lens through which historical facts are viewed is "exchanged" for a more fitting one. Temporal distance and a somewhat more "detached" perspective may also lead to the revision of past interpretations. Therefore, I understand the term "revisionism" as an effort to update the interpretation of historical facts in the light of new findings (e.g., the opening of archive collections, the release of formerly classified material, etc.). Hence, the revision of history is dependent on the availability of sources, and on the researcher's position in time and space.

Albeit the term historical revisionism has acquired a pejorative meaning, implying manipulation and abuse, I do not view it as something negative *per se*. And even though David Irving can be termed a historical revisionist (or more precisely a "Holocaust revisionist"), I nevertheless contend that not all historical revisionists are of Irving's *contour*.[6] Irving's case, which certainly represents the extreme end of the scale, may however serve us in the attempt to define historical revisionism.[7] Levy, who also does not view historical revisionism as something intrinsically negative, notes how the "hunger for memory" observable since the 1980s has been accompanied by a proliferation of historical revisionism, and that its objective is to question the foundational myths of the nation.[8] "More specifically, the object of historical revisionism is to debunk those mythical substructures upon which collective identities rely. By attacking these mythological foundations, revisionists thematize issues that were not previously discussed, and render them intelligible for rational debate."[9]

While Levy studies France, Germany, Israel, and the US, I turn to Central Eastern Europe to address the question of whether this region is witnessing a specific kind of historical revisionism (that is, if the surge of historical revisionism has been exceptionally strong there). I begin my answer to this question with Shari J. Cohen's pertinent analysis of the "amorphous nature of these societies emerging from communist domination." Cohen notes it is important to recognize "the lack of unifying ideologies, a devastating legacy left by the 50 or 70 year experience of Leninist domination. These are societies trying to create new polities without common standards of moral or historical judgment."[10]

In my description of the landmarks of post-Soviet Estonian historical culture, I illustrate how the experience of alternating military occupations and the legacy of two totalitarianisms, makes the assessment of the past a highly complicated matter.

MEMORY POLITICS OR DIFFERENT USES OF PUBLIC HISTORY

Apart from historians rewriting history for and within the academic domain, there are many different societal groups using history for their ends in the public sphere. The term "user" signifies intermediaries such as politicians and teachers, disseminating historical facts, as well as the wider audience of consumers (e.g., newspaper readership, students, etc.). In addition, local historians produce history outside of mainstream academia. The term "use" implies that, alongside ethically and morally decent ways of utilizing history, misuses or abuses also exist. This is intimately connected to the question of principles, rules, and standards of "history production," and to whose or what ends historical facts are employed.[11] However, uses of history cannot be equated with manipulation or deception *per se*.[12] Gallerano holds that the "public use" of history is "all that developed outside of the domain of scientific research in its strictest sense, outside the history of historians which is usually written by scholars and intended for a very limited segment of the population."[13] However the academic domain does not exist in isolation from other ideological and political currents in the society that surrounds it.

I argue that historical revisionism is more connected to the public use of history than confined only to the scientific community, or more precisely, it is situated at the interface of the two and targeted (more) towards a wider public. It is in the public sphere that different societal groups attempt to gain recognition for their privately held memories (individual or group); it is this struggle for public recognition which is intrinsically connected to questions of authorship, authenticity, custodianship and ultimately identity.[14] The different dimensions of history emerge in this "rational debate" over the past. I will identify four dimensions of public history that I hold to be relevant to the topic of historical revisionism (whereby I understand these differentiations to be only of ideal typical nature, as in practice all dimensions overlap in various ways).

MORAL DIMENSION

The moral dimension of history is a reaction to past insults, and can be found in the endeavor of a political elite to put right historical wrongs. In the public discourse surrounding Estonia's accessions to NATO and the European Union, the narrative of "being wronged by history" appeared in moralizing arguments of betrayal and retribution. For instance, it was occasionally stated that Western Europe bears a moral responsibility towards Estonia (since the Allies did not intervene and spare them their fate in 1944/45).[15]

IDEOLOGICAL DIMENSION

The use of history by intellectuals for the national cause can be defined as an ideological dimension of history (for the purpose of national regeneration, for example). Such an ideological take on history was prevalent in the program of the Estonian People's Front (In Estonian, *Eestimaa Rahvarinne,* or RR), mobilizing mass-support for Estonia's independence. Both the ideological and the moral dimensions of history are linked to ideas of absolute truth. Here, history is not a gradually evolving process, but a story of mistakes that need rectifying. Quintessentially this presupposes history as a metaphysical entity that is intrinsically moral. But can history be wrong or right in the first place?[16]

POLITICAL DIMENSION

The political dimension denotes the rhetorically convincing use of historical arguments to tackle or attack existing socio-political shortcomings. In this way, historical arguments are employed in a comparative, metaphorical fashion (often taken out of their original context). An overbearing political dimension translates into an inflationary use of historical arguments in the public arena (for instance in political propaganda). The concept of politics of history (In German, *Geschichtspolitik*), which views history as fundamentally political and focuses on the formation and imposition of historical interpretations and models of identification in the official domain, is useful in highlighting the fact that history is essentially political.[17] In the same vein, Gallerano insists that "history is used above all as an instrument of the day-to-day political battle."[18] Both the ideological and political dimensions of history are employed to claim and legitimize political power. I argue that historical revisionism is intimately linked to the ideological and political dimensions of history.

EXISTENTIAL DIMENSION

Fourthly, history plays a pertinent role for the identity of a community (for example "remembering in order not to forget"—In Hebrew, *Zahor Lo Tishkah*). When a society is facing external or internal pressures of cultural homogenization (caused for example by inter-ethnic conflict, foreign occupation, etc.), the existential dimension of history becomes more pronounced. As a counter-history it will be largely confined to the private or semi-private sphere (for instance the opposition movement and dissident circles in Soviet Estonia). The example of the heated conflict over memorial monuments to different veteran groups, discussed in a later section, demonstrates that the existential use of history can also be played out in the public sphere.

In what follows, I will delineate different landmarks of the historical culture in post-Soviet Estonia, while paying close attention to the different dimensions of public history as previously outlined.

The entry hall of the Estonian Occupation Museum (2003)

In the main entry hall of the Estonian Occupation Museum two massive iron locomotive *replicas* can be found serving as a gateway to the exhibition. The models are identical copies of each other, except that one displays a red star, whereas the other bears the swastika. An artistic expression, which places both regimes on parallel tracks, raising the pertinent question of the dangers inherent in historical comparison.

THE ESTONIAN OCCUPATION MUSEUM: A CLAIM FOR VICTIMHOOD

The Estonian Occupation Museum provides a case in point of the political dimension of history and the quagmires that historical comparisons often entail. Battered suitcases, prison doors, aluminum cutlery, a refugee boat, a range of trivial objects of daily use, as well as letters and newspapers, constitute the core of the exhibition.[19] In the words of one interviewee, who was involved in planning the Museum from the very start, it "has to be like a monument or a tombstone for the many people who have not returned. And I believe that for the people who still live, but went through this period, this [museum] would be something to make them feel a little proud; that something like this is built for them."[20]

The museum documents mainly the suffering that Estonians endured at the hands of the Soviets between 1940/41 and 1944–1991, while paying little attention to the victims of the Holocaust in Estonia or questions of indigenous collaboration with the foreign regimes. This focus is consistent with the fact that the repression by the Soviet authorities stands out as *the* main public concern regarding Estonia's recent past.[21] This only changed under international pressure, leading to a "prescribed public remembrance" of the events surrounding the German occupation.[22] Why public debate about the occupations in post-1991 Estonia mainly concerned the Soviet terror, while Estonian collaboration during the Nazi occupation was hardly touched upon, can in part be understood as an overreaction against the long-endured bias in Soviet historiography, which focused mainly on the atrocities committed during the Nazi occupation of Estonia.[23] A further cause may lie in Russia's failure to acknowledge the events of 1939–41 (specifically, the recognition of the annexation of Estonia in 1940 as an illegitimate act).

Equivalents to the Estonian Occupation Museum can be found in Riga (the Documentation Centre of Totalitarianism, TSDC, established in 1998) and in the Museum of Genocide Victims located in the cellars of the former KGB headquarters in Vilnius (founded in 1992).[24] It appears that in post-Soviet societies an idiosyncratic logic or perspective is operational: the fact that these societies experienced both the Nazi and the Soviet occupations leads to a specific interpretation of history different from that which prevails in Western European countries, which were "only" occupied by Nazi Germany. For if one were to pass by a "museum of occupation" in Amsterdam, Paris, or Oslo, one could conclude from the name alone that the museum concentrates on mass-deportations of Jews, communists, and anti-German résistance fighters; but the curators of the

Estonian Occupation Museum clearly adhere to a different logic. Here, it is the "national suffering" of ethnic Estonians during the various occupations that takes center stage (that is, mainly the Soviet occupations).[25]

At the opening of the museum the Russian Foreign Ministry issued a statement that the museum's creation was informed by a political bias, in equating fascist Germany and the former Soviet Union.[26] Although it is crucial to avoid the pitfalls of historical comparison, such as attempting to relativize individual or collective suffering and injustices by means of such comparison, it is also necessary to bear in mind that comparison deals with both resemblance and difference, and that to compare does not mean to justify. Hence, the crimes committed in the name of Hitler's Germany cannot be explained by the atrocities committed in the name of Stalin, or *vice versa*.[27] In the mainstream academic debate in the former FRG, comparative approaches to understanding the totalitarianisms of Stalinism and Hitlerism were frowned upon, and left on the fringes.[28] After the break-up of the Soviet bloc and the German reunification, direct comparisons between the systems became more *en vogue*; this was particularly the case in the debates emerging in newly independent Eastern Europe. In the public debate in post-Soviet Estonia, there was little hesitation about comparing the two systems, which would indicate that it is not the victims of the Nazi occupation (that is, Jewish survivors or communist sympathizers) who dominated the debate, but victims of Stalinism and those that believed that the Nazi occupation was the lesser of two evils.[29] In response to a speech by the Latvian President Vike-Freiberga (at the International Forum on Preventing Genocide in Stockholm in 2004) Ephraim Zuroff, head of the Jerusalem office of the Simon Wiesenthal Centre, complains that some political leaders utilize the destruction of European Jewry as a background to speak about other tragedies, such as communist crimes. More specific, Zuroff opines that the mass deportations of Latvians were not a case of genocide, and warns of a false symmetry that upgrades communist crimes by placing them on an equal footing with the Holocaust.[30]

THE ESTONIAN INTERNATIONAL COMMISSION FOR THE INVESTIGATION OF CRIMES AGAINST HUMANITY

Whereas the museum's primary objective is to collect and exhibit artefacts, memoirs and eyewitness accounts to document the periods of occupation, the Estonian International Commission for the Investigation of Crimes against Humanity (hereafter "Commission"), was established by the Estonian government in 1998 to produce objective research reports on the same periods, clearly tailored towards an international readership.[31] It was decided at the outset that a team of researchers selected by the Commission's board would first investigate crimes against citizens of Estonia (and on the territory of the Estonian Republic) committed during the German occupation, and subsequently explore crimes committed during the Soviet occupations. The report attributes overall responsibility for the crimes committed during the German occupation to the Germans, but it identifies individual Estonians who served in the Estonian military units, Estonian Police Battalions, and Estonian Security Police, stating that they shared responsibility through their own actions in and outside of Estonia.[32] Moreover, the Commission holds all members of the Estonian Political Police responsible for war crimes, and asserts that members of the Estonian self-government were also responsible for war crimes committed in Estonia. It is noteworthy that the Commission debunks the myth of a "just war" of the Estonian auxiliary police (In Estonian, *Omakaitse*, or *OK*) in 1941 by emphasizing that the bulk of the killing of alleged communists during the early stages of the German occupation happened at the hands of the Estonian auxiliary police, and that, in assisting the *Einsatzkommando* 1 A, the *OK* played an active role in the extermination of the local Jewry in 1941–42.[33] The report also mentions that the majority of members of the "destruction battalions" were ethnic Estonians, thus touching on another taboo—that of the fratricidal war in Estonia.[34] The report ends on the broader note that historical events made Estonia a "victim nation," but states that this "does not preclude acts of perpetration."

According to its statutory report, the Commission is not intended to be a fully-fledged "Truth Commission." Former President Lennart Meri, who headed the Commission until 2001, explained its two-pronged approach: "It reflects our hope in Estonia, that shining the bright light of truth on some of the tragedies of the past will not only contribute to reconciliation within our society and its further reintegration into the international community of nations, but also prevent the repetition of such tragedies elsewhere."[35]

From this it is evident that the Commission is not a juridical or prosecutorial body, which is why it did not initiate the tracking down of those few Estonian perpetrators still alive, who were identified in the report on the German occupation (published online in 2001), in order to extradite and try them. However, one may argue that the Commission is not "just" a scholarly body of politicians and journalists, since it is a state-funded institution. Hence, the question remains as to why the Commission did not instruct the relevant governmental body to follow up these cases. In this context Zuroff rebuked the contemporary Estonian Security Police for not investigating the suspected criminals identified in the Commission's report. Already in autumn 1991, he made a failed attempt to arrest the Estonian Evald Mikson (who was living in Iceland at the time) for war crimes committed during the Nazi occupation of Estonia.[36] More recently, Zuroff presented the Estonian Security Police with a list of 16 members of the 36th Police Battalion, who according to the Commission's report participated in the execution of Jews in Belarus in 1942; but, contrary to the Commission's findings, the Estonian Security Police concluded that they had no evidence to confirm this indictment. In obvious frustration, Zuroff then announced a reward of US $10,000 to anyone providing information leading to the arrest of these men.[37] His effort to place an advertisement reading "during the Holocaust, Estonians murdered Jews in Estonia as well as in other countries" in local newspapers, however, came to nothing.[38] Consequently, in his reports for the years 2001 and 2003, Zuroff classified Estonia as making "insufficient and/or unsuccessful efforts to prosecute perpetrators of the Holocaust."[39]

Compared to the objectively written report of the Commission, the paper of a younger Estonian historian (who worked in the Commission's research team on the German occupation) presented at a conference in Sweden on "Collaboration and Resistance in Estonia 1940–44," seemed slightly more biased, as he deliberately only included the genocide of Estonian Jews, while choosing not to deal with the fate of those thousands of European Jews who were deported to Estonia to perish in the camps there.[40] This limitation allowed him to claim that less than 1,000 Estonian Jews were killed in Estonia during the German occupation. Moreover, he suggested that the "evacuation" of approximately 500 Estonian Jews to Russia by the Soviets can be termed the "first act of the Holocaust." All this led him to conclude that Estonia, although it was the first country to declare itself "free of Jews" (in German, *judenfrei*), was also the country in which the smallest number of Jews was exterminated under German occupation. His presentation stands as an example of a highly selective and ethno-centric approach to the study of the Holocaust in Estonia. At the same conference, an American historian of Lithuanian origin acknowledged that Lithuanians needed to settle accounts with their past, but that this could only happen in their own time and in their own way; above all he said that they needed to discuss it among themselves in their own language, as many Lithuanian words (and concepts) cannot be translated into English and are thus fundamentally unintelligible to outsiders. This is the argument for a "closed discourse"; and possibly a consequence of long-term foreign rule.[41]

Shari J. Cohen notes that the difference between Eastern and Western Europe and the USA shows when it comes to the interpretation of the Holocaust.[42] The uproar caused by the then newly appointed American ambassador to Estonia, Joseph M. De Thomas, when he drew attention to the fact that since 1991 no Estonian war criminal had been prosecuted for crimes committed during the Holocaust, sustains this claim. De Thomas recommended that the Holocaust needed wider recognition as part of Estonia's national history.[43] His remarks were however rated as "interference in the internal affairs of Estonia" by the Estonian Justice Minister, who replied that De Thomas' statement was like "breaking in through an open door, since only a few states have done as much work as Estonia in investigating the crimes of the Holocaust."[44] De Thomas' comments were not entirely unfounded, for as recently as October 2000 the Estonian Minister of Education declared that a Jewish Holocaust Day in schools was not required. This opinion was only revised in 2002, when the Estonian government declared 27 January Holocaust Day in schools.[45] This incident illustrates how Estonian politicians can act as if they were under attack when it comes to the internationally-voiced demand for education in and research on the Nazi occupation of Estonia.[46] This defensive reaction may be understood to stem from the fact that during the Soviet period Estonians (along with the other Baltic nationalities) were collectively branded as "fascists" and "collaborators"; there is a tradition of defiance against these kinds of allegations.[47]

EMBLEMATIC DIMENSION

The Commission's work may be seen as an attempt at restoring Estonia's moral standing in the international community (that is, as a strategy of whitewashing), which would substantiate the idea that the Commission's carefully-worded and well-balanced report may not reflect the predominant opinion among Estonian historians, or indeed of Estonian society at large.[48] It may therefore be described rather as an "emblematic" use of history, leading us to the fifth dimension of public history, that is, the emblematic dimension. The moral use of history can be labeled emblematic when the discussion of certain historical facts remains mostly on the surface. For instance, a fundamental settlement with the Soviet legacy through lustration or a "Truth Commission" has not been achieved in post-Soviet Estonia.[49] Another example of the emblematic use of history in Estonia is the recently introduced "Holocaust Day" which lacks meaning for most Estonian pupils since the Holocaust plays such a minor part in most family narratives and in the official narrative.

WHEN PRIVATE MEMORY GOES PUBLIC:
FISTICUFFS OVER MONUMENTS

During the Soviet period, narratives of fighting side-by-side with the Germans against the Red Army were passed on as essentially unquestioned heroic stories of national resistance in the private realm of many Estonian families. However, not all the privately held counter-memories that resurfaced in the public domain of newly independent Estonia could be integrated into the official history in the long run. The memory of the veterans who fought in the German army is an example of an unofficial account that became part of the public memory after 1991, but was pushed back into the private sphere thereafter. It is this phenomenon that will be elaborated in subsequent sections.

Earlier it was mentioned that a different regional logic prevails in societies which experienced both the Nazi occupation and the Soviet regime. Enn Sarv's recollections on the situation of Estonians in early 1944 reflect this specific outlook on the past predominant among Estonians:

> In order to obtain weapons, [Estonian] men were forced to fight in German uniform ... but they considered themselves an Estonian army. They had managed to gain the right to wear a coat of arms with the colors of the Estonian national flag on their sleeves. In February, Estonian SS fighters removed the SS symbols from their collars without authorization and replaced them with the emblem of the Estonian Cross of Freedom ... Our main enemy, the Soviet Union, was about to invade Estonia, once again aiming to destroy our nation: so the War had become our own War.[50]

Another Estonian interviewee (a professional historian and politician born in 1960) related that his father and both his uncles fought in the German army. In response to my question about whether his father joined the German army voluntarily, he clarified:

> To fight against the Russians of course! You know pretty well that the Germans had been our historical enemy and we Estonians didn't like them very much. But only one year, 1940–41, made us love the Germans so much and greet them as "liberators." Nazis as "liberators," isn't it awful? But it only gives you an idea what the communist occupation had been like. Not that we are Nazis or Nazi-minded, no, never![51]

He insisted that they did not expressly fight for the Germans or on the German side, but that they had no other choice. This is the line of argument the veterans themselves take. So for instance, Ilmar Haalviste, a Waffen SS veteran, exemplified this particular Estonian standpoint when he stated: "At the end of the day there was no right or wrong side. The War was thrust upon us. We were on our side, defending our homes."[52]

The Lihula monument to Estonian soldiers in the German army

The Lihula monument depicts a soldier wearing a German army helmet and carrying a gun, with the order of the Estonian Cross of Freedom on his collar.

THE MEMORIAL STONE IN PÄRNU: A SYMBOL OF RESISTANCE

In July 2002, a privately-funded memorial stone depicting an Estonian soldier in Waffen SS uniform was put up at the Estonian sea resort town of Pärnu. After attracting a negative response from the national government, the memorial was removed and town officials ordered its redesign and the replacement of its inscription, which originally read "to all Estonian soldiers who fell in the Second World War to liberate their homeland and to free Europe in 1940–45."[53] A local historian, Leo Tammiksaar (born in 1962), who runs an organization called the "Estonian SS Legion Museum" (in Estonian, *Eesti SS Leegioni Muuseum*) since the early 1990s, is behind the memorial.[54] The inference from the original inscription and from Tammiksaar's public statements is that he believes the Estonian legionaries prevented the Red Army from occupying the whole of Europe.

THE 'LIHULA CONTROVERSY'

The Pärnu monument was altered and re-erected in the Estonian village cemetery of Lihula in August 2004. The local authorities and about 2,000 people who witnessed the unveiling ceremony wanted—in the words of the former dissident and historian Tiit Madisson and mayor of the Lihula parish, "to honor those who chose the lesser evil."[55] Whereas the monument still depicts an Estonian soldier in German uniform, the altered inscription is now "to the Estonian men who fought in 1940–45 against Bolshevism and for the restoration of Estonian independence."[56]

A fortnight after its inauguration, the police removed the monument in the face of an enraged, stone-throwing crowd of several hundred. After the removal only the base of the memorial remained, where a simple plaque was installed, reading "at this place the monument to the Estonian men used to stand 20.08.04–02.09.04."[57] The national government maintained that it was not appropriate "to build a monument that may be interpreted as an attempt to commemorate totalitarian regimes that had occupied Estonia."[58] The announcement of the Estonian Foreign Minister Kristiina Ojuland expressed a similar view: "Estonia must not isolate itself from the international community and damage its reputation … Local inappropriate action often results in very serious and far-reaching international consequences … Estonia … acknowledges the need to commemorate the fallen. This must be done in a manner that does not bring forth past evils to poison the future."[59]

At the same time the Estonian government offered its cooperation in setting up a more apposite memorial.[60] In a general response to the fisti-cuffs over the Lihula monument, it established yet another commission to decide on the official representation of Estonian contemporary history, whose long-term objective is to "persuade the international community to condemn the crimes of the communist regime."[61]

The position of the Estonian government on the occasion of the re-burial of Alfons Rebane, an anti-Soviet partisan (and later a commander of the Estonian Legion) in 1999 was equally ambiguous. For even though the government contributed (financially) towards a reburial ceremony with full military honors, only two MPs and the commander of the Esto-nian Defense Forces attended the event. Most representatives of the Esto-nian government may have feared international criticism and thus avoided a public appearance.[62]

THE "ESTONIAN FREEDOM FIGHTERS' ASSOCIATION"

On 6 July 6 2004 about 1,500 Estonian veterans commemorated the 60th anniversary of the battles against the Red Army. This public annual cele-bration in Tallinn has been organized by the "Estonian Freedom Fighters' Association" since the early 1990s.[63] During the course of the celebration, the Estonian government was pressed to attribute the status of "Freedom Fighters" to those Estonians who fought against Soviet occupation, in recognition of their claim to have fought for Estonia's freedom and de-mocracy.[64] In their appeal the veterans explicitly sought state protection against accusations from Russian and Jewish organizations which labeled them fascists.[65] The veterans demand public rehabilitation of their status; hence their identification as "Freedom Fighters" in reference to the name of the veterans of the Estonian War of Independence (1918–20). Also during the summer of 2004 the Estonian Freedom Fighters' Association planned to put up a monument in the district of Maarjamäe (located on the outskirts of Tallinn), which was to include the names of 16 Estonian units who fought as part of the Wehrmacht and a map indicating the sites of battles involving SS units against the Red Army.[66] However, in April 2005 the government decided against the unveiling of the monument, originally planned for 8 May 2005.[67]

CHANGING INTERPRETIVE FRAMEWORKS

In sum, the contested monument to the Estonian soldiers who fought in the German army brought to light how counter-memories can enter into the official representation of the past, but can then be pushed back into the private sphere once the official interpretive framework changes. In the course of a strengthening orientation towards the West, the specific Estonian interpretation of the Second World War clashed with the interpretive framework underlying the Western discourse on the topic. It can be concluded that, compared to the early 1990s, a reorientation took place in the Estonian public by the end of that decade which no longer allowed the Estonian legionaries public space for their commemoration.[68] Consequently, the odd situation occurred that the individual memories of Estonians who fought in the German army were once more confined to the private sphere.[69]

THE BRONZE SOLDIER STATUE

The removal of the Lihula monument unleashed a wave of vandalism against Soviet-built memorials all over the country.[70] In recent years the Bronze Soldier—a prominent Second World War memorial, known as the "monument to the liberators of Tallinn," commemorating Soviet soldiers who died fighting against the German army, has become a field of commemorative combat over the revision of Estonia's recent past.[71] It was vandalized with paint on the morning of 9 May 2005—the 60th anniversary of "Victory Day," and on numerous occasions thereafter.[72] 9 May became the focal point of attention for Red Army veterans and Estonian legionaries, all of whom claim to have fought for the "Estonian cause."[73] But whereas for the Red Army veterans the date marks the "liberation" of Estonia from Nazi occupation and Fascism, it represents the continuing occupation and the "Long Second World War" for many Estonians.[74] Hence many Estonians publicly request the removal of this monument, arguing that it serves as a reminder of five decades of Soviet rule in Estonia; while for many Red Army veterans the removal implies the revision of the results of the Second World War.[75]

The furore about the Bronze Soldier is indicative of the fact that the memory of those Estonians who fought in the Estonian Corps (Red Army) was pushed to the margins of the national narrative of post-1991 Estonia. Forgetting that (ethnic) Estonians fought as Soviet soldiers, many Estonians understand the Bronze Soldier to honor only the Russian soldiers (while equating Soviet with Russian).

The Bronze Soldier Statue

The Bronze Soldier at the foot of Tõnismägi in central Tallinn, which allegedly contains the ashes of fallen Soviet soldiers, was erected in 1947 (formerly with an eternal flame burning in front of the memorial). It became the concourse for the annual meetings of Red Army veterans on May 9 and September 22 (that is, on "Victory Day" and on the "Day of the Liberation of Tallinn from Fascism").

To this day the official canon on how to remember the fallen remains unresolved in Estonia; nor is it decided whether the fallen on all warring sides shall be honored, or only selected groups. In an attempt to end this divisive and somewhat ethnocentric interpretation of the past, the chairman of the Russian Faction of the Reform Party, Sergei Ivanov, suggested replacing the Bronze Soldier with a monument to all soldiers who fell in the Second World War.[76] Ivanov's proposal thus includes all soldiers who fought in the armed forces and seems to be based on the assumption that soldiers generally are victims of their sovereign.[77] Furthermore, we would have to examine whether Ivanov's suggestion is born of humanitarian intent or whether he is in fact attempting to relativize the war crimes committed by soldiers of either side.[78] We need to be clear that the memorial in mind would only concern soldiers who fought in the war; because it is yet another matter to erect a monument to all victims of war and tyranny in Estonia (see for instance in the case of the New Guard House in Berlin, [in German, *Neue Wache*]), which would unite perpetrators and victims of the war and of totalitarian regimes in their suffering and thus perilously blur the line between them.[79] The current Estoninan Prime Minister Andrus Ansip has repeatedly spoken in favor of the removal of the Bronze Soldier as "Monuments must unite people, but the monument in question [the Bronze Soldier] is dividing people."[80] However, his main coalition partner, the Centre Party under Edgar Savisaar, is against the relocation of the Soviet-era memorial. Hence the Bronze Soldier became a key issue in the elections on 4 March 2007.[81]

The "battle over monuments" in Estonia (and other Central and Eastern Europe societies) has a *longue durée* dimension, in that parts of monuments erected during the interwar period (and symbolizing independent statehood) were rescued and hidden in the countryside during the foreign occupations.[82] It was related to me that candles were regularly lit at the remaining pediments of monuments in memory of Estonian soldiers who fought in the War of Independence which had been dismantled after the Soviet takeover. These were understood as silent acts of resistance.[83]

IN CONCLUSION

In this article I have argued that historical revisionism is intimately linked to the ideological and political dimension of history and that it tends to be more connected to the public use of history as it is targeted towards a wider public and not just to the scholarly community.

I examined three landmarks of Estonian historical culture: whereas the Estonian Occupation Museum aims at cementing the notion of Estonian suffering, the Lihula monument and the Estonian Freedom Fighters' Association claims are linked more to ideas of national resistance. Through the example of the Estonian legionaries, I demonstrated how the revision of history is continuously contested and how monuments as "sites of memory" can turn into "contested terrain," because their destruction or removal causes a "dislocation" or "displacement" of the respective group memories.[84] Ultimately these monuments are so fiercely contested, because they are sources of group identities (that is, the existential dimension of history); we can thus speak of displaced group memories or identities. These battles over monuments are battles between competing interpretive frameworks, that is, between the specific official and local Estonian points of view, the Western reading of the Second World War, and lastly pro-Russian, and outdated Soviet views of the past.

I end by pointing out that I consider further comparative research in the iconography of cultural memories in post-Soviet and post-socialist societies to be very fruitful.

NOTES

1 Something I will later refer to as the "existential dimension" of history.

2 D. Levy, "The Future of the Past: Historiographical Disputes and Competing Memories in Germany and Israel." *History and Theory* 38, No. 1, (1999): 51–66, 66.

3 This article is based largely on Chapter Seven of my doctoral thesis, entitled *Historical Culture, Conflicting Memories and Identities in Post Soviet Estonia*, forthcoming in Berghahn Books (in the series on Making Sense of History). It examines the debated codification of an official memory in contemporary Estonia, while exploring how the experience of long-term occupation impacted on the formation of post-Soviet identities. The study used life story interviews as its primary source: between 1996 and 2003. I interviewed over 40 historians of Estonian, Russian and Estonian-Russian background, questioning them about their childhood, choice of profession, war memories, narratives of resistance, suffering and shame.

4 I employ the concept of "historical culture" (In German, *Geschichtskultur*), first introduced by Jörn Rüsen, as it offers an integrative approach to the study of collective memory and history by understanding both phenomena as expressions of "historical culture." In short, "historical culture" includes every articulation and contestation of "historical consciousness" (In German, *Geschichtsbewußtsein*) and all the ways in which "historical memory" is processed in the daily life of a society. The concept of "historical culture" includes both processes of "history production" and the moral standards operative in the relevant society. J. Rüsen and F. Jäger "Erinnerungskultur" [Memory culture] in *Deutschland TrendBuch. Fakten und Orientierungen* [Germany book of trends: facts and orientations], K.-R. Korte and W. Weidenfeld, eds., (Opladen: Leske & Budrich, 2001), pp. 397–428, 399; J. Rüsen, "Was ist Geschichtskultur? Überlegungen zu einer neuen Art, über Geschichte nachzudenken" [What is historical culture?], in *Historische Faszination. Geschichtskultur Heute* [Historical Fascination], J. Rüsen, K. Füßmann, et al., eds., (Köln: Böhlau Verlag, 1994), pp. 3–25.

5 On the different dimensions of history and its public use, see J. Rüsen and F. Jäger, "Erinnerungskultur," p. 406; Nicola Gallernano, "History and the Public Use of History," F. Bedarida, ed., The social responsibility of the historian, *Diogenes Library*, No. 168 (Oxford–New York: Berghahn Books, 1994): 85–102; K.-G. Karlsson, *Historia som vapen: Historiebruk och samhällssupplösning i Sovjetunionen och dess efterföljarstater 1985–1995* (History as Wappen) (Stockholm: Natur och Kultur, 1999), pp. 57, 218–232; Karlsson, K.-G. "History in Swedish Politics—the 'Living History' Project," in *European History: Challenges for a Common Future*, A. Pok and J. Rüsen, et al., eds., (Hamburg: Körber Stiftung, 2002), pp. 145–162; K.-G. Karlsson, U. Zander, et al.

Echoes of the Holocaust: Historical Cultures in Contemporary Europe (Lund: Nordic Academic Press, 2003).

6 E. Menasse, *Der Holocaust vor Gericht: Der Prozess um David Irving* [The Holocaust in court. The case of David Irving] (Berlin: Siedler Verlag, 2000).

7 That is, where is the border between legitimate reexamination of history and rewriting history in a politically motivated manner, while changing widely established historical facts?

8 Levy, "The Future of the Past," pp. 62–63.

9 Levy, "The Future of the Past," p. 65.

10 S. J. Cohen, *Politics without a Past. The Absence of History in Postcommunist Nationalism.* (Durham and London: Duke University Press, 1999), p. 2.

11 In the light of Cohen's assessment of post-communist societies, these common standards of "history production" may be weak or non-existent.

12 T. Todorov, "The Abuses of Memory," *Common Knowledge* 5 (1996): 6–26, 15.

13 Gallerano, "History and the Public Use," p. 85. According to Gallerano, the public use is to a large extent based on the means of mass-communication and encompasses the use of history in schools, museums, cultural associations, political parties, etc.

14 And to what might be translated as "definitional authority" (in German, *Definitionsmacht*).

15 Cf. T. H. Ilves, "Estonia and the State of Change in European security," a paper delivered at Chatham House (London: 4 May 1999).

16 An over-moralization of history can also be found in the public discourse on Germany's recent past during the 1990s.

17 E. Wolfrum, *Geschichtspolitik in der Bundesrepublik Deutschland: Der Weg zur bundesrepublikanischen Erinnerung 1948–1990* (The politics of history in the FRG: The path to a memory of the Federal Republic of Germany 1948–1990) (Darmstadt: Wissenschaftliche Buchgesellschaft, 1999), pp. 13–38.

18 Gallerano, "History and the Public Use," p. 100.

19 Otherwise the Occupation Museum relies on new media, including video testimonies and a series of seven CD-ROMs covering roughly the period from 1940 to 1987, as well as the Estonian independence movement. See www.okupatsioon.ee.

20 Simon, interview (Tallinn: 7 June 2002). The interview was conducted before the Occupation Museum was inaugurated in 2003.

21 Elsewhere, I sustain the argument that it is the narrative of sole victimhood, which leaves little space for another people's suffering, which forms an integral part of Estonian national identity.

22 Namely the work of Efraim Zuroff (the head of the Jerusalem office of the Simon Wiesenthal Centre), pressure from Russia and pressure applied to Estonia in the course of the EU and NATO accession processes (in connection to this, the example of the Holocaust Day is discussed in a later section).

23 R. J. Misiunas, "Soviet Historiography on World War II and the Baltic States, 1944–1974" in *The Baltic States in Peace and War 1917–1945*, eds., V. S. Vardys and R. Misiunas (University Park – London: Pennsylvania State University Press, 1978), pp. 173–196.

24 For historical revisionism in post-Soviet Latvia, see Eva-Clarita Onken, "Revisionismus schon vor der Geschichte: Aktuelle lettische Kontroversen um die Judenvernichtung und Kollaboration 1941–1944" [Revisionism prior to history: current Latvian con-

troversies on the Holocaust and collaboration 1941–1944], *Galut-Nordost*, Sonderheft 1 (special issue) (1998).

25 This is the overall tenor of a publication displayed at the Estonian Occupation Museum in 2003, which contains a collection of speeches by the former Prime Minister Mart Laar, Tunne Kelam, and Enn Sarv, see M. Laar, and T. Kelam, et al., "International Conference on Crimes of Communism" Tallinn 14.06.00 (www.isamaaliit.ee/isamaa2/eng_4_2.html). The Museum Dungeon of the KGB in Tartu, which was termed the 'Gray House,' is another site to remember the Estonians' struggle for freedom (and their suffering). This museum was established in 2001, that is, two years prior to the inauguration of the Occupation Museum; similarly, its collection lacks any reference to the site's usage during the German occupation. See www.tartu.ee/linnamuuseum.

26 M. Tarm, "The Gift: An American of Estonian Descent Funds a new Museum that Recounts a Nation's Tragedy—and her own," in *Baltic City Paper* (September 2003), 12.

27 Todorov, "The Abuses of Memory," pp. 16–19.

28 Cf. H. Arendt, *Elemente und Ursprünge totaler Herrschaft* [The origins of totalitarianism, 1951] (Munich: Pieper, 1986); D. Beyrau, "Nationalsozialistisches Regime und das Stalin-System. Ein riskanter Vergleich." [National Socialism and Stalinism: A precarious comparison.] *Osteuropa* 50, No. 6 (2000): 709–729; E. Nolte, *The Three Faces of Fascism* (London: Weidenfeld & Nicolson, 1965); S. Creuzberger and I. Mannteufel, et al., "Kommunismus und Terror. Das "Schwarzbuch des Kommunismus"—Hauptthesen und Argumente" [Communism and Terror: The "Blackbook of Communism"—main theses and arguments]. *Osteuropa* 50, No. 6 (2000): 583–584; Dan Diner, ed., *Ist der Nationalsozialismus Geschichte? Zu Historisierung und Historikerstreit* [Is National Socialism history? About historization and the historians' debate] (Frankfurt: S. Fischer, 1988).

29 This is when we follow Todorov's list of four possible responses to the comparison of the two totalitarianisms. It helps to identify the standpoint of the individual employing the comparison: 1) "Hitler's hangmen" favor the pairing with Stalinists because it serves to excuse their own actions; 2) Hitler's victims oppose a pairing, because they are aware that the "hangmen" use it as an excuse; 3) "Stalin's hangmen" oppose a pairing, because it is used against them as an accusation; 4) Stalin's victims favor the pairing, because they can use it as an accusation (Todorov, "The Abuses of Memory," pp. 16–19).

30 E. Zuroff, "Misleading Comparisons of the 20th-century Tragedies" in *The Baltic Times* (19 February 2004); E. Zuroff, "Lifting the Shadow of a Bloody Past" in *The Baltic Times* (4 March 2004).

31 The clear focus on an international public is also reflected by the international composition of the Commission's board, with politicians and scholars from Germany, the UK, Finland, Denmark and Russia (that is, Arsenij Rosinsky, the head of *Memorial*). It is noteworthy that there are only a few trained historians among the board members. Former President Meri's initiative was supported by leading Jewish organizations in the US, which is mirrored in the person of Nicholas Lane, Chairman of the IR commission of the American-Jewish Committee, also a member of the Commission's board. It needs to be stressed that comparable commissions were set up in the other Baltic States (also in 1998), so that we may speak of a regional post-Soviet phenomenon.

32 By its statutory report the Commission refrains from assigning "collective guilt."

33 The report stresses that 1200 of the 40,000 members of *OK* were involved in killings.

34 These destruction or shock battalions fought side-by-side with regular Soviet troops carrying out Stalin's scorched-earth policy in the face of the approaching German troops in 1941.

35 See the Commission's homepage, www.historycommission.ee.

36 E. Zuroff, *Beruf: Nazijäger. Die Suche mit dem langen Atem: Die Jagd nach den Tätern des Völkermordes* [Profession: Nazi hunter. A search that requires a long breath: hunting for the perpetrators of the Holocaust] (Freiburg: Ahriman-Verlag, 1996), pp. 318–321; cf. R. Kruus, ed., *People be Watchful!* (Tallinn: Estonian State Publishing House, 1962).

37 S. Toth, "Cursory Nazi probe rejected," in *The Baltic Times* (25–31 July 2002): 3.

38 "Wiesenthal Center ad left unprinted," in *The Baltic Times* (30 January 2003).

39 In April 2001, Estonia belonged to "category D" (BNS "Juudikeskus peab Eestit kehvaks natsiuurijaks" [The Jewish Centre considers Estonia to be a bad Nazi researcher]) in *Postimees* (20 April 2001). In 2003 Estonia remained in this category, joined by Austria, Finland, France and the UK ("Estonia gets Low Marks in Nazi Hunting") in *The Baltic Times*, (1 May 2003); BNS "Reinsalu disputes Nazi-hunt findings," in *The Baltic Times*, (31 August 2003).

40 Meelis Maripuu's paper reads "the present article is only concerned with the fate of the local Jewish community during the Second World War; while the destiny of those European Jews deported to Estonia in 1942–44 is not addressed" (Maripuu, Meelis "Kollaboration und Widerstand in Estland 1940–1944" [Collaboration and resistance in Estonia 1940–1944], a paper presented at the conference on '*Reichskommissariat Ostland.* Collaboration and Resistance during the Holocaust,' Stockholm & Uppsala, Sweden, (18–21 April 2002).

41 My usage of the term "closed" ought not to be confused with Karl Popper's concept of the "closed society."

42 Cohen, *Politics without a Past*, pp. 11f.

43 In his article De Thomas states "the fact that the Soviet occupation did more direct harm in Estonia, however, does not negate the fact that the Holocaust happened here too." J. M. De Thomas, "Past, Present and Future," in *Eesti Päevaleht,* (28 May 2002) http://estonia.usembassy.gov/holocaust_eng.php.

44 "Estonian government puzzled at US ambassador's Holocaust statement." in *Leta Daily News Review* (30 May 2002).

45 "Lieber braun statt rot?" [Better Brown than Red?] in *Newsletter of the Swiss Baltic Chamber of Commerce* (Tallinn: 27 October 2000). 25 March and 14 June are National Days of mourning in remembrance of the mass-deportations during the Soviet periods.

46 K. Brüggemann, "Von der Renationalisierung zur Demontage nationaler Helden. Oder: Wie schreibt man estnische Geschichte?" [From re-nationalization to the demolition of national heroes: Or how does one write Estonian history?], *Osteuropa* 7 (2001): 810–819.

47 Cf. Vardys and Misiunas, eds., *Baltic States.*

48 In her review of the final 1,300-page report of the Commission (published in English in 2006), Eva-Clarita Onken concludes that it fails to take notice of the social context in which the findings had been published (online) over the last six years, that is, its reception among the wider Estonian public. Moreover, Onken notes a rather positivistic understanding of history as "true facts" in the individual contributions (and consequently a

lack of analysis); see Eva-Clarita Onken, "The Politics of Finding Historical Truth: Reviewing Baltic History Commissions and their Work," *Journal of Baltic Studies* 38, No. 1 (2007).

49 Apart from declarations, such the statement of the President of the Riigikogu, Toomas Savi, on 18 February 2002 on the crimes of the occupation regime in Estonia. T. Savi, "Statement of the President of the Riigikogu on the Occupation Regime in Estonia" in Euro *University. The Monthly Survey of the Baltic and Post-Soviet Politics*, No. 7 (109) (2001/2): 3–4.

50 E. Sarv, "Our Duty of Remembering," a paper delivered at an International Conference on Crimes of Communism (Tallinn, 14 June 2000): 36. See www.isamaaliit.ee/isamaa2/eng_4_2.html.

51 Oskar, interview (Tallinn, 01.10.03).

52 "Veterans: Views from the East." in *BBC News Week* (9 May 2005) (See http://news.bbc.co.uk/2/hi/europe/4530273.stm). By comparison the veterans of the Red Army in Russia vehemently deny such a claim.

53 BNS, "History Buff Building SS Legion Museum in Pärnu," in *The Baltic Times* (3 June 2004); Agence France-Presse, "Plans halted for WWII memorial," in *The Baltic Times* (25–31 July 2002), 3; Melanie O'Connell, "Pärnu to Commemorate Freedom Fighters Again," in *The Baltic Times* (31 August 2003).

54 A. Gunter, "Monumental Needs and Rethinking Estonia's past," in *The Baltic Times* (10 June 2004).

55 BBC, "Estonia Unveils Nazi War Monument," in *BBC News World* Online Edition (20 August 2004).

56 A. Gunter, "Riot Police Help Remove Controversial WWII Monument," in *The Baltic Times* (9 September 2004).

57 M. Kolb, "Looking for the Truth Behind Lihula," in *The Baltic Times* (27 April 2005).

58 "State Removes Controversial Monument by Force," in *The Baltic Times* (02.09.04).

59 Välisministeerium (Estonian Foreign Ministry), "Press Release: Statement by Foreign Minister Ojuland Concerning the Lihula Monument," (3 September 2004).

60 "State Removes Controversial Monument by Force," in *The Baltic Times* (2 September 2004).

61 A. Gunter, "Estonia Sets its History Straight," in *The Baltic Times* (1 November 2004); Kolb "Looking for the truth;" From Wire Reports "Controversy Erupts Around Historical Commission," in *The Baltic Times* (18 May 2005).

62 M. Huang, "Doing it Half Right," in *Central Europe Review* 1, No. 2 (5 July 1999).

63 M. Shafir, "Analysis: Estonian War Veterans Provoke Russian Reaction," in *Radio Free Europe, Radio Liberty* (RFE/RL) (22 July 2004). The "Estonian Freedom Fighters' Association" represents Estonians who fought in divisions of the Waffen SS (particularly soldiers of the 20th division of the Waffen SS, that is, the Estonian Legion) and as anti-Soviet partisans (that is, the "Forest Brethren"). Likewise in neighboring Latvia, the veterans of the Latvian SS Legion (the "National Soldiers' Association") organize an annual public march to the Freedom Monument in the centre of Riga on 16 March.

64 BNS, "Freedom Fighters Demand Historical Clarification," in *The Baltic Times* (8 July 2004).

65 Staff and wire reports "Freedom Fighters Appeal for Help, Evaluation of WWII Events," in *The Baltic Times* (5 August 2004).

66 J. Postcom Staff, "Estonia Plans to Unveil Memorial to SS Veterans," in *Jerusalem Post*, Online Edition (22 May 2004). The Estonian Legion *per se* cannot be termed a criminal organization, since in 1949–50 a UN commission investigated the Estonian and Latvian SS (the so-called Baltic Legions) and found these military units to be neither criminal nor Nazi collaborators. However, the 16 Estonian units include the 36th Estonian Division of the Waffen SS, which the Estonian International Commission for the Investigation of Crimes against Humanity had identified as having committed crimes against humanity.

67 "Tallinn decides against unveiling monument to Estonian Nazi troops," in *Estos in the News, Itar-Tass* (27 April 2005). After the German troops withdrew from the city of Narva in 26 April 1944, soldiers of the Estonian Legion tried to bring the advancing Red Army to a halt at Sinimäe. It is to the graves in Sinimäe that Estonian Waffen SS veterans, or legionaries, come to commemorate their battle on 8 May, a day *before* Victory Day (S. Stepanov, "Victory Day Opens Old Wounds," in *The Baltic Times* [16 May 2002]).

68 U. Seaver and Küllike Roováli "Pärnu sai SS-vormis 'Euroopa vaduse kaitsja' bareljeefi," [Pärnu got a memorial plaque for the "protector of Europe's freedom" dressed in SS uniform] in *Postimees* (23 July 2002); U. Seaver and M. Ojakivi "Pärnu võttis SS-vormis sõduriga ausamba maha," [Pärnu removed the statue of the soldier in SS uniform] in *Postimees* (24 July 2002).

69 Gunter, "Riot Police."

70 Even though the inscription (in Russian and Estonian) reads "To the fallen of the Second World War" the statue depicts a soldier in Soviet uniform, clearly defining the meaning of the monument (S. L. Myers, "Debate Renewed: Did Moscow Free Estonia or Occupy it?" in *The New York Times* [25 January 2007] See www.bafl.com/news).

71 J. Tanner, "War monument in Estonia vandalized," in *Seattle Post-Intelligencer* (9 May 2005); From wire reports "Candle Vigil Throws Kind Light on Bitter Monument," in *The Baltic Times* (15 September 2004).

72 J. Alas, "May 9 Protestors Call for Removing Bronze Soldier Statue," in *The Baltic Times* (10 May 2006); Joel Alas, "Brawl Breaks Out in Shadow of the Bronze Memorial." in *The Baltic Times* (24 May 2006). On 9 May 2006 the controversy reached a new height when Estonian nationalists clashed with Soviet veterans and members of the Russian-speaking community waving Soviet flags (Joel Alas, "Coalition Split over Bronze Soldier," in *The Baltic Times* [17 January 2007])

73 Evidence for a different perception of European history came to light during the 60th anniversary of the end of the Second World War, when the Estonian and Lithuanian leaders did not travel to Moscow for the celebration on the 9th of May. The Latvian president attended the ceremony, using the publicity to demonstrate the Baltic view on the events of the Second World War. J. Vosswinkel, "Der 8. Mai 1945. Wo Russen Täter waren" (8 May 1945. Where Russians were the Perpetrators), in *Die Zeit* (4 May 2005), 19.

74 The dispute prompted members of the Russian Duma to push for sanctions against Estonia. Agence France-Presse, "Russia slams removal of WWII memorial," in *The Washington Times* (22 January 2007). The Russian Foreign Minister Sergei Lavrov called upon the other European countries not to permit "this kind of blasphemous attitude towards the memory of those who fought against Fascism." TBT staff, "Russian

Foreign Minister Opposes Sanctions Against Estonia," in *The Baltic Times* (30 January 2007).

75 From Wire Reports, "Russian-speaking NGOs to Hold Roundtable on Bronze Soldier," in *The Baltic Times* (7 June 2006).

76 Michael Walzer argues along these lines: M. Walzer, *Just and Unjust Wars: A Moral Argument with Historical Illustrations* (New York: Basic Books, 2000). Other scholars in just war theory—such as David Rodin: D. Rodin, *War and Self-Defense*, (Oxford: OUP, 2003), take a slightly more liberal stance, in that they allow for the fact that soldiers can be held responsible on an individual basis, because they have some freedom of choice even in the exceptional situation of war.

77 In his case possibly more with the intention to relativize the war crimes committed by Soviet soldiers. I believe the purpose of relativizing the extent of a group's suffering or the gravity of the crimes committed by that group is that of whitewashing.

78 O. Bartov, *Mirrors of Destruction: War, Genocide, and Modern Identity* (Oxford: OUP 2000): 39. In 1993 the *Neue Wache* was rededicated as the central memorial site for the victim of war and tyranny. The plaque on the right side of the entrance reads "The *Neue Wache* is the site of memory and remembrance of the victims of war and tyranny." Subsequently, those nations and civilians who suffered and perished are listed in the same breath with fallen soldiers and with innocent victims of war (that is, killed at home, in captivity, and due to expulsion). The next section lists Jews, Sinti and Roma, homosexuals, and the mentally handicapped. Then those killed due to their religious or political beliefs are mentioned, followed by a paragraph on resistance fighters. The final section is dedicated to women and men persecuted and killed due to their resistance to the post-1945 totalitarian dictatorship. This is an extremely interesting example of an attempt to do justice to many different (that is, competing) victim groups, but the juxtaposition of victims of different periods and regimes—and here I agree with Bartov's assessment, is highly problematic Cf. P. Reichel, *Politik mit der Erinnerung: Gedächtnisorte im Streit um die nationalsozialistische Vergangenheit* [Politics of remembrance: Sites of memory in the battle over the Nazi past] (Frankfurt am Main: Fischer, 1999).

79 "Grave Mistakes," in *The Baltic Times* (17 January 2007).

80 J. Alas, "Coalition split." In an attempt to resolve the dispute the Estonian parliament accepted a bill banning the display of Soviet and Nazi symbols that might incite hatred in late 2006. J. Alas, "Free Speech Questioned as Estonia Prepares to Ban Soviet, Nazi Symbols," in *The Baltic Times* (6 December 2006). Furthermore the parliament adopted the "War Graves Protection Act" on 10 January 2007 to establish the legal basis for the removal of the statue. A commission on war burial sites was soon established to decide (along with the parliament) whether a monument contradicts public interest or if it is located in an inappropriate public place. Lastly, the parliament considers a draft law on renaming 22 September as "Day of Mourning," V. Socor, "Bronze Soldier Set to Leave Tallinn as Last Soviet Soldier," in *Eurasia Monitor Daily*, Jamestown Foundation (12 January 2007).

81 A similar emotional attachment can be witnessed with regard to forbidden books, indicative of the existential dimension of history.

82 Oskar, interview (Tallinn: 1 October 2003).

83 Every collective memory is anchored (and unfolds) in a spatial framework (as well as in a social framework). See: M. Halbwachs, *La topographie legendaire des évangiles en Terre Seinte. Étude de mémoire collective* [The Legendary Topography of the Gospels

in the Holy Land], (Paris: Presses universitaires de France, 1941); M. Halbwachs, *La Mémoire collective*, (1950) [Collective memory] (New York: Harper & Row, 1980); M. Halbwachs, *Les cadres sociaux de la mémoire* [Social frames of memory] (Paris: Librairie Felix Alcan, 1925); P. Nora, *Zwischen Geschichte und Gedächtnis* [Between history and memory] (Berlin: Wagenbach, 1990); P. Nora, ed., *Realms of Memory: Rethinking the French Past, Conflicts and* Divisions, Vol. I, (New York: Columbia University Press, 1996); P. Nora, ed., *Realms of Memory: The Construction of the French Past,* Traditions, Vol. II, (New York: Columbia University Press, 1997).

About the Authors

Eva Hahn was a research fellow at the Collegium Carolinum in Munich until 1999. Since then she has worked as an independent historian in Oldenburg, Germany. She is the author of numerous studies on the intellectual history of Central Europe in the 19th and 20th centuries, see www.bohemistik.de/evahahn.

Hans Henning Hahn is Professor of East European History at the Carl von Ossietzky University in Oldenburg. He specializes in Polish and Czech history, concentrating on historical research on national stereotypes and German attitudes to East European nations. Among his recent publications are *Politische Mythen im 19. und 20. Jahrhundert in Mittel- und Osteuropa,* Heidi Hein-Kircher and Hans Henning Hahn, eds., (Marburg: Verlag Herder-Institut, 2006) and *Nationale Wahrnehmungen und ihre Stereotypisierung. Beiträge zur Historischen Stereotypenforschung*, Hans Henning Hahn, Elena Mannová, eds., (Frankfurt am Main: Peter Lang Verlag, 2007)

Owen V. Johnson is Associate Professor of Journalism and Adjunct Professor of History at Indiana University. He is writing a book on media and nation in 20th-century Slovakia. He previously wrote *Slovakia 1918–1938: Education & the Making of a Nation* (New York: Columbia University Press, 1985).

Georgiy Kasianov is the Head of the Department of Contemporary History and Politics, Institute of Ukrainian History, National Academy of Sciences of Ukraine.

Katya A. M. Kocourek studied the contemporary history of East-Central Europe and Russia at the universities of London and Oxford. Her current research concerns the political legitimacy of Czechoslovak state ideology, particularly in interwar Czechoslovakia (1918–38). She has published essays and articles on themes of Czechoslovak and Russian history in the 20th century. She was founder-editor of the journal *Central Europe* (2002–04) at the School of Slavonic and East European Studies (SSEES), University College London.

Michal Kopeček is a senior research fellow at the Institute of Contemporary History, Prague. He has specialized in modern intellectual history and nationalism in East Central Europe, Communism and transition studies, and the history and theory of historiography. Apart from publishing various articles he is one of the editors of the series of volumes *Bolševismus, komunismus a radikální socialismus v Československu* [Bolshevism, Communism and Radical Socialism in Czechoslovakia] (Prague: ÚSD-Dokořán, 2003–2005) and of the *Discourses of Collective Identity in Central and Southeast Europe (1770–1945): Text and Commentaries* (Budapest, New York: CEU Press, 2006ff)

Ferenc Laczó is a doctoral student at the History Department of Central European University, Budapest. His main research interests are political ideologies and nationalism, modernity and urbanism in East Central Europe (more specifically the symbolism and perceptions of capital cities), and the history of Communism in East Central Europe (especially cultural life, dissidence and opposition, and the legacy and memory of Communism)

Ingo Loose studied contemporary history and Slavonic languages in Hamburg, Warsaw, Moscow and Berlin. He is a lecturer in the department of Contemporary History, Humboldt University of Berlin. His fields of interest are contemporary Polish history and the history of the Holocaust in Eastern Europe; in 2005 he received the Prix de la Fondation Auschwitz—Jacques Rozenberg, Brussels. His recent publications include "Credit Banks and the Holocaust in the *Generalgouvernement*, 1939–1945," in: *Yad Vashem Studies* 34 (2006), pp. 177–218; *Credits for Nazi Crimes. German credit banks in Poland and the looting of the Polish and Jewish population, 1939–1945* (Munich: 2007) (forthcoming).

András Mink, historian and journalist, is Senior Research Archivist at the Open Society Archives, Budapest, and editor-in-chief of the liberal monthly *Beszélő*. His areas of interest are the history of Hungary after 1945 and historiography. He has authored a number of articles and edited several volumes on Hungarian history, most recently *The Defendant: the State. The Story of the Hungarian Helsinki Committee.* (Budapest: Hungarian Helsinki Committee, 2005)

Vladimir Petrović is a research associate of the Institute for Contemporary History in Belgrade and doctoral candidate at the History Department of the Central European University in Budapest. Currently he is researching the nexus between historical narratives and legal procedures.

Rafał Stobiecki is Professor at the Chair of the History of Historiography of Łódź University. His fields of interest include the history of modern historical thought with special emphasis on the historiography of the communist period and Polish historiography in exile. Author of numerous books, most recently *Bolszewizm a Historia. Próba rekonstrukcji bolszewickiej filozofii dziejów* [Bolshevism versus history. An attempt to reconstruct the Bolshevik philosophy of history] (Łódź: Wydawnictwo Uniwersytetu Łódzkiego,1998); *Klio na wygnaniu. Z dziejów polskiej historiografii na uchodźstwie w Wielkiej Brytanii po II wojnie światowej po 1945 r.* [Clio in exile. On Polish émigré historiography in Great Britain after 1945] (Poznań: Wydawnictwo Poznańskie, 2005); co-author with Jarosław Kita of *Słownik biograficzny historyków łódzkich* [Biographical dictionary of Łódź historians] (Łódź: Ibidem, 2000); *Jerzego Giedroycia rozrachunki z historią i polityką* [Jerzy Giedroyc's coming to terms with history and politics] (Łódź: Ibidem, 2005).

Aviezer Tucker teaches philosophy at Queens University, Belfast. His main fields of interest are the philosophy of historiography, epistemology, philosophy of science, and social and political philosophy and theory. He has published *Our Knoweldge of the Past: A Philosophy of Historiography* (Cambridge: Cambridge University Press, 2004) and *The Philosophy and Politics of Czech Dissidence from Patocka to Havel* (Pittsburgh: Pittsburgh University Press, 2000). He is now editing *The Blackwell Companion to the Philosophies of Historiography and History.*

Meike Wulf is a post-doctoral research fellow at the Centre for East European Language Based Area Studies (CEELBAS) at the School of Slavonic and East European Studies, London (UCL SSEES). She received a BA from the University of Münster, a MA from SSEES, and a PhD from the Government Department (LSE). She studied and taught at the Universities of Münster, Uppsala, Konstanz, Tallinn, as well as at BEEGS (Stockholm), and the KWI (Essen). Her research interests center on memory studies, life story research, generations, nationalism, civil society, multiculturalism, identity politics and contemporary East European history and politics (i.e., the Baltic States).

Name Index

Subject Index